The Population of Europe

THE MAKING OF EUROPE

Series Editor: Jacques Le Goff

The *Making of Europe* series is the result of a unique collaboration between five European publishers – Beck in Germany, Blackwell in Great Britain and the United States, Critica in Spain, Laterza in Italy and le Seuil in France. Each book will be published in all five languages. The scope of the series is broad, encompassing the history of ideas as well as of societies, nations and states to produce informative, readable, and provocative treatments of central themes in the history of the European peoples and their cultures.

Also available in this series

The European City
Leonardo Benevolo

The Rise of Western Christendom:
Triumph and Diversity 200–1000 AD
Peter Brown

The European Renaissance
Peter Burke

The Search for the Perfect Language
Umberto Eco

The Distorted Past: A
Reinterpretation of Europe
Josep Fontana

The Origins of European
Individualism
Aaron Gurevich

The Enlightenment
Ulrich Im Hof

The Population of Europe
Massimo Livi Bacci

Europe and the Sea
Michel Mollat du Jourdin

The Culture of Food
Massimo Montanari

Religion and Society in Modern
Europe
René Rémond

The Peasantry of Europe
Werner Rösener

States, Nations and Nationalism
Hagen Schulze

European Revolutions 1492–1992
Charles Tilly

In preparation

Democracy in European History
Maurice Agulhon

Migration and Culture
Klaus Bade

Women in European History
Gisela Bock

Europe and Islam
Franco Cardini

The European Family
Jack Goody

The Industrialization of Europe
Jurgen Kocka

The Law in European History
Peter Landau

The University in European History
Jacques Le Goff

The First European Revolution,
900–1200
R. I. Moore

The Frontier in European History
Krzysztof Pomian

The Birth of Modern Science
Paolo Rossi

The Population of Europe
A History

Massimo Livi Bacci

Translated by Cynthia De Nardi Ipsen
and Carl Ipsen

First published in Italian as *La popolazione nella storia d'Europa* by Gius. Laterza & Figli in 1998. First published in English by Blackwell Publishers Ltd 2000, and by three other publishers: © 2000 Beck, Munich (German); © 1999 Critica, Barcelona (Spanish); © 1999 Editions du Seuil, Paris (French).

2 4 6 8 10 9 7 5 3 1

Blackwell Publishers Ltd
108 Cowley Road
Oxford OX4 1JF
UK

Blackwell Publishers Inc.
350 Main Street
Malden, Massachusetts 02148
USA

British Library Cataloguing in Publication Data

A CIP catalogue record for this book is available from the British Library.

Library of Congress Cataloging-in-Publication Data

Livi Bacci, Massimo.
[Popolazione nella storia d'Europa. English]
The population of Europe : a history / Massimo Livi-Bacci ; translated by Cynthia De Nardi Ipsen and Carl Ipsen.
p.   cm. — (The Making of Europe)
Includes bibliographical references and index.
ISBN 0–631–20078–9 (hb : alk. paper) 0–631–21881–5 (pbk: alk paper)
1 Europe—Population—History. I. Title. II. Series.
HB3581.A3L5813   1999
304.6'094—dc21   99-29297
                                                                    CIP

Typeset in 11 on 12.5pt Sabon
by G & G Editorial, Brighton

This book is printed on acid-free paper

Contents

List of Tables   vii
List of Figures   ix
Series Editor's Preface   xi

1   Numbers   1
    Factors of constraint and factors of choice   1
    A millennium of demographic development   5
    Slow change in old regime societies   12
    Interpretive choices   16

2   Space   18
    Geography and environment   18
    The conquest of space before the Black Death   21
    Again eastward and southward   28
    Settlement intensification and land reclamation   30
    Consolidation   35

3   Food   40
    Population and nutrition   40
    Nutrition, infection, and mortality   42
    Bread and its accompaniments   45
    Famine and hunger   51
    Long-term nutrition and mortality   56
    Paradoxes and reality   59

4 Microbes and Disease   61
   Lives on the brink   61
   A world in motion   64
   The plague: a four-handed game   70
   The final match   75
   Demographic losses   80
   Other factors and the road to normality   84

5 Systems   91
   Demographic systems   91
   England, France, and Germany   95
   Marriage   99
   Fertility   107
   More on infant mortality   112
   Migration   116
   Equilibrium and transformations   122

6 The Great Transformation (1800–1914)   126
   A frame of reference   126
   Demographic expansion: numbers and interpretations   132
   Two months per year: increasing life expectancy   140
   Infant mortality yet again   147
   The advent of birth control   151
   Outside of Europe   158

7 The End of a Cycle   164
   Demography in the twentieth century:
      mortality and fertility   164
   Demography in the twentieth century:
      migration, structures, models   169
   Politics   172
   Economics   178
   Values   183

Further Reading   190

Index   214

List of Tables

1.1   Population of selected European countries,
      1500–1900   8 & 9

1.2   Doubling and doubling time for selected
      European populations, 1550, 1700, 1800   10

2.1. Urban population as a percentage of total for
      countries and regions, 1500–1800   36

2.2   Average latitude and longitude of cities newly
      arrived at a population level over 50,000,
      1200–1800   38

4.1   Percentage of deaths from smallpox, selected
      European populations, eighteenth century   88

5.1   England, Germany, and France: a comparison
      of systems   94

5.2   Legitimate fertility rates in selected European
      countries, seventeenth and eighteenth centuries   110

5.3   Infant and young mortality in selected European
      countries, second half of the eighteenth century   113

6.1   Per-capita gross domestic product in selected
      European countries, 1820–1913   128

6.2   Population of major European countries and
      average annual growth, 1800–1913   132 & 133

6.3   Demographic indices for selected European
      countries, 1800–1913 (per 1,000 inhabitants)   134

6.4   Life expectancy at birth in selected European
      countries, 1750–1915   135

6.5   Average number of children per woman (total
      fertility rate) in selected European countries,
      1800–1910   136

6.6   Marital fertility in selected European countries   154

7.1   Population of selected European countries,
      1920–2000   165

7.2   Life expectancy (men and women) in major
      European countries, 1920–94   166

7.3   Average number of children per woman in
      selected European countries, 1921–95   168

7.4   Per-capita gross domestic product in European
      countries, 1913–92 (1990 dollars)   180

List of Figures

1.1	European Population, 1000–2000	6
1.2	Timing of doubling of 1800 populations	12
1.3	Population and grain prices in Europe, 1200–1800	15
2.1	Founding of cities in central Europe	23
2.2	Steps in the *reconquista* of the Iberian peninsula, 900–1500	24
2.3	Land reclamation, coastal areas and internal lakes, in the Netherlands, 1100–1950	33
2.4	Cities with over 12,000 inhabitants, 1500–1800	37
3.1	Per-capita daily consumption of bread and grains in selected European areas, fourteenth to twentieth centuries	49
3.2	Indices of grain prices and deaths in England, France, and Tuscany	54
4.1	Spread of the plague in Europe, 1347–53	73
4.2	Annual deaths in Siena (partial series), fourteenth and fifteenth centuries (period average = 100)	82
4.3	Population change in the Holy Roman Empire during the Thirty Years War	86

4.4 Intensity of mortality crises in northern Italy,
central-southern Italy (Mezzogiorno), and
Tuscany, 1590–1749   89

5.1 Low nuptiality Europe, high nuptiality Europe,
and Hajnal's line, end of the eighteenth century   102

5.2 Age at first marriage, England and France,
seventeenth to nineteenth century   104

5.3 Age at first marriage for women in Tuscany,
1350–1800   106

5.4 Temporary migration systems in western
Europe, end of the eighteenth century   117

5.5 Selected extra-European emigrations in the
modern era   120

6.1 Distribution of European provinces by date of
onset of fertility decline   155

6.2 European emigration 1846–1924 (five-year
averages)   159

Series Editor's Preface

Europe is in the making. This is both a great challenge and one that can be met only by taking the past into account – a Europe without history would be orphaned and unhappy. Yesterday conditions today; today's actions will be felt tomorrow. The memory of the past should not paralyze the present: when based on understanding it can help us to forge new friendships, and guide us towards progress.

Europe is bordered by the Atlantic, Asia, and Africa, its history and geography inextricably entwined, and its past comprehensible only within the context of the world at large. The territory retains the name given it by the ancient Greeks, and the roots of its heritage may be traced far into prehistory. It is on this foundation – rich and creative, united yet diverse – that Europe's future will be built.

The Making of Europe is the joint initiative of five publishers of different languages and nationalities: Beck in Munich; Blackwell in Oxford; Critica in Barcelona; Laterza in Rome; and le Seuil in Paris. Its aim is to describe the evolution of Europe, presenting the triumphs but not concealing the difficulties. In their efforts to achieve accord and unity the nations of Europe have faced discord, division, and conflict. It is no purpose of this series to conceal these problems: those committed to the European enterprise will not succeed if their view of the future is unencumbered by an understanding of the past.

The title of the series is thus an active one: the time is yet to come when a synthetic history of Europe will be possible. The books we shall publish will be the work of leading historians, by no means all European. They will address crucial aspects of European history in every field – political, economic, social, religious, and cultural. They will draw on that long historiographical tradition which stretches back to Herodotus, as well as on those conceptions and ideas which have transformed historical enquiry in the recent decades of the twentieth century. They will write readably for a wide public.

Our aim is to consider the key questions confronting those involved in Europe's making, and at the same time to satisfy the curiosity of the world at large: in short, who are the Europeans? where have they come from? whither are they bound?

Jacques Le Goff

1

Numbers

Factors of Constraint and Factors of Choice

At the beginning of this past millennium the population of continental Europe – from the Urals to the Atlantic – numbered somewhere between 30 and 50 million; a modest figure for so vast a territory, roughly 10 million square kilometers, much of it well-suited to settlement and cultivation but still abundant in open and relatively unclaimed spaces. Over the next thousand years leading up to our day, the population of Europe has grown by a factor of ten or twenty, conquering the continent's open spaces and covering it with a dense network of settlements and a highly-developed urban system.

This great transformation did not take place gradually, but in alternating periods of growth, stagnation, and regression; and while we are familiar with the general pattern, the mechanisms behind it are less clear. Populations in fact have a remarkable capacity for varying the rhythm of their growth over time as the bionatural characteristics of human beings interact with the constraints of the environment. A few examples: in 1328 , the total number of hearths, or family units, in the districts (*baillages*) of Caux, Rouen, and Gisors was 164,519, divided into 1,891 parishes. Four centuries later, in virtually the same area, there were 165,871 hearths spread among 1,908 parishes. This remarkable stability of population and its distribution over time – considering that the intervening centuries included the dramatic upheavals caused by the Black Death and the Hundred Years War – can be explained by the relatively fixed nature of resources and their distribution. Rigidity of this sort is characteristic of many rural populations in which the available resources, mostly land, are more or less fixed. Several hundred kilometers to the east, beyond the Rhine, German censuses reveal instead an almost fourfold population increase for the industrial districts (*Kreise*) of Dusseldorf, Arnsberg, Aachen, and Münster over less than half a century; between 1861 and 1910 they grew from 1.5 to 5.8 million. What is especially significant about this increase is that only a small part of it was the result of immigration. We can instead reasonably assume that the population grew in response to an increased demand for labor and a rise in real income during a period of rapid economic growth. Further south, in the heart of Tuscany the population of Prato and the surrounding countryside declined from 26,000 inhabitants at the beginning of the fourteenth century to just over 8,000 in the first quarter of the fifteenth century, following the plague cycle initiated by the Black Death.

These three localized cases of relatively small populations – one stable, one growing, and one declining – are mirrored on a large scale as well. For a variety of complex reasons, the population of the Netherlands between 1650 and 1800 remained surprisingly steady, while forces similar to those which drove the growth of the industrial *Kreise* in Germany caused the population of England to quadruple in the nineteenth century (from 8.9 to 32.5 million). In eastern Europe – between the Vistula and the Urals – population growth on the scale of England's was instead the result of a great land surplus rather than industrialization. In the case of population decline, the century marked by the 1348 plague cycle saw the population of almost all of Europe decline sharply by somewhere between one-quarter and one-third. On the other hand, Ireland's precipitous population decline (from 8.2 to 4.5 million in the 60 years after 1841) derived from the demographic saturation of a collapsing agricultural system that culminated in the Great Famine and mass emigration.

There are good explanations for each of the local and national cases mentioned above: stationary rural population in the face of fixed resources and their rigid distribution; rapid increase accompanying the creation of new resources through industrialization or the opening of new frontiers; and demographic decline following epidemics or environmental crises. Two general points, however, need to be stressed. The first point is that the capacity or potential for growth, tied to the biological characteristics of the human species, is, as far as we know, fixed and does not vary from period to period or population to population. In other words, the essentially biological potential for reproduction and survival is a constant. What do instead vary as a function of environment, quality of life, and social factors are their concrete manifestations, namely births and deaths. For this reason, and this brings us to our second point, the history of population presents us with cases of both sustained growth and sustained decline, and indeed every imaginable scenario in between.

How is it then that given a single shared premise – the bionatural characteristics of the human species – we encounter such widely differing outcomes? In the simplest of terms we might say that demographic transformations are the result of a clash between the forces of constraint (linked to the environment and its resources in the broadest sense) and the forces of choice (socially and culturally determined and tied to individual, family, and collective demographic behaviors). The rules of this contest are not fixed because the interaction between choice and constraint alters them, but in general those rules change relatively gradually, which facilitates their study.

Among the factors of constraint, we can identify climate, space, land, settlement patterns, disease, energy, and food. These forces are interdependent to varying degrees but share two characteristics: their importance in relation to demographic change and their own slow rates of change. With regard to demographic change, the mechanisms are fairly straightforward and also well demonstrated. Space determines not only settlement patterns, density, and mobility, but also availability of land. Food, raw materials, and energy resources all derive from the land and are important determinants of human survival. Climate determines the usefulness of space, imposes limits on human settlement, and is linked to patterns of disease. Diseases, in turn, are linked to nutrition, and affect reproduction and survival directly. Space and settlement patterns are linked to population density and the transmission of diseases. These brief comments should already suggest the complexity of interrelationships and interactions among the forces of constraint.

The second characteristic of the forces of constraint is their permanence (space, climate, disease) or slow rate of change (land,

energy, food, settlement patterns). Permanence in this case is not
to be taken literally. Space can be created (take the example of land
reclamation) or destroyed (erosion); climate has long cycles; and
almost all diseases reappear over time or vary in their virulence.
Instead, let us consider permanence in terms of the time frame used
in demographic analysis – a generation or at most the length of a
human life. In general, these forces are relatively fixed and can be
modified by human intervention only very slowly. On the other
hand, food, natural resources, and energy supplies can of course be
increased by expanding cultivation or introducing new technology;
improved clothing and housing can moderate the effects of climate;
and measures to prevent infection and the spread of diseases can
limit their impact. Nonetheless, the cultivation of previously
unfarmed land, the development of new technology, better protection from climate, and the prevention of the spread of disease do
all take time. In the short and medium term (and often in the long
as well) a population must adapt to and live with the forces of
constraint.

The process of adaptation implies a degree of behavioral flexibility that allows a population to adjust its size and rate of growth
to the forces of constraint described above. This flexibility is in
some cases automatic, in some socially determined, and again in
others is the result of explicit choices. An example of automatic
adjustment is a reduction in height and weight in response to a
subsistence crisis. Such adaptations, within certain limits, do not
necessarily have negative effects on physical efficiency, health, and
survival. Beyond those limits, alimentary deprivation leads to
increased mortality, which might be selective (and so improve the
survival of future generations) but is not, by definition, adaptive.
Another type of adaptation which is almost automatic, and in any
case independent of human action, is the permanent or semi-
permanent immunity developed by those infected by certain
pathogens, such as smallpox and measles; or again, the mutual
adaptation of pathogen and human host that in the long term
brings about a sort of "domestication" of an initially violent
disease, like syphilis.

What is of particular interest to us, however, is what happens to
the pace of population growth as a result of changes in individual
and group behavior. In particular, we shall concentrate on those
powerful accelerators and decelerators of growth much studied by
demographers: nuptiality, a sort of "right" to reproduce; rhythm
of reproduction, which responds to both predominantly natural

factors, such as the duration of breastfeeding, and voluntary ones such as abortion and birth control; and mobility and migration, which shape settlement geography and size.

This is a study of long-term dynamics and attempts to follow two distinct but intertwined paths through many centuries. The first path traces the system of constraints that over time has conditioned demographic events. Three basic components shall be discussed: space and the availability of land; food production and nutritional regimes; and epidemiology. The second path focuses on the ways the demographic "system" works, or better still, on its different typologies. The components of the "system" – nuptiality, fertility and reproduction, mortality, mobility and migration – are subject to laws of operation and links of interdependency. How quickly variations in a population occur, and the changes in its structure and form, are dependent on the laws which govern the operation of the system. As we have already noted, the system of constraints is essentially rigid, not because the laws of operation are fixed in time (for example, the epidemiological component is extremely volatile) but because human intervention produces change only very slowly. The demographic system instead is variable, given its dependence on the changing adaptive choices of a population over time.

A Millennium of Demographic Development

It is only from the end of the Middle Ages that estimates of European population growth begin to be based on something more than guesswork. The curve in figure 1.1 traces a pattern of growth generally agreed upon, but whose accuracy rapidly deteriorates as we go back in time. The oldest detailed and reliable document that has come down to us is the *Domesday Book*, a land registry survey made in 1086 for almost all of present-day England which also includes a count of population. This document has allowed us to estimate that population to be about 1.1 million, give or take a margin of 20 percent. The degree of uncertainty is clearly much higher for those areas where quantitative evidence is more limited or else lacking altogether. Figure 1.1 also indicates some of the factors of constraint and measures of adaptation that have shaped long-term population growth.

The major phases of European population history are well-known and we shall discuss them in greater detail later on. There

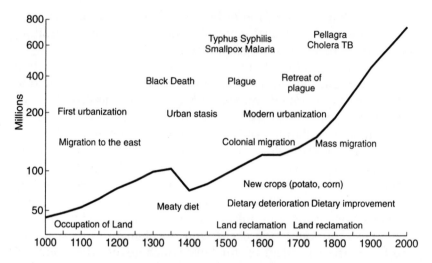

Figure 1.1   European population, 1000–2000

is no disputing that population grew steadily between the beginning of the millennium and the thirteenth century. New lands were
cultivated; population spread, especially to the east of the Elba and
the Oder rivers; thousands of new castles and villages were founded
and the walls of the major cities enlarged (see chapter 2). Other
signs point to a slowdown in growth by the end of the thirteenth
century, almost certainly the result of decreasing returns on land
newly cultivated in response to increased demand and population,
and more frequent subsistence crises – such as the severe crisis
around 1320 – and the resulting demographic crises. The effects of
the virulent European plague cycle begun in 1347 are well documented. Successive waves of the epidemic, which lost impetus in
the first half of the fifteenth century, dramatically reduced the
population of Europe. Only the magnitude of the decline is debat-
able. In the ensuing 150-year recovery, population once again came
to exceed pre-plague levels; lands were resettled and intensively
exploited; movement to the east began again; Europe for the first
time exported population as America became an outlet; and the
urban framework was fortified. The renewal lasted until the end of
the sixteenth century and then yielded to the crises of the seventeenth century: the Thirty Years War, a new plague cycle, and
serious subsistence crises. In the following century, the population
of Europe entered the modern era as plague vanished from the
continent, industrialization created new energy sources and the

means to produce resources, and important openings were made – not only to America in the west but also to the Urals and beyond in the east – which allowed for the departure of human resources and the arrival of material ones.

This overview – which for the moment I shall adhere to – requires some further elaboration. First, let us consider the nature of growth, meaning not just demographic increase or decline but also density of settlement and type of land use. Over the very long term there are two clear directions. One goes from southeast to north and northwest or from an original eastern Mediterranean nucleus to the Atlantic periphery. The other runs from west to east and represents a gradual penetration outward from the heart of Europe – the Rhine axis – to the open lands of Poland and Russia. A second consideration regards the transformation of Europe from an importer of people in the Middle Ages to an exporter in the modern and contemporary eras, becoming once again an importer at the close of the millennium. Finally, let us make an observation regarding long-term development patterns that can easily be discerned from the slope of the curve in figure 1.1. If we roughly divide the millennium into three periods separated by moments of stagnation or recession – the first ending with the end of the plague cycle, the second with the seventeenth- century crises, and the third with the present-day zero or negative population growth – then we find that the phases of population growth are very different. Population less than doubled in both the first period (1000–1400) and the second (1400–1700), while there was an approximately sixfold increase in the third period (1700–2000).

As I have already observed, it is only in the modern "statistical" era that one begins to encounter population figures that are something more than daring guesswork. Table 1.1 lists population figures from 1550 to 1900 for five countries (England, France, the Netherlands, Spain, Italy) which in 1550 represented approximately 52 percent of the population of Europe excluding Russia. For the period between 1700 and 1900 five other countries are added (Norway, Sweden, Ireland, Germany, Russia) which, together with the first five, made up between two-thirds and three-fourths of the population of Europe from the Atlantic to the Urals. These estimates for population size, distribution, and intensity of growth begin to offer some interpretative tools over the long term. For example, we see: faster growth in the peripheral Atlantic, Baltic and eastern regions of Europe as compared to the French-Italian-Iberian nucleus; an acceleration in the second half of the eighteenth

Table 1.1 Population of selected European countries, 1500–1900

Year	Ireland	England	Norway	Sweden	Netherlands	France	Germany	Russia	Italy	Spain	Europe
Total inhabitants (millions)											
1500	–	–	–	–	1.0	–	–	–	9.0	–	84
1550	–	3.0	–	–	1.3	19.5	–	–	11.5	5.3	97
1600	–	4.1	–	–	1.5	19.6	–	–	13.5	6.7	111
1650	–	5.2	–	–	1.9	20.3	–	–	11.7	7.0	112
1700	2.5	4.9	0.52	1.37	1.9	22.6	16	16	13.6	7.4	125
1750	3.2	5.8	0.64	1.78	1.9	24.6	17	25	15.8	8.6	146
1800	5.3	8.6	0.88	2.35	2.1	29.3	24.5	39	18.3	10.6	195
1850	6.6	16.6	1.41	3.48	3.1	36.3	35.4	60	24.7	14.8	288
1900	4.5	30.4	2.24	5.14	5.1	40.6	56.4	109.7	33.8	18.6	422
Percentage of European total											
1500	–	–	–	–	1.1	–	–	–	10.7	–	–
1550	–	3.1	–	–	1.3	20.1	–	–	11.9	5.4	41.8[1]
1600	–	3.7	–	–	1.4	17.7	–	–	12.2	6.0	40.9[1]
1650	–	4.7	–	–	1.7	18.1	–	–	10.4	6.3	41.1[1]
1700	2.0	3.9	0.4	1.1	1.5	18.0	12.8	12.8	10.9	5.9	69.4[2]
1750	2.2	3.9	0.4	1.2	1.3	16.9	11.6	17.1	10.8	5.9	71.4[2]
1800	2.7	4.4	0.4	1.2	1.1	15.0	12.6	20.0	9.4	5.5	72.3[2]
1850	2.3	5.8	0.5	1.2	1.1	12.6	12.3	20.8	8.6	5.1	70.3[2]
1900	1.1	7.2	0.5	1.2	1.2	9.6	13.4	26.0	8.0	4.4	72.6[2]

Table 1.1 continued

Year	Ireland	England	Norway	Sweden	Netherlands	France	Germany	Russia	Italy	Spain	Europe
Annual rate of growth per thousand											
1550–1600	–	6.3	–	–	3.6	0.1	–	–	3.2	4.8	2.7
1600–50	–	4.8	–	–	4.5	0.7	–	–	-2.9	1.0	0.2
1650–1700	–	-1.1	–	–	0.3	2.2	–	–	3.0	1.0	2.2
1700–50	4.9	3.1	4.3	5.3	0.3	1.7	1.2	8.9	3.0	3.1	3.1
1750–1800	10.1	8.0	6.2	5.5	1.5	3.5	7.3	8.9	2.9	4.2	5.8
1800–50	4.4	13.2	9.5	7.9	7.7	4.3	7.4	8.6	6.0	6.6	7.8
1850–1900	-7.7	12.2	9.3	7.8	10.3	2.2	9.3	12.1	6.3	4.6	7.6
1550–1700	–	3.3	–	–	2.8	1.0	–	–	1.1	2.3	–
1700–1900	2.9	9.1	7.3	6.6	4.9	2.9	6.3	9.6	4.6	4.6	6.1

Notes [1] 5 countries as percentage of European total; [2] 10 countries as percentage of European total

Source: See note to table 1.2

Table 1.2 Doubling and doubling time for selected European populations, 1550, 1700, 1800

Country	1550[1]		1700[1]		1800[1]	
	Year of doubling	Years elapsed	Year of doubling	Years elapsed	Year of doubling	Years elapsed
England	1760	210	1810	110	1850	50
Netherlands	1825	275	1870	170	1886	86
France	1900	350	1920	220	1985	185
Italy	1840	240	1870	170	1886	86
Spain	1800	250	1850	150	1922	122
Norway	–	–	1827	127	1881	81
Sweden	–	–	1820	120	1886	86
Ireland	–	–	1795	95	never	–
Germany	–	–	1838	138	1889	89
Russia	–	–	1780	80	1875	75
Austria-Hungary	–	–	–	–	1902	102
Switzerland	–	–	–	–	1904	104
Portugal	–	–	–	–	1923	123
Europe	1800	250	1835	135	1890	90

Note: [1] Years in the columns are those when the population for the year heading the column doubled. Years elapsed are the number of years between the two dates. Population estimates after 1800 are taken from official national sources and from G. Sundbärg, *Aperçus statistiques internationaux*, Imprimerie Royale, Stockholm 1908.

Sources: For the other data (in some cases elaborated by the author) the following sources were used. England: A. E. Wrigley and R. Schofield, *The Population History of England, 1541–1871*, Arnold, London, 1981; B. H. Slicher van Bath, "Historical Demography and the Social and Economic Development of the Netherlands." *Daedulus*, Spring 1968, 609. France: J. Dupâquier and B. Lepetit, "La Peuplade." In J. Dupâquier ed., *Histoire de la population française*, vol. II: De la renaissance à 1789. PUF, Paris, 1988. Italy: L. Del Panta, M. Livi Bacci, G. Pinto, E. Sonnino, *La popolazione italiana dal medioevo a oggi*, Laterza, Rome-Bari, 1996. Spain: J. Nadal, *La población española, siglos XVI a XX*, Ariel, Barcelona, 1984. Sweden: D. S. Thomas, *Social and Economic Aspects of Swedish Population Movements*, New York, 1941. Norway: S. Dyrvik "Historical Demography in Norway: A Short Survey, 1601–1801." *Scandinavian Economic History Review*, 20, 1, 1972. Germany: J. J. Sheenan, *German History, 1770–1866*, Clarendon Press, Oxford, 1950. Ireland: K. H. Connell, *The Population of Ireland (1745–1845)*, Clarendon Press, Oxford, 1950. Russia: estimates for European territory, 1914 borders, based on F. Lorimer, *The Population of the Soviet Union: History and Prospects*. League of Nations, Geneva, 1946.

century and throughout the nineteenth; the development of England demographically from a small to a large country; and the ever greater importance of Russia.

The same data also shows that before the nineteenth century, which is to say in the demographic "old regime" when resources like food, raw materials, and energy were all directly linked to the availability of land, a doubling of the population led to fundamental social changes. In the absence of accumulation and an improved standard of life, a demographic doubling in fact signified a roughly twofold increase in demand for food, raw materials, primary resources, and energy, and consequently required greater production without significant changes in technology and productivity. Table 1.2 gives the years when a series of European countries doubled their populations following 1550, 1700, and 1800. For Europe as a whole, the 1550 population doubled in 1800 after two and one-half centuries; the 1700 population doubled in 1835; and only 90 years elapsed before the 1800 population achieved the same.

We have reliable data about population growth after 1550 for five countries. The earliest case for a doubling of population is England, after two centuries, and the latest is France after three and one half. In a sampling of ten countries, the earliest doubling of the 1700 population takes place in Russia, after 80 years, and the latest is after 220, again in France. Finally, for the 13 countries whose 1800 populations are shown, the earliest doubling takes place in England after only 50 years. The latest doubling – that of Ireland – has yet to occur, as that country today barely maintains its 1800 population level as a result of the interruption in growth sustained in the mid-nineteenth century due to the Great Famine and emigration. The message in any case is clear: in the old demographic regime, when four-fifths of the population depended on the land for their livelihood, the time it took for a population to double was between two and three centuries; whereas beginning in the eighteenth century, industrialization reduced this time period to about a century.

Figure 1.2 offers us a clearer picture of growth at the beginning of the contemporary age by depicting the geographic component of the 1800 population doublings. We are working with large aggregates here, and subnational groupings are made only for a few large nations. The results are interesting: in certain peripheral areas such as England and southern Russia population had already doubled before 1850, while in others, such as Scotland and eastern

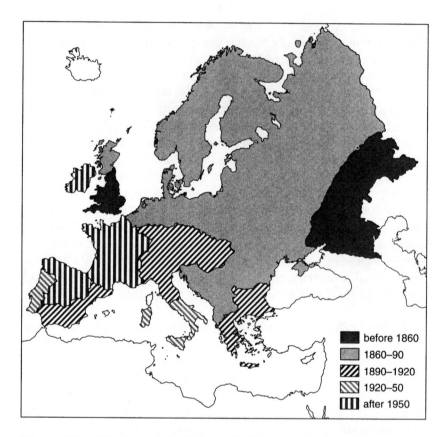

Figure 1.2   Timing of doubling of 1800 populations

Russia, it did so by 1870, and the Scandinavian, German, Polish, and Baltic populations doubled by 1890. In most of the Mediterranean and France much more time was needed; until after the first World War in some cases and even after the second World War in others.

Slow Change in Old Regime Societies

The old demographic regime, which lasted more or less until the start of the Industrial Revolution, was characterized by slow growth over long periods of time and by the remarkable stability of its mechanisms. In chapter 5 I shall discuss these characteristics in greater depth, but for the moment I should point out that "slow" needs to be understood here in relation to the growth rates for the past 50 years, when poor countries have experienced annual rates of increase between 2 and 4 percent, at least an order of magnitude greater than that of European populations in the medieval and early modern periods. Yet in fact, a sustained increase of two or three per 1,000 – which leads to a doubling in two or three centuries – cannot be divorced from a comparable rate of economic growth, certainly considerable for systems with little capital and relatively fixed technological capabilities.

A few figures will help to clarify these statements. Old regime societies were essentially agricultural, and so agricultural progress drove gradual social change. It is reasonable to estimate that roughly three-fourths to four-fifths of the workforce were engaged in farming. In Sweden and Finland, Russia, Austria and Hungary, Spain, Portugal, and Ireland – countries that industrialized late – censuses from the second half of the nineteenth century reveal proportions of nearly this size, between two-thirds and four-fifths. For earlier periods, estimates are even higher: 80 percent in France at the start of the eighteenth century and in Sweden by the middle of that same century; 75 percent in Austria in 1790; 78 percent in Bohemia in 1756; 72 percent in the United States in 1820. And as we shall see in chapter 2, these figures are consistent with the prevailing low levels of urbanization. In Europe as a whole less than 6 percent of all people lived in cities bigger than 10,000 inhabitants in 1500, and in 1700 still fewer than 9 percent did. Those who lived in small villages or in the countryside were mostly peasants, share-croppers, and small landowners. This population was bound to the land, and its survival and progress relied upon developments in farming. In this case, the obstacles to growth were not related to workforce but to capital (primarily the availability of land) and a relatively stagnant technology. A large part of the demographic history of Europe is inextricably tied to the history of settlement and the occupation of new territories: beginning with the Germanic colonization of the east between the eleventh and thirteenth centuries right through to the massive transoceanic migrations to the Americas. While it has been both costly and difficult to acquire land throughout the modern era, nonetheless land hunger could drive costly land reclamation projects. Moreover, once the peoples of Europe had settled most of the continent, there remained only one seemingly unavoidable check on their power to master the environment: the availability of energy. As Carlo Cipolla has observed, "the fact that the main sources of energy other than man's muscular work remained basically plants and animals must have set a limit to the possible expansion of the energy supply in any given agricultural society of the past. The limiting factor in this regard is ultimately the supply of land." It was the introduction of the steam engine, an inanimate energy converter, that ultimately supplied a new source of energy; and that, perhaps, was the most significant difference between the early modern era and the contemporary one.

The pace of technological progress is also fairly slow, though already in the Middle Ages there were important geographical differences in productivity linked not only to natural factors but to different agricultural methods. This observation is supported by one of the few available measures of productivity for the early modern world, namely the harvest-to-sowing ratio for grains, the primary foodstuff. The great agricultural historian Slicher van Bath has shown that yields were definitely on the rise at the beginning of the seventeenth century in the agriculturally advanced countries of England and the Netherlands, with ratios of 7:1 in the sixteenth century, 9:1 in the late seventeenth, and 10:1 in the late eighteenth. Meanwhile yield remained steady (around 7:1) in France, Italy, and Spain between 1500 and 1800, and steady, though lower (around 4:1), in northern, eastern, and central Europe. The inevitable outcome of relatively stable productivity is the impossibility of increasing production when the land under cultivation is fixed. Productivity in turn influences nutritional levels, yet another factor of constraint for demographic growth. In general, following the crisis of the late Middle Ages – which coincided with a shrinking population and a richer diet – nutritional levels seem to have declined, only beginning to recover in some areas in the eighteenth century, and in other outlying, poorer ones not until the nineteenth, if not the twentieth. By employing what may seem exaggerated generalizations – and so overlooking the progress resulting from improvements in cultivation, the introduction of new crops, development of livestock raising, specialization, and the contribution of trade – we can see that the major demographic trends unfolded in a context where stability dominated, though change indeed occurred and was important.

In figure 1.1 we can see that the major demographic cycles since the late Middle Ages have been strongly conditioned by disease, a factor largely independent of human living conditions. But these cycles have also been closely linked to economic forces that influence demographic systems and force them to change. Historical wage and price series reveal fundamental changes that are linked to the great demographic cycles, as revealed in figure 1.3, taken from Slicher van Bath. This model is typically Malthusian: during the negative phase of a demographic cycle – for example, the century after the Black Death or the seventeenth century – the decline or stagnation of population, and so demand, leads to a reduction of prices and at the same time an increase in the demand for labor, and so wages. Between the mid-fourteenth and mid-fifteenth centuries, for example, wheat prices were more than halved, only to later rise again. As Slicher van Bath writes: "Then came the recession of the fourteenth and fifteenth centuries. The population had been reduced by epidemics, and because the area of cultivation was now larger than necessary for the people's sustenance, cereal prices fell. Through the decline in population, labour became scarce, so that money wages and real wages rose considerably." Strong demographic recovery in the sixteenth century reversed the situation: increasing demand forced up the price of grain and other foods while real wages declined, a trend which

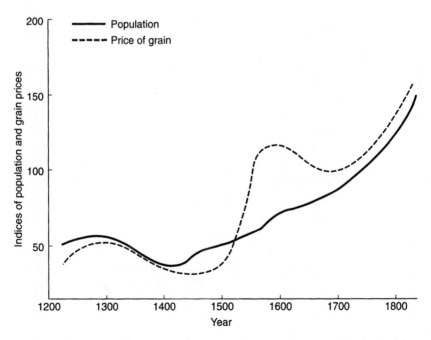

Figure 1.3 Population and grain prices in Europe, 1200–1800 (1721–45 = 100)

reached a critical point at the beginning of the seventeenth century. The demographic slowdown of the seventeenth century and the catastrophic decline of the German population as a result of the Thirty Years War are among the causes of a new inversion of the cycle (accompanied by declining demand and prices and increasing wages) that continued until the mid-eighteenth century, when demographic growth reversed the situation once again.

Interpretive Choices

We have several options – each reasonable though not all practical – to choose from in attempting to draw a coherent picture of the development of the population of Europe. Our path to understanding both how a demographic system works and how it changes over time is to examine the interaction between the forces of constraint and the forces of choice described above. Our choice of sources and interpretations are in keeping with this approach. In the ensuing discussion, macro and aggregate features are privileged over micro and individual ones; general trends are preferred to particular moments or events; and broad distinctions or geographical uniformities take precedence over localized analyses. This approach has certain obvious advantages and disadvantages. A macro or aggregate analysis tends to reconstruct components and mechanisms of the demographic system with reference to population as a whole. It is based on the estimate or measure of the sum of population events. Microanalysis instead depends on genealogies and family reconstitutions and ties demographic events to specific individuals. A name-based micro study permits a detailed reconstruction of the mechanisms of formation, growth, and dissolution of individual families. The reconstitution process however is painstaking and requires the availability of complete birth, marriage, and death records by name (only possible from the seventeenth century on); and it can only be used for small groups, such as families who stay in one place (family reconstitution in the face of emigration is either very difficult or impossible). In this way typical behaviors are examined in great detail, but there always remains some doubt whether they apply to a population as a whole. Henry and Gautier developed nominative family reconstitution in their study of the village of Crulai in Normandy. They managed to reconstruct everything the curious demographer could possibly want to know about fertility, as well as important details regarding nuptiality and mortality, but confessed to knowing almost nothing about numerical changes in the group (though they were inclined to assume that population was a fairly stationary 1,000 through the seventeenth and eighteenth centuries). The total population of early modern France, then, and its fluctuations are still mostly conjecture, despite the great work done in the field of historical demography. To be sure, we have come a long way since Montesquieu, the Maréchal de Saxe, or Mirabeau, who in the eighteenth century still thought the population of France to be in decline. A preference for macroanalysis derives from the desire to give a coherent picture of the facts – or hypotheses – regarding the key demographic trends, beginning with population size. The study of individual behaviors may then be minimized, but is not completely ignored. Nor is the motive behind this choice solely that of simplifying a vast topic. It derives instead from the fact that the major factors of constraint – land availability, space, food resources, disease – are highly dependent not so much on the range of behaviors of different segments of the population as on the acceleration, density, and growth of the population as a whole. Individual behaviors – which micro-analysis describes so well – are often produced out of a vice of contrasting forces: demography on the one side and the factors of constraint on the other.

For a similar reason, I have preferred to look at major trends as opposed to the more refined study of historical events (with the exception of crises, to which I dedicate considerable space), and to use geographical data from large areas rather than small. Ideally this work might constitute the preface to a demographic study of the great variability of demographic behaviors seen in the light of a specific time and place.

2

Space

Geography and Environment

Human beings, like other living species, need space for procuring the resources necessary for survival, for numerical growth, and for social organization. This need was especially strong in old demographic regimes when populations were almost completely dependent upon the land for food, natural resources, and energy. Though seemingly a commonplace, this connection is virtually ignored in studies of population history, apparently because it smacks of biological or natural determinism. And yet the history – and not just the demographic history – of the peoples of Europe is tied in many ways to the conquest of space. As Malthus wrote: "plenty of rich land, to be had for little or nothing, is so powerful a cause of population as to overcome all other obstacles." We need then to assign just importance to the relationship between population and space; and in particular to four specific points.

The first regards the natural characteristics of the European space: its dimensions, environmental conditions, accessibility, and uses. For our purposes, I will highlight only those geonatural features that are particularly connected to population. The second point involves the occupation of uninhabited or sparsely populated lands, still abundant in the early centuries of the millennium. The third point I shall treat is the settlement and rendering productive of land that though available previously had not been actively occupied or exploited: deforestation, land reclamation, and swamp draining. Finally, the fourth point involves the intensification of occupation and exploitation of lands for both agricultural production and settlement. The second, third, and fourth points are closely linked, and though they are logically successive stages of a process, in practice they often occured simultaneously. Our discussion of population and space will touch on several demographic themes including mobility, migration, settlement patterns, and urbanization; themes to which we shall return in greater detail later on.

Up until the Industrial Revolution – a period I shall often refer to as the "old regime" in order to distinguish European demographic behavior prior to the transformations of the contemporary era – humans were almost entirely dependent upon space and land. As Cipolla writes, "It is safe to say that until the Industrial Revolution man continued to rely mainly on plants, animals, and other men for energy – plants for food and fuel, animals for food and mechanical energy, and other men for mechanical energy. . . There is no evidence for precise quantitative assessments, but on the basis of general traits one may venture to say that eighty to eighty-five percent of the total energy income at any time before the Industrial Revolution must have been derived from plants, animals, and men."

Continental Europe occupies roughly 10 million square kilometers and is well defined on the west by the Atlantic Ocean; on the south by the Mediterranean Sea, the Black Sea, the Caucasus mountains, and the Caspian Sea; and on the north by the Arctic Ocean. To the east its border is less clear: the chain of the Ural mountains and then the Ural river to the Caspian Sea. It is in any case a conventional border: the Ural mountains form a barrier that is both easily identified and easily penetrated, while to the south a wide entryway extends for several hundred kilometers to the Caspian Sea, the initiation of a series of steppes that stretch uninterrupted for thousands of kilometers all the way from China to the northern shore of the Black Sea. This huge expanse "narrows" to about 600 kilometers at the entrance to Europe, and it is through this great portal that for thousands of years the great migrations that shaped European population passed.

The European continent is in reality the western end of the much larger Eurasian land mass. It lies between longitudes 10° west and 50° east and latitudes 35° and 70° north and is characterized by a number of features that have been important for its population history. The first is climate, the east–west differences as much as the north–south. Of overriding importance in this regard is the moderating effect of the Atlantic Ocean, which gradually recedes as one travels east. Winter temperatures, for example, along a single latitude generally grow colder as one moves east while those along a single longitude tend to remain stationary (within certain limits) as one moves north to south. For example, the winter temperatures in Bergen, Norway and Lyon, France – on the same meridian but 1,500 kilometers apart – are basically the same. West of the Venice – Hamburg line the average temperature in January, the coldest month of the year, is above 0° C, including the Norwegian coastal area near the Arctic circle. East of that line the January average rapidly decreases and reaches -15° C along the line of the Urals. This gradient entails a complex series of climatic characteristics that help to explain historic population movements. Initially that movement flowed from southeast to northwest (towards more northern lands, but ones moderated by the influence of the Atlantic) and only later, and relatively recently (in the last millennium), from west to east toward climatically more hostile lands. In addition, climate affects the length of the agricultural growing season, which can be approximated by the time between the last frost of one "winter" and the first of the next. In southern Europe that season extends to more than 300 days while in the northern parts of Russia it lasts only two or three months.

Another important characteristic that has been conducive to European settlement is the extensive coastline in proportion to the overall surface area of the continent, owing in part to its extensive internal seas: the Mediterranean Sea, the Black Sea, and the Baltic Sea. A geographical measure of the accessibility of internal spaces, the European ratio between coastline and surface area is considerably higher than in other continents. Similarly, Europe's extensive and rich hydrographic network facilitates the penetration of the continent: one has only to think of important rivers such as the Volga, the Danube, and the Rhine. The exploitation of rivers and coastline opened up the continent to both people and things.

The fact that Europe has relatively few high mountains is another geographical feature relevant to our discussion. The truly mountainous areas of the continent – altitudes above 1,000 meters – account for barely 7 percent of the total surface area while roughly two-thirds of that total is below 300 meters. The average altitude in Europe is less than 300 meters, as compared to almost 600 meters in the Americas and over 1,000 meters in Asia. The high mountain ranges that do exist in Europe have contributed more to dividing up the population of Europe than impeding its spread, while the major theater of European population over the last thousand years has been the great European plain that extends from the north of France through all of northern Europe to the great open spaces of Russia.

We need then to keep in mind the following: a moderate climate that varies as much east – west as it does north – south and exercises an important influence on settlement patterns and agriculture; the great accessibility and penetrability of the continent; and the existence of a vast and almost uninterrupted plain (of good soil) that favored migrations and the settling of peoples.

The Conquest of Space before the Black Death

Until the eighteenth century European agriculture responded to the need to feed a growing population by expanding the area farmed and so production. Traditional methods of crop rotation and long fallow periods kept yields low; productivity was basically stagnant, as the more or less fixed ratio between seed and harvest for those grains that satisfied the bulk of nutritional needs testified. A majority of the population was necessarily nutritionally self-sufficient, a situation that made specialization, division of labor, and the development of large-scale trading difficult. Of course there were notable exceptions: both Flanders and the Po Valley, for example, achieved high levels of productivity. But since there is no reason to believe that nutritional levels improved between the beginning of the millennium and the eighteenth century, it is likely that the tripling of the population during that period corresponded to a similar expansion of cultivation, or an even greater one in the case of decreasing yields.

In the centuries preceding the Black Death of the fourteenth century, the demographic settlement of the continent acquired the outlines of a relatively stable system, though any notion of stability of course requires qualification. The great blending of populations in Europe caused by migrations from outside the continent did not end in the ninth century when nomadic peoples coming from the steppes settled down in Hungary, nor in the thirteenth century with the Christian *reconquista* of the Iberian peninsula. It continued in the open spaces of the eastern steppes up to the eighteenth century and with the ebb and flow of Turks in the Balkans. Nevertheless, major immigration into Europe basically ceased by the end of the

Middle Ages; the frontier marking the limit of permanently and densely inhabited lands had shifted well to the east; and the urban framework of the continent had taken shape.

The early centuries of the new millennium saw intense population movement to the east for the purpose of settling, a process that continued, in spite of demographic decline caused by the Black Death, with varying rhythm right up to the nineteenth century. That movement consisted of Germanic groups gradually recovering territories occupied by ethnic Slavs during the preceding millennium. In addition to this major eastern thrust there were lesser migrations in other directions as well: from north to south following the *reconquista* of the Iberian peninsula; northward by the Scandinavians; and southward in Russia in search of more stable borders.

The initial phase of the great movement eastward began on a large scale in the eleventh century and ended with the plague of the fourteenth century. Population basically followed three paths: to the south following the natural path of the Danube river in the direction of the Hungarian plain; in the center into the lowlands of Thuringia, Saxony and Silesia, north of the central mountains of Bohemia; and finally to the north along the Baltic coast, avoiding the German swamps and forests that hindered migration and settlement, a migration that led to the eventual founding of cities like Rostock and Königsberg. Slavic settlement was pushed to the east and penetrated by the Germanic lands of Austria to the south, Silesia in the center, and Pomerania and Prussia to the north. Nor was this penetration limited to these relatively saturated regions (which nonetheless maintained Slavic elements), but divided and fragmented, extending into the Baltic provinces, Volhynia, Ukraine, Transylvania, Hungary, and still further east.

Led by princes – such as the Margrave of Meissen – bishops, and, later, the knights of the Teutonic Order, the colonization process was well financed. In the eleventh and twelfth centuries colonization reached beyond the line of the Elba and Saale rivers, the eastern limit of the Carolingian empire and of Germanic settlement. During the twelfth century Holstein, Mecklenburg, and Brandenburg were all settled, and in the thirteenth the migration penetrated eastern Brandenburg, Pomerania, Silesia, and northern Moravia, going beyond the Oder river. The settlement of Prussia, extending beyond the Vistula, peaked in the fourteenth century. Germanic expansion instead did not penetrate Bohemia, the interior of Pomerania, and Lusazia. Eastern expansion continued even after the declines

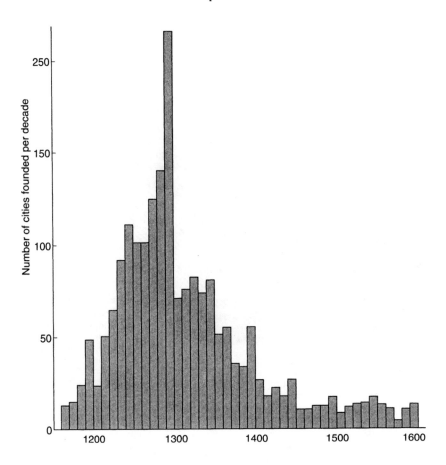

Figure 2.1 Founding of cities in central Europe

Source: N. J. C. Pounds, *An Historical Geography of Europe*, Cambridge
University Press, Cambridge, 1990 (from W. Abel, *Gestichte der deutschen
Landwirtschaft*, Stuttgart Ulmer, 1962), p. 46

and abandonments that accompanied the long demographic crisis
of the fourteenth and fifteenth centuries. As we see in figure 2.1 the
rhythm of the colonization process can be followed by tracing the
founding of new cities, a process that peaked around 1300.

This *Drang nach Osten* was by no means the only large scale
colonization effort of the Middle Ages. The *reconquista* of the
Iberian peninsula saw Christians penetrate southward into areas of
Arab domination, a process basically completed when Ferdinand
III (the Saint) took Seville in 1248. Only Granada and its small

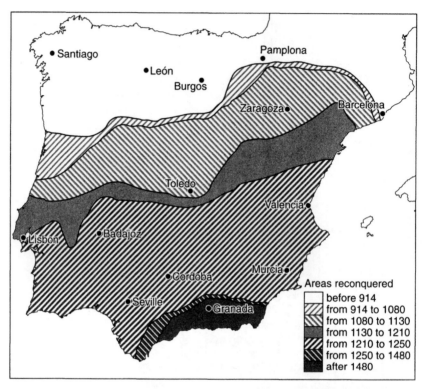

Figure 2.2 Steps in the *reconquista* of the Iberian peninsula, 900–1500

Source: D. W. Lomax, *La Reconquista*, Editorial Crítica, Barcelona, 1984

surrounding territory held out until 1492. The *reconquista* (figure 2.2) was accompanied by the founding of villages and the gradual cultivation of the territories surrounding them. After the fall of Seville, a Royal Commission presided over by Bishop Segovia Raimundo distributed the captured land and resources to Christians. The territories of the Christian kingdom, however, were ample and sparsely populated; they were peopled not so much out of land hunger as for political and military reasons. The loose network of settlements, especially in the territories of the Crown of Castile, were prone to instability, or had been founded at the expense of older ones. The attempt to repopulate the Guadalquivir Valley during the thirteenthth century in fact failed; the problem, it seems, was too much land in relation to population, a problem perhaps exacerbated by inadequate equipment and organization.

At the other end of Europe, Scandinavians expanded beyond the continent into marginal and difficult climatic zones. In the ninth century, the Norwegians, unified by Harald the Fairhaired, occupied Iceland. The *landnamabok*, an exceptional document that dates to around 930, reveals a sizable settlement of 30–35,000 people. Norwegians also settled on the Shetland and Orkney Islands and later established an unstable settlement in Greenland. In addition to these few daring episodes, we can trace the gradual agricultural settlement of the Baltic Islands, Scania, and central Sweden.

These various movements helped to create a fairly stable settlement network for continental Europe that even the depopulation following the Black Death – visible in the great number of villages abandoned- could test but not completely upset. Much of European space came to be occupied not only politically but also physically, by hamlets, villages, castles, and cities in a structure which proved to be stable and resistant.

The medieval population movement outlined in the preceding pages raises many important demographic questions. The first regards the dimensions of the migration, for which our sources are largely conjectural. Kuhn has studied the various available documents – censuses, cadastres, village foundation, etc. – and estimates that in the twelfth century about 200,000 people left old Germany for lands between the Elbe and the Oder. The thirteenth-century migration wave that populated Pomerania and Silesia was probably of similar dimensions. According to Aubin, between 1200 and 1360 about 1200 villages were founded in Silesia and 1400 in eastern Prussia, corresponding to a total 60,000 farms and about 300,000 people. These numbers are relatively small but derive from a modest total Germanic population of about 6 million in 1200. Even assuming that these estimates are well below the true figures and that the population movements were two to three times greater in size, we are still left with a moderate migration of not more than one per 1,000 per year. Nevertheless, the impact of that "founding" migration was great considering that by the end of the nineteenth century its descendants, the Germanic population east of the Elbe – Saale line, was about 30 million.

At this point we must ask some important questions. First of all: can the eastern migration be considered – as it traditionally has been – as a movement driven by land hunger following increased agricultural density in the sending areas, that density itself the result of vigorous demographic growth? There are reasons to question this traditional explanation: in fact, the density of the sending areas (especially at the beginning of the movement) was still low; the migration itself was modest in relation to the vigorous natural growth of the time; and there were still some relatively open areas near to home. In reality, the emigration wave seems to have several more likely explanations: the high level of organization and technology of the departing population in relation to the less advanced indigenous Slavs in the destination areas; highly favorable conditions for peasant settlement; and, not least of all, the fairly short distances between the two areas. The German immigrants had ploughs, axes, and tools for deforesting and cultivating difficult terrain, while the Slavs hunted, fished, and practiced itinerant farming, abandoning their fields once they had exhausted their fertility. Aubin describes the circumstances and characteristics of an immigration which was organized and planned by the clergy and aristocracy, the knightly orders (Templars and Teutonic knights), and the major religious orders (Cistercian and Premonstratensian monks). In particular he cites: (a) the ability to plan and choose lands, and to measure and divide them, taking into account both water supply and flood risks (these lands were mostly uncultivated); (b) the capital to finance the travel of the migrants, feed them until the first harvest, and distribute seed, tools, and raw materials; (c) the existence of colonization entrepreneurs who mediated between landowners and peasants; (d) the typical allocation per family of a 20-hectare farm or *hufe* (17 hectares for the Flemish or small model and 24 hectares for the large or Frankish model) and an average establishment of a 200–300-person village (scattered houses were the exception); and (e) the fact that the land was free of encumbrances for many years and could be willed, sold, or abandoned.

The existence of such favorable conditions and the necessity of using recruiting agents has led Aubin to believe that the supply of land far exceeded the demand:

> The great extension of the movement is only explained by the fact that colonists bred colonists; for all over the world settlers have big families. Migration from Old Germany in many cases slackened early. Conditions of tenure in the colonized areas also encouraged this colonization by colonists' families. Law or custom favoured the undivided inheritance of peasant holdings; so there were many younger sons without land.

If we follow this line of thinking, then the hypothesis is no longer plausible that strong demographic growth (which there was) as well as land hunger led to emigration. Instead it seems that the process was self-propulsive, favored by an abundance of land and the superior organization and technology of the colonists as compared to the transient and agriculturally less sophisticated indigenous population. The possibility of trading a small farm in one's native land for a property of 20 odd hectares must have been appealing. These favorable conditions in turn generated strong demographic growth in the colonizing groups and so new waves of emigration. The colonization process then may not have required sizable migrations over long distances, but, instead a continuous forward march by new and numerous generations descended from the original colonists.

Moreover, the importance of a "foundation" effect exercised by certain migratory movements that take place under favorable conditions is well documented. For instance, France made a minimal effort to populate the St. Lawrence River Valley in Canada. And yet today's 6 million French Canadians are, for the most part, the direct descendants of the 15,000 pioneers that emigrated from northwest France in the seventeenth century, of which only about 5,000 managed to establish families in the New World. Favorable conditions for survival, high nuptiality and fertility, and abundant resources made their rapid multiplication possible. There are of course contrary examples: the attempt of the grand duke of Tuscany to settle the Italian Maremma in the eighteenth century with colonists from Lorraine failed almost immediately, largely because of high mortality caused by malaria; and the king of Spain's attempt to settle Germans in the Sierra Morena during that same century was no more successful.

The colonization to the east instead had lasting results. A stable and prosperous class of landowning farmers developed: a political and social order was established which had a positive impact also on the indigenous population; marketplaces were expanded, opening channels of export to the west, so that by 1250 Brandenburg exported grain to Holland and England which allowed for agricultural specialization in those countries.

Again Eastward and Southward

Despite the fourteenth- and fifteenth-century plague catastrophe, subsequent population decline, and the abandonment of lands and villages, population continued to move eastward. The settlement frontier was in constant flux with numerous fringe areas and islands beyond it. The colonization of conquered Slavic lands became an integral part of seventeenth- and eighteenth-century Prussian and Austrian territorial politics. Following the Thirty Years War, Germanic colonists from Silesia and Brandenburg settled in Pomerania. Frederick II of Prussia acquired Silesia in 1740 and planned to Germanize it with a large transfer of colonists. It is estimated that between the late seventeenth century and the end of Frederick II's reign (1786), 430,000 people migrated into the expanded Prussia and this contributed to the striking growth of that state and the ultimate Germanization of its territories. Meanwhile migration to Hungary proceeded apace, and Fenske estimates a population transfer between 1689 and the end of the eighteenth century of about 350,000 persons. Yet another channel, encouraged by Catherine the Great of Russia, flowed toward the Volga regions. The empress, anxious to consolidate her eastern territories, initiated a true immigration policy in 1762–4 that lasted to the end of the century. Still others currents moved in the direction of the Black Sea at the end of the century. Poland, too was an important destination.

The colonization of the lower Volga river valley deserves further comment. The imperial census of 1897 records roughly 400,000 inhabitants of German origin (less returnees, assimilations, etc.) in the Samara and Saratov districts (which include the Volga colonies). Here is another example of the great impact a small group of colonists can make; the original 27,000 settlers – who, again, arrived between 1762 and 1764 – multiplied by a factor of at least 15 in the space of little more than four generations, testimony to the growth potential of well-planned settlements with good land and adequate organizational and technical abilities.

The other trajectory of conquest and settlement, especially in the eighteenth century, lay within the Russian empire and pointed southward in the direction of the Black Sea. In addition to the Volga colony, 1764 witnessed colonization of the province of New Russia (between the Bug and Donets rivers), then the southern frontier of the Empire. This movement took root following the defeat of the Turks in the Russo-Turkish war of 1768–74 and with the encouragement of Potemkin, appointed governor of New Russia and Azov, following the annexation of Crimea in 1783. McNeill writes, "By 1796, therefore, when the Empress Catherine II died, the Russian flood had engulfed the once-formidable Tartar society, reducing the remnant to a culturally decapitated, economically impoverished and politically helpless enclave. All the vast steppe region north of the Crimea and west of the Don had been occupied by landlords and settlers." The area was still intermittently and sparsely inhabited:

> Yet new towns had arisen (Kherson in 1778; Nikolaev in 1788; Odessa in 1794) and throve as administrative centers and grain ports; and with urban life the manifestations of higher culture – flavored by a distinctly cosmopolitan tincture owing to mixture of Greeks, Bulgars, Poles, Jews and a few western Europeans – soon appeared. In short, civilization in the Russian style came in with a rush all along the northern Black Sea coast and hinterland.

It is estimated that between 1724 and 1859 the Russian population of the New South grew from 1.6 to 14.5 million thanks to immigration from central and northern Russia towards the fertile black lands and steppes of the south. Nonetheless, at the end of the eighteenth century the demographic density of this vast land remained modest – no more than 7–8 inhabitants per square kilometer.

Finally, concern over security convinced Austria to send colonists from a variety of places – though primarily Germans – to establish agricultural settlements in the border area with the Ottoman Empire, particularly along the Danube, from where it meets the Sava to the Iron Gate. In this case too, an abundance of land, careful planning, good farming techniques, and the introduction of new crops (potatoes and tobacco) contributed to successful immigration. By the end of Maria Theresa's reign, immigration had all but ceased as almost all the available land had been subdivided among colonists who had successfully transplanted a Germanic society to the southeastern border of the empire.

By the end of the eighteenth century, both the political–military and demographic conquest of space on the continent had come to an end. No open and uninhabited spaces remained except to the far north. Nor were there sparsely and randomly inhabited areas that could serve as potential targets for migration and settlement. The human geography of Europe had stabilized and only violent military upheavals would be able to change it.

Settlement Intensification and Land Reclamation

The growth of European population relied not only on the appropriation of space, discussed above, but also on the intensification of its occupation, the recovery of uncultivated lands, and on land reclamation. I call this process *intensification*, a more general category that includes agricultural intensifications; historically it has been associated with periods of demographic expansion and increased demand for land and production, especially food production. This intensification process was in turn a function not only of regional environmental characteristics but also of age of settlement, population density, and the ways in which territory was settled.

Prior to the Industrial Revolution, agricultural methods placed real limits on population density, and so demographic expansion. An increase in population – in the absence of a decrease in standard of living (almost impossible given the already low level of subsistence of the majority of the population) – could only occur if the amount of cultivable land available was increased or if that land were farmed more efficiently (greater productivity per unit of land). It was mainly by means of the first alternative (more cultivated land) that over time an equilibrium – albeit an unsteady one – between population and resources was maintained. Yet in much of Europe west of the Venice–Hamburg line – excluding the Iberian peninsula – significant expansion was not possible through the complex settlement processes which we have already discussed. In eleventh-century England – the era of the *Domesday Book* – the organization of space seems already to have been fairly consolidated. As Adam Smith noted, the number of parishes in the English Midlands was nearly the same in the *Domesday Book* (1,288) as it was in the 1801 census (1,311). In the Lowlands, the eleventh-century distribution of district parishes has remained more or less the same right up to the present day. Similar observations can be made with regard to France, southern Germany, and especially Italy. In Roman times, Italy had reached a level of density that defined an organizational scheme, which while it has undergone reform has never been fundamentally altered.

In the absence of great empty spaces it became necessary to work within the bounds of already organized territories and recover land, clear forests and woodlands, expand cultivation, dry up bogs and marshes, and reclaim coastal areas. According to Slicher van Bath's calculations, given a yield/seed ratio of 5:1, it takes one hectare of land to feed one person for one year. So if we allow for a possible doubling of the population of Italy between 1000 and 1300, reaching a pre-Black Death high of 12 million, then over those three centuries 6 million additional hectares of land would have had to be cultivated. This figure is equivalent to roughly one-fifth of the total surface area of the country, or the sum of three large regions such as Venetia, Emilia, and Tuscany. Considered in still another way, the collectivity would have had to bring another 20,000 hectares of land per year under cultivation, at no small effort. These figures are only guidelines – they could be doubled or halved – but help to give some idea of the intensity of the phenomenon.

There were three principal ways to gain more farmland: by expansion into neighboring areas by individual farmers who cleared woodlands or transformed uncultivated lands; by the founding of villages or castles by nobles, orders of knights, monastic orders, or municipalities, and the planting of the areas surrounding or between settlements; and by the reclamation of swampy areas and other land not generally suitable for farming. Those cases of new lands tilled through spontaneous initiative, largely individual, have little in the way of documentation. By comparison, the founding of castles, free villages, hamlets, etc. that marked organized stages in a settlement process is better studied. Beginning in the eleventh century, village foundation – population centers dependent on a city, a monastery, or a nobleman – is well documented in Normandy and in western and central France. In Aquitaine, especially from the twelfth century, the peopling of new areas revolved around the foundation of *castelnaux*, that were dependent on a nobleman's castle, *sauvetés*, or villages under the protection of the Church, and especially from the thirteenth century, *bastides*, or villages planned for a few dozen families or more. Between 350 and 400 of these have been identified. In the north the new agglomerations were called *villeneuves*: between the eleventh and fourteenth centuries about 500 were founded in the Paris Basin. In Languedoc, instead, the expansion of castles prevailed.

In Italy the founding of free villages and *villenuove* was intensive in the north, especially in Piedmont and Lombardy, but also fairly diffuse throughout the rest of the country. Pinto writes:

Even though new villages and castles were founded first for political and military reasons, there is no doubt that as the phenomenon
became more widespread it led to the expansion of cultivated space
and a better distribution of population throughout the territory. In
most cases, the population expansion drew off demographic surplus
from nearby areas. Though sometimes the newly arrived came from
more distant regions" (for example, Germans in the Alpine valleys
and Lombards in the south).

In this case too, the majority of new settlement took place in the
eleventh to thirteenth centuries. According to Sereni, out of the
8,000 settlements whose origins have been reconstructed, approximately 2,700 were either pre-Roman or Roman, another 1,100
were founded up through the tenth century, and then 945 in the
eleventh, 1,014 in the twelfth, 886 in the thirteenth, and 217 in the
fourteenth. Naturally, the demographic crisis following the Black
Death, which caused the population of Europe to decline and settlements to vanish, arrested this process. New villages did continue to
be founded, but never again with the same vigor as before. In Sicily,
for example, 130 new feudal villages were founded primarily in the
central and western areas and for the most part between the end of
the sixteenth and the middle of the seventeenth century. The stim-
ulus for this expansion was strong demographic growth in the
sixteenth century and a rapidly increasing demand for wheat, both
domestic and for export. Similar processes characterized other
parts of Europe as well: England, southern Germany, and also
Scandinavia where village foundation began later and was still
intense in the sixteenth and seventeenth centuries. There was,
moreover, a concern common to many states to consolidate open
spaces, especially border areas, by means of the encouragement and
organization of settlement, a true spatial policy.
    Another means of acquiring more arable land was to transform
swamps, marshlands, and moors that were otherwise unfarmable.
During the expansion of the late Middle Ages land reclamation
seems to have been a less important method for acquiring land fit
for cultivation. A salient exception was certainly the case of the
Netherlands where the reclamation of land from the sea and the
drying up of internal lakes has proceeded at a brisk pace for a
millennium. Figure 2.3 illustrates, in 25-year increments, the
progress of land recovery beginning in 1100.
    Many factors have influenced the progress of land reclamation
and transformation over time in the Netherlands: changes in sea

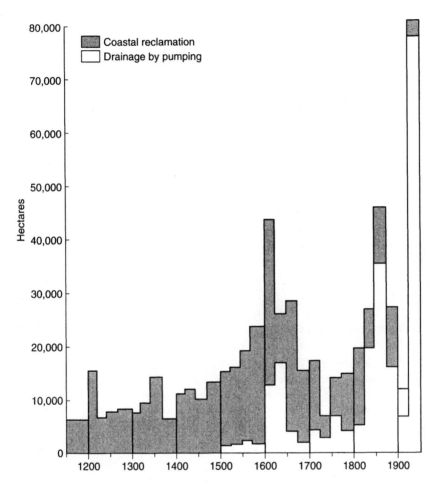

Figure 2.3   Land reclamation, coastal areas and internal lakes, in the Netherlands 1100–1950

Source: P. Wagret, *Polderlands*, Methuen, London, 1968, p. 76

level, fluctuating agricultural prices, available technology and capital, and so forth. However, cycles in population history are also important: recession following the Black Death; subsequent recovery peaking in the first quarter of the seventeenth century; depression again until the second half of the eighteenth century; and the subsequent rapid growth that peaked in the mid-nineteenth century. Land recovery then proceeded rapidly: between 1550 and 1650, for example, when 162,000 hectares of arable land were reclaimed and population increased by approximately 600,000.

Even this expansion did not guarantee self-sufficiency as the region imported grain, mainly from eastern Germany and also France. Even given their relatively high yields, the recovered lands theoretically were capable of feeding only about half of the additional population. Such was the technical expertise of Dutch engineers and laborers that they lent their skills to the rest of Europe: in the Middle Ages they pioneered reclamation along the banks of the Elbe and in the bogs of Brandenburg, and then, beginning at the end of the sixteenth century, carried out projects in England, France, Germany, and Italy.

The case of the Netherlands is certainly unique both for the size of the area recovered and the duration of the project: an entire millennium. Yet land reclamation has been a traditional and often important way to meet the demand for land and food in periods of demographic growth; a way, albeit a costly one, to loosen the constraints on demographic growth imposed by the limits of space. In the Po River Valley of Italy, especially in the second half of the twelfth and the thirteenth centuries, cities in Lombardy, Venetia, and Emilia financed their own projects to recover land and control the rivers. Medieval projects to reclaim land and to protect areas from the sea and river flooding took place in England, in Lincolnshire and Norfolk, in France along the Loire, and in Germany on the Elbe. Land reclamation took on larger proportions during the demographic recovery that followed the crisis of the fourteenth and fifteenth centuries. In England the Draining Act of 1600 was aimed at the productive recovery of hundreds of thousands of acres of wetlands. The most ambitious project among the many undertaken was the reclamation of the Fenland, especially the area of Bedford Level. Lancashire, Norfolk, and Essex were also intensively drained. Similar work was carried out in France along the northern coast with the help of Dutch workers and also along the malarial and swampy coasts of Provence and Languedoc. And in Italy reclamation activity took off again as well, especially in the Po River Valley in the sixteenth and early seventeenth centuries. Aymard writes, "To the west the first rice paddies were created in the eastern part of Piedmont between Novara and Vercelli, but the greatest activity was in the east; massive and surprising transformations took place on either side of the Po: in the Venetian *terra firma*, in the Duchies of Parma, Reggio, Mantua, and Ferrara, and in Emilia." The most impressive undertaking was perhaps that of the Great Reclamation of the Polesine of San Giovanni in 1580 by the Este family; more than 30,000 hectares of land were reclaimed as farmland, although not all of it endured.

The demographic reawakening of the second half of the eighteenth century went everywhere hand-in-hand with the revival of reclamation projects. In England vast expanses of moorland were turned into farmland; malaria was eliminated from the lowlands of the Trent and the Humber; and in Lincolnshire 70,000 hectares of marsh were reclaimed as arable; while in Huntingdonshire, Suffolk, and Cambridgeshire the peat-bogs were improved. In Italy, the Tuscan reclamation projects in the Val di Chiana and the Maremma are the most well known. In Germany reclamation took place in Schleswig-Holstein and, following the partition, in the Polish regions of the Donetsk Valley between the Oder and the Vistula. In the Netherlands, where land reclamation reached a historic low in the second quarter of the century, new projects were subsequently undertaken, as they were in the French Poitou, in Catalonia, and in Ireland.

Reclamation projects differed in quality and often met with failure and reversals of fortune. Yet together they followed the major population cycles, and the resulting increase in farmland required an enormous investment of capital, labor, and organizational capabilities.

Consolidation

One aspect of intensified occupation of space was the development of an urban network, crucial to the stabilization and consolidation of settlement. Demographic size is the criterion normally used to define an urban center, though there are a host of other criteria that would be preferable: the percentage of the labor force that is non-agricultural, the presence of specialized professions, and population density. In table 2.1 urbanization is measured according to whether a city has more than 10,000 inhabitants, a level that guarantees the above characteristics. In figure 2.4, instead, a slightly higher limit of 12,000 is used. The level chosen is arbitrary, though one should keep in mind that if the threshold is too low one risks diluting the concept of city or urban population by the inclusion of relatively rural and nonspecialized centers.

An increasing level of urbanization is a sure sign of a population's stability. The birth of an urban structure requires a densely settled rural hinterland that produces a large enough surplus to generate

Table 2.1 Urban population as a percentage of total for countries and regions, 1500–1800

	1500	1550	1600	1650	1700	1750	1800
1 Scandinavia	0.9	0.8	1.4	2.4	4.0	4.6	4.6
2 England and Wales	3.1	3.5	5.8	8.8	13.3	16.7	20.3
3 Scotland	1.6	1.4	3.0	3.5	5.3	9.2	17.3
4 Ireland	0	0	0	0.9	3.4	5.0	7.0
5 Netherlands	15.8	15.3	24.3	31.7	33.6	30.5	28.8
6 Belgium	21.1	22.7	18.8	20.8	23.9	19.6	18.9
7 Germany	3.2	3.8	4.1	4.4	4.8	5.6	5.5
8 France	4.2	4.3	5.9	7.2	9.2	9.1	8.8
9 Switzerland	1.5	1.5	2.5	2.2	3.3	4.6	3.7
10 Northern Italy		15.1	16.6	14.3	13.6	14.2	14.3
11 Central Italy	12.4	11.4	12.5	14.2	14.3	14.5	13.6
12 Southern Italy		11.9	14.9	13.5	12.2	13.8	15.3
13 Spain	6.1	8.6	11.4	9.5	9.0	8.6	11.1
14 Portugal	3.0	11.5	14.1	16.6	11.5	9.1	8.7
15 Austria-Bohemia	1.7	1.9	2.1	2.4	3.9	5.2	5.2
16 Poland	0	0.3	0.4	0.7	0.5	1.0	2.5
Region							
1–6 Northwest	6.6	7.2	8.2	10.9	13.1	13.6	14.9
7–9 Centre	3.7	4.0	5.0	6.0	7.1	7.5	7.1
10–14 Mediterranean	9.5	11.4	13.7	12.5	11.7	11.8	12.9
15–16 East	1.1	1.2	1.4	1.7	2.6	3.5	4.2
	5.6	6.3	7.6	8.3	9.2	9.5	10.0

Note: Inhabitants of cities with populations over 10,000 per 100 total inhabitants
Source: J. De Vries, *European Urbanization, 1500–1800*, Cambridge (Mass.), Harvard University Press, 1984

trade and leave the city free to specialize its production and function. Urban centers rarely arise in nomadic or semipastoral economies, or in sparsely populated areas. In addition, they help consolidate a population and the settlement of space, as once they have been founded they may suffer relative decline but rarely disappear; such at least has been the experience of the last few centuries. For Europe in 1800 (excluding Russia and the Balkans), de Vries has identified 364 cities with populations of at least 10,000. Fifteen other cities had populations over 10,000 at some time after 1500 but no longer by 1800. These cities did decline in size and import-

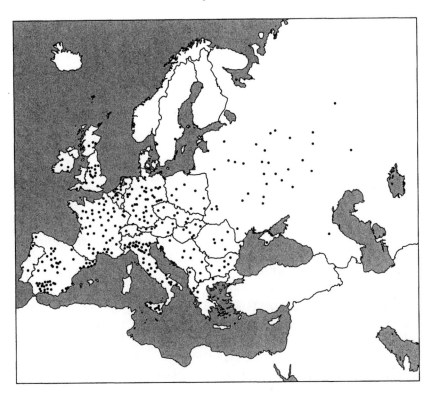

Figure 2.4   Cities with over 12,000 inhabitants, 1500–1800

Source: P. Bairoch, J. Batou, P. Chèvre, *La population des villes européennes de 800 à 1850*, Droz, Geneva, 1988

ance but they represent a small percentage of the 1800 group – barely one in 25 – and a larger though still modest percentage – one in ten – of the 154 cities that had populations greater than 10,000 in 1500. Table 2.1 traces the evolution of urbanization between 1500 and 1800 in Europe (again excluding Russia and the Balkans). The proportion of the population living in cities larger than 10,000 inhabitants grew from 5.6 percent to 10 percent in the period, though with important regional variations: slower in the Mediterranean (already more urban than the rest of Europe in 1500); and faster in the west and north. In 1500, urbanization was very limited in the Celtic fringe of the British Isles, in Scandinavia, Poland, Austria, and Bohemia (between 0 and 2 percent); average in England, France, Germany (3 to 4 percent) and Spain (6 percent); high in Italy (12 percent); and highest in the

Space

Table 2.2 Average latitude and longitude of cities newly arrived at a population level over 50,000, 1200–1800

Date	Latitude	Longitude	Number
1200	42°04'	3°00'	7
1300	43°30'	10°08'	6
1400	46°50'	2°90'	6
1500	45°15'	7°53'	10
1600	46°43'	6°34'	10
1700	51°40'	5°57'	9
1800	49°96'	6°05'	24

Netherlands (18 percent). In 1800, by contrast, northwest Europe (at 15 percent) was more urban than the Mediterranean region (13 percent), while Scandinavia, Germany, Austria-Bohemia (5 percent) and Poland lagged behind. Urban growth, however, was not constant in the period. There was a growth spurt between 1550 and 1650 and a falling off in the early part of the eighteenth century.

Figure 2.4 represents – for all of Europe – the location of cities with populations greater than 12,000 between 1500 and 1800. It gives a clear picture of the urban network; fairly weak east of the Adriatic Sea and of the Venice–Szczecin line, and north of the straits that separate the Scandinavian peninsula from the rest of the continent. Over time urbanization spread along a south–north axis: by examining those cities that exceeded the 50,000 mark each century – the "great cities" – we find that they lie increasingly to the north. In 1200, the seven cities with populations greater than 50,000 included three in Spain (Cordova, Granada, and Seville), two in Italy (Palermo and Venice), plus Paris and Cologne. Their average latitude is 42°. Over subsequent centuries the cities reaching the 50,000 benchmark were more and more northerly, as demonstrated by table 2.2.

Between 1200 and 1700 the average latitude rises notably – approximately from the level of Rome to that of London – while longitude remains in the relatively narrow meridian strip between Paris and Hamburg. This shift illustrates the penetration of large-scale urbanization to the north. Of the 25 cities that in 1500 had populations greater than 50,000, just five were located north of the 50° parallel; in 1800 28 out of 61 were. In the case of the Atlantic and northern "periphery" (Ireland, Scotland, Scandinavia), in

1500 there were only two cities with populations greater than 10,000; in 1600 there were three; in 1700 there were seven; and by 1800 there were twenty-two.

The end of the eighteenth century signaled the end of a long process of occupation and consolidation in Europe. The eastern thrust had ended and the push northward had reached its natural limit. The southeastern border at the Asiatic steppes was defined by the settlement of a significant rural population. The urban network had spread and intensified. The demographic acceleration of the eighteenth century stimulated the demand for agricultural products, and throughout the continent forests and uncultivable land gave way to farming or grazing. In England at the end of the seventeenth century there were 8 million hectares of pasture and farmland – the eminent political arithmetician Gregory King estimated 4.45 million hectares of farmland (reduced to 3.6 million by Davenant) and 4.05 million hectares of pasture – and over 11 million by 1800. In France farmland increased by about a third between mid-eighteenth century and the mid-nineteenth, and similar increases can be documented elsewhere. Yet we find ourselves already in a vastly different world: technology and mechanization have made it possible to farm land previously uncultivable or abandoned; energy resources have multiplied; industrialization has expanded resources. Space has ceased to be a factor that limits growth; in the century to come it will expand dramatically with the colonization of great open lands in North and South America, Siberia, and still farther afield. Moreover, while demographic growth to the end of the eighteenth century had found limited, though important, outlets outside the continent and so had to rely primarily on European space, in the nineteenth century mass emigration emerged as an important response to the upheaval that resulted from both demographic and economic transformations.

3
Food

Population and Nutrition

The relative abundance or scarcity of food determines the growth cycle of every living species. Biologists and naturalists are well aware that availability of food in the natural world depends on a matrix of climate, epidemiology, competition between species, and predation. This matrix is complex, and even the most sophisticated mathematical models fail to adequately reproduce it. The fact that humans are able to produce and store their food adds a further complication. Nonetheless, human growth has always depended on food supply, especially in rural societies whose members, in addition to clothing and sheltering themselves, labored primarily to keep hunger at bay. This rule also held for much of the small percentage of the population who lived in cities: shopkeepers, shophands, artisans, and laborers indeed spent almost all of their earnings on food. As late as the nineteenth century, two countries well in the vanguard of culture and science – France and Germany – still had not fully resolved the food problems of their populations. While nutritional levels were generally adequate in those years free of war or climatic catastrophe, times of scarcity and famine saw caloric intake decrease dramatically.

Even before Malthus, Adam Smith in 1776 made the following famous observation regarding the close link between availability of resources and demographic development: "every species of animal naturally multiplies in proportion to the means of their subsistence, and no species can ever multiply beyond it." By subsistence, Smith undoubtedly meant the basic material requirements for survival, and above all food. A couple of decades later, Malthus reiterated: "food is necessary to the existence of man" and "the power of population is indefinitely greater than the power in the earth to produce subsistence for man." Here, subsistence still meant primarily food, and the scarcity or absence of it led to "vice" (prostitution, acts against nature, abortion) and "misery," and consequently to high infant mortality and disease. While backbreaking labor, inadequate clothing, and poor shelter certainly all contributed to "misery," its leading cause was still lack of food. David Ricardo, in 1817, concurred: "in those countries where the laboring classes have the fewest wants, and are contented with the cheapest food, the people are exposed to the greatest vicissitudes and miseries." Moreover, he observed – like others before him – that it was the low price of food in America and its high price in Europe that accelerated demographic growth in the former and slowed it down in the latter.

The Malthusian model inexorably links population with resources. The potentially geometric growth of population strains the relationship between resources and people to the dangerous point where repressive checks intervene: famine, disease, and war reduce population size and reestablish a balance with available resources until the negative cycle begins once again, unless the population finds some other way to limit its reproductive capacity. This "preventive" and virtuous check exists in the delay or forgoing of marriage, practices that reduce the reproductivity of populations wise enough to apply them. In Malthus' day voluntary birth control or contraception, the usual preventive check in today's world (see chapter 7), was neither respectable nor widely practiced. The fate of a population then depended on the battle between the repressive checks and the preventive ones, between reckless and responsible behavior, between the forces of constraint or the forces of choice.

Nourishment emerges as a powerful factor of constraint in the history of European population, at least up until the nineteenth century. Over the course of many centuries, changes in the standard of living for the vast majority of the population were closely linked to the availability of food. Indeed, the need for more resources lay behind the conquest of new lands and the adoption of new and more intensive methods of cultivation. And frequently pre-Industrial Revolution demography has been explained in light of a simplified Malthusian model based on the following three premises: (1) nutritional levels depend upon the availability of food; (2) levels of nourishment determine mortality not only in the short term – the connection between famine and death is obvious – but also in the long term as malnutrition creates conditions that favor the rise of life-threatening diseases; (3) shifts in mortality largely determine the fluctuations and cycles of population growth, as the combination of a lack of birth control and stable nuptiality made for a relatively constant birth rate in old regime societies, and so fertility had little bearing on variations in the rate of increase. While this interpretation until recently still found authoritative support, it has not held up in the face of historical evidence. The first premise is the least problematic as there does indeed exist a relationship between food supply and nutritional levels. However, while overall sustenance may appear sufficient, its poor distribution can create obvious inequalities, and disease itself – despite adequate nourishment – can produce nutritional insufficiencies. The second premise while true in principle – a population that is malnourished is on average a population with higher mortality – is false in practice: structural factors and epidemics (plague for example) not linked to nutritional factors have historically determined major mortality levels and cycles. The final premise is even more tenuous than the second as historical demographic studies have revealed that "natural" fertility, in the absence of birth control, can reach levels that are substantially different in different populations and time periods, confirming the existence of significant variations in marriage practices. In the long term then, births as well as deaths have influenced the rate of population growth.

Nutrition, Infection, and Mortality

Adequate nutrition for a healthy organism must provide it with sufficient energy to maintain normal metabolic processes, insure growth, sustain physical activity, and maintain body temperature. Pregnancy and breastfeeding require additional energy, as does recovery from illness. Energy needs then vary according to sex, age, body weight, state of health, level of activity, and local climate. A healthy adult body must take in the same amount of energy as it expends in order to avoid either losing body tissue because of a caloric deficit or accumulating body fat because of an excess. If we apply currently accepted caloric standards to historical populations, then an average daily consumption of 2,000 calories per person (a bit more in the active summer period and a bit less in the winter) should provide sufficient nourishment, at least in terms of energy. One, however, needs to keep in mind that the average calorie count does not take into account either the quality or variety of food, nor its distribution. In particular, it masks those instances of dramatic inequality when a significant portion of the population did not attain the average level.

A normal diet should also include adequate amounts of protein, vitamins, and minerals. The absence of these basic nutritional elements can lead to disease even when total caloric requirements are met. A lack of protein – present in animal products such as meat and fish but also in legumes – causes such devastating childhood diseases as marasma (wasting disease) and kwarshiorkor, two leading causes of high mortality in developing countries (and to a lesser degree in historical Europe). A deficiency of vitamin A causes blindness, while too little vitamin D, found in animal and vegetable fats, leads to rickets, a disease that John Graunt observed in children in seventeenth-century London. Too little Vitamin C causes scurvy, once the scourge of ships' crews the world over, while a lack of niacin is responsible for pellagra, a disease that spread through much of southern Europe in the eighteenth and nineteenth centuries. Of the minerals, too little iodine is at the root of goiter and cretinism, once prevalent in mountainous regions including the Pyrenees, the Alps, and the Carpathians. In general, though, the nutrients essential for healthy survival can be found in a wide variety of foods and of cultural, climatic, and economic contexts, so that a satisfactory and balanced diet is possible almost everywhere. Dietetic shortages and imbalances instead occur primarily in areas with extreme climates (for example, among the Inuit and Lapps who inhabit extremely cold and remote lands and have disproportionately high-fat diets), in special organizational contexts (the absence of Vitamin C that leads to scurvy at sea), or during periods of famine or social unrest. In these instances deficiencies may become chronic and block the natural ability of humans to adapt to their nutritional resources.

Science confirms what common sense dictates, namely that a close relationship exists between nutritional levels and infectious diseases and their virulence. The high mortality of the past was linked primarily to the rise, spread, and severity of infectious diseases, and the role of malnutrition was mainly that of lowering an organism's defenses and so favoring the infection. In the most general of terms, a poorly nourished population is more susceptible to infectious diseases and less able to resist their spread, severity, and impact. Another general claim is that in a traditional high-mortality regime, the transition from malnutrition to adequate nutrition (and vice versa) – the result, for example, of changes in agricultural productivity – could bring improvement (or deterioration) in mortality levels. A third generalization, however, does not hold up to scrutiny: namely that an inverse relationship exists between nourishment levels and infection and mortality. In fact, not only does no relationship exist beyond the threshold of malnutrition and sufficient nutrition, but indeed the opposite relationship exists in the case of hypernutrition, which spawns its own pathologies.

In any case, we cannot injudiciously assume a connection between nutritional level and mortality when interpreting historical demography. The difficulty of estimating, with any certainty, nutritional levels and their fluctuations in historical European populations is discussed below, but even if we could know them precisely, it would still be difficult to evaluate their effect on mortality. In fact, while malnutrition on the one hand hastens the process of infection, on the other hand it can also be a symptom of that same infection. For example, it is well known that diarrhea – one of the more widespread infectious conditions in populations suffering from high infant mortality – makes it difficult to take in and absorb nutrients, and so is a major cause of malnutrition. Infectious disease and mortality, on the one hand, and nutrition, on the other, are retroactively linked; both result from a general state of backwardness and poverty. Nor is it easy to measure the net effect that variations in food and nutritional supply have had on past mortality; the two concepts are not equivalent because of the effect of preservation and preparation methods on wastage and losses.

There are other problems involved in assessing the impact of nutrition on mortality. The first, and more general, is the difficulty in gauging the minimum nutritional level below which there is a greater risk of contracting disease, and therefore a greater risk of dying. While the risk of death increases precipitously below an extremely low threshold, slight or moderate malnutrition has a negligible effect. In addition, not all infectious diseases are "sensitive" to malnutrition. In fact, nutritional deficiencies can not only depress a human body's defenses, they can also in some cases inter-fere with the metabolic and reproductive processes of an attacking micro-organism. So in some cases malnutrition acts as an antago-nist rather than a protagonist, thereby limiting the damage caused by infection.

The link between nutrition and mortality appears minimal, if nonexistent, for some of the main infectious diseases that have influenced mortality levels in the past. For example, nutritional deficiency seems to have had little or no effect on the rise and spread of plague, smallpox, and malaria. By contrast, it has played an important role in the history of many intestinal and respiratory illnesses, but an uncertain and variable one for other important infections such as typhus, diphtheria, and others. Many accepted truths then in the field of population history need to be reassessed. It is certainly reasonable to maintain that malnutrition aggravates chances for survival when combined with other factors that favor the spread of infection and negatively influence their outcome (poor hygiene, poverty, ignorance); however, these factors aside, the role of malnutrition is not uniform for the reasons cited above. It has even been proposed that "there is some support for the thesis that calculated mild undernutrition and leanness may be an animal's greatest physical asset, producing longer life, fewer malig-nancies, reduced mortality from inherited susceptibility to auto-immune disease and perhaps fewer infections."

Bread and its Accompaniments

We do not know much about the basic dietary trends of past European populations. While episodic and anecdotal information abounds, there is little reliable basic knowledge. It is therefore diffi-cult to determine with any certainty whether European populations continually struggled with a scarcity of food resources or instead lived more or less above the danger zone, or perhaps alternated between periods of comfortable plenty and of dire hardship. Agricultural history is rich in details about cultivation techniques, yields, land management, and price trends, but poor in providing information about the changes in production required to evaluate consumption levels. There are nevertheless several ways to measure dietary changes over time: estimates of food budgets for a number of communities and of their caloric intake; levels of consumption of staples like bread and meat; the dietary contribution of new crops such as potatoes and corn; comparison of wage and price trends as indicators of buying power; and variations in height as an indicator of nutritional status.

Food budgets and calorie counts are based on records of purchases by families and institutions and on estimates of production destined for consumption. These estimates are problematic for we have no idea how much food was home-produced or how much food spoiled, was wasted, or thrown out. We also have no information about the accumulation or depletion of stock and it is difficult to calculate the calorie content of foods when we know little about their quality, or methods of preparation, not to mention the questionable nutritional value of wine, beer, and spirits. Moreover, the figures indicate average levels of consumption and so do not reflect the impact of social inequalities on one's "access to food." There are relatively few reconstructions of overall diets in the past, a total made still smaller when special cases (royal households or the households of higher nobility and clergy) are eliminated. These special cases help us to understand the lifestyle of the upper classes, but are not particularly useful for our purposes. Take the sixteenth-century court of King Erik of Sweden – with an average per-capita consumption of 6,500 calories a day- or the seventeenth-century household of Mazzarino (7,000 calories) or the Duke Magnus and his court (higher still). These estimates are mind-boggling, if not gout-inducing, though one can take some comfort in the thought that a significant surplus of this food must have made its way into the servants' households and so helped to satisfy the hearty appetites of their families.

Food budgets for certain specialized groups – military (rations for the navy), civil, religious (monasteries), charitable (hospitals, hospices) and penal (prison) – are also of limited interest for our discussion. Although these communities often kept reliable records – though who is to say that the products acquired were consumed exclusively by those entitled to them? – they are too specialized to be representative of the general population. So the 5,000 daily calories for each student at the Borromeo College in Pavia in the seventeenth century cannot have been the norm for the average inhabitant of that city with his grain-based diet. If the patients of the hospital in Caen received 3,000 daily calories in 1725, it was probably because their health was so poor that they required additional nutrition; and if the soldiers and sailors of Venice, Tuscany, Sweden, Russia, France, and England received food rations in excess of 3–4,000 calories a day – appropriate to the heavy exertion of their military or navigational activities – it was certainly not the case that the civil populations enjoyed similar diets, though some do claim that rations of this sort were the norm and not the exception. If from these studies of special and certainly privileged groups we move on to other studies of larger collectivities, or smaller ones nonetheless made up of "common people," the results are likely to be of greater potential demographic significance. An inventory of caloric totals for groups from many European countries between the fourteenth and twentieth centuries produces some interesting conclusions. The results, important for their value as surveys of a hidden and little-known world, suggest caloric levels generally higher than, and indeed in some cases even double, the 2,000 daily per-capita level I have suggested as adequate for an old-world population. The only instance of a level below 2,000 calories is for France in 1780–90 and 1803–12, as estimated by Toutain, although even he revised it upwards for 1780–90. Morineau increased the total to over 2,000 calories using persuasive arguments and maintaining that food supply in France, from the end of Louis XIV's reign to that of Louis Phillipe, was sufficient, though stationary. If we want to lend credence to the more remote historical studies – such as those for Norfolk day-laborers in the fourteenth and fifteenth centuries, royal serfs in sixteenth-century Sweden, or wage-earners in fifteenth- and sixteenth-century Languedoc – then we can say that food in those centuries was abundant and even greatly exceeded required levels. The lowest levels, close to the minimum requirement, are instead encountered at the end of the eighteenth and beginning of the nineteenth century in France and England. As compared to this admittedly hazardous comparison, we are on surer ground when we observe, citing a variety of indicators, that both living conditions and food supply deteriorated in the seventeenth and eighteenth centuries in various parts of Europe.

Another important gauge is the consumption of bread, flour and other grains. Grains dominated traditional diets because of their long shelf-life, versatility, and most importantly, economy. Calorie for calorie, bread is indisputably the least expensive food. In a Florentine household in the second decade of the seventeenth century, 1,000 calories from meat cost between five and 17 times (depending on the type of meat) as much as 1,000 calories from bread. Again, calorie for calorie, fresh fish cost 55 times more than bread; pickled fish 15 times more; eggs seven times more; cheese four to seven times more; and sugar ten to 20 times more, according to how refined. Only wine (nutritionally valuable only in small quantities), oil (used only as a condiment) and beans (fairly rare at the time) had a cost to calorie ratio comparable to bread. Cheapness then explains the historic popularity of grains on European tables. In prosperous Antwerp at the end of the sixteenth century, approximately four-fifths of household income was spent on food, and half on bread. Three centuries later, between 52 and 95 percent of family budgets from various Italian provinces was spent on bread. The modest dietary well-being of Europeans therefore depended largely on the availability of grains.

Figure 3.1 summarizes the estimates I have been able to put together for the approximate consumption or average availability of bread and grains, generally in excess of half a kilogram a day. Only the values for England and the Netherlands at the beginning of the nineteenth century are slightly lower, though these populations were fairly well fed and the potato, particularly in the Netherlands, had by then largely replaced bread. Rations of one kilogram or more are frequent, particularly in earlier periods. In Italian cities between the fifteenth and eighteenth centuries, or in non-urban areas around Siena and in Sicily in the seventeenth century, or in eighteenth century Piedmont, bread consumption ranged between 500 and 800 grams a day. If we use the lower figure – 500 grams of bread per day – the caloric value is roughly 1,250 calories, while 500 grams of wheat correspond to about 1,600 calories: respectively, two-thirds and three-quarters of the hypothetical daily requirement of 2,000 calories. To take an example, the "average" requirement could be satisfied by a 500 gram loaf of bread (1,250 calories), together with 100 grams of black olives (250 calories), and 100 grams of cheese (100 calories), half an onion and a bit of fresh fruit or vegetables. Indeed, that combination constituted the normal Mediterranean diet from the time of Homer until virtually the present day.

The above applies of course to normal years, ones free of famine. According to Ferdinando Galiani in his *Della Moneta* (1751), the availability of grains in the Kingdom of Naples never dipped more than 25 percent below the average, even in very bad years when, in any case, reserves helped in some measure to attenuate the crisis. Clearly, though, food shortages following from meager harvests, coupled with rising prices and consequent poverty, compounded the negative effects for the poor.

What can we say about the "quality" of past diets? One indicator, albeit an indirect one, is meat consumption. There is a

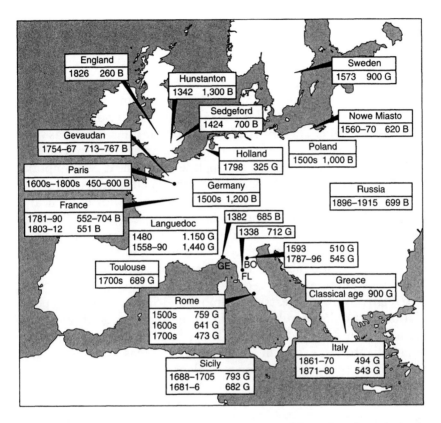

Figure 3.1 Per-capita daily consumption of bread and grain in selected European areas, fourteenth to twentieth centuries

Note: Each box includes: locality or area, era or years, daily consumption in grams; B = bread, G = grain.
Source: M. Livi Bacci, *Population and Nutrition*, Cambridge University Press, Cambridge, 1991, p. 90

compelling argument that meat consumption was relatively high during the last two centuries of the Middle Ages and well into the sixteenth century, gradually tapering off to a record low around the beginning of the nineteenth century, and beginning to rise again during the course of that century – and in some areas only in the twentieth century – though at different paces in different areas. The principal advocate of this theory is Wilhelm Abel, following on Gustav Schmoller's nineteenth-century studies. The process of *Wüstungen* (land abandonment) that accompanied the plague cycle of the Middle Ages underlay the conversion of large cultivated areas into pasture, and so increased stock-breeding and meat-eating. In late medieval Germany, according to Abel, meat consumption exceeded 100 kilograms annually per person, while subsequent crises reduced that figure to a low of 14 kilograms at the beginning of the nineteenth century. Standard economic laws were at work. The demand for grains was relatively inelastic and varied little in relation to income; instead it declined along with population following the plague. The demand for meat on the other hand was very elastic and post-Black Death real wage increases led to a strong increase in its consumption. The high levels of meat consumption found in medieval Germany and the subsequent trend seem to be supported also by information from Poland (an exporter of meat), Sweden, the Netherlands, and England. "They eat plentifully of all kinds of flesh and fish," observed Sir John Fortescue about the English in the fifteenth century. There is in fact little doubt regarding both the abundance of meat at their tables and its later decline. Meat consumption in fourteenth- and fifteenth- century Italy was also relatively high, at least in Piedmont and Sicily. A declining population and reduced cultivation freed up wide tracts of land that favored raising flocks and herds. The decline in meat consumption in later centuries, except in wealthier urban areas, is confirmed by the low levels of consumption prevalent almost everywhere well into the twentieth century. In some areas though – England, Flanders, and perhaps some parts of eastern Europe – meat consumption remained relatively high. It is also likely that traditional stock-raising areas with a regular export trade – such as the Tyrol, Switzerland, Denmark, southern Sweden, and, further east, Hungary, Podolia, Moldavia and Walachia – had higher than average meat consumption. Moreover, the increase in livestock export from east to west after the fifteenth century coincided with a decrease in stock-raising in the west, in turn a response to the pressure of demographic growth, so that not even the modest and declining demand for meat could be met. At the end of the seventeenth century, Gregory King estimated that out of a population of 5.5 million English, 1.6 million ate meat daily, 0.7 million ate it five times a week, 3 million once a week, and 0.2 million never. Average annual consumption in England at the time was around 33 kilograms per person, much lower than the 100 kilograms for Germany two or three centuries before, but twice as high as that estimated for the beginning of the nineteenth century. This long-term trend also applied to the consumption of other animal-derived products – butter, eggs, cheese, lard – and to game.

That meat consumption was very low in most of Europe in the nineteenth century is well established. According to Toutain's estimates, no more than 20 kilograms per capita per year were consumed in France between 1780 and 1834, after which the level began to rise a little. In post-Unification Italy, estimated meat consumption was even lower: 13 kilograms for 1861–70; a kilogram or two more in 1901–10; and reaching 30 kilograms annually only in the 1930s. In the spring of 1787 while traveling in Sicily, Goethe and his companions feasted liberally on artichokes and the like, but upon reaching Caltanisetta were not sure where or how to cook a hen purchased along the way, testimony to the Sicilians' unfamiliarity with meat at the time. For rural communities in Italy, as for much of the Mediterranean, meat was a rare luxury, often reserved for holidays, until well into the twentieth century. And in those regions, mortality reduction occurred in the absence of improved diet.

Famine and Hunger

Although long-term European dietary trends are difficult to reconstruct, details abound regarding short-term oscillations in food supply. "City fathers, take pity on us, show charity, and give us grain for the love of God, that we and our families may not die of hunger." This plea, directed at Florentine administrators during the famine of 1329, and others like it were repeated innumerable times up through the nineteenth century. Famines were all too common in Europe and no generation managed to escape them, some experiencing several. Other less explicit, though no less eloquent, indicators also help us understand the relationship between food and mortality. In particular, the comparison proposed by Jean Meuvret in 1946 between the price series for commonly consumed staples and mortality statistics enables us to systematically examine the relationship between the short-term fluctuations of both. The argument goes that preindustrial European populations were, for the most part, great consumers of grains which, in the form of bread, biscuits, porridges and the like, represented the dietary mainstay of the great majority. In the case of a poor harvest, usually caused by bad weather, prices rose and anyone obliged to purchase flour or bread suffered a dramatic reduction in buying power and, in extreme cases, had to go without. One alternative to scarcity was to substitute inferior grains for high-quality ones, but if production was particularly bad that year then there was likely to be a shortage of all grains. For many, reduced availability of foods meant a deterioration of health and, eventually, death from starvation or more often from epidemic infection. A sudden rise in prices then would be followed by a rise in mortality. Of course famines had other demographic consequences as well: a decline in marriages and conceptions and, almost always, a great increase in the migration of wandering and hungry beggars, a phenomenon which could play a role in the onset of epidemic cycles.

While the logic of this argument is strong, it does have some weaknesses. In the first place, while price trends reflect the market value of wheat or other grains, we have no way of knowing what percentage of each family's food resources were bought on the open market (and so must have declined when prices rose sharply) and how much was directly produced and consumed, or bartered or received in exchange for labor. Price fluctuations are therefore an imperfect gauge of the availability of food and its consumption. In addition, the onset of an epidemic was more often the social consequence of famine, rather than the bionatural one. Famine swelled the already conspicuous mass of beggars and vagrants. More people migrated to towns, and packed the poorhouses, hospitals, and hospices, thus facilitating the spread of epidemic infections, typhus for example. In 1602 Giovan Battista Segni, an eyewitness to famine in Bologna, recounted

> [one] would hear the cries of the crowd, would see the poor justly rioting, the wretched rend the air with their wailings, the country-folk exclaim till their lungs are to bursting, the hospitals fill up, the droning of wretched voices at the doors of the rich, the squares in an uproar, the foodstores and stalls swarming with distressed and wretched people.

In other words, the ideal conditions for the rise and spread of an epidemic. In the last great famine in the western world, the Irish Famine which began in 1845, many of the deaths were caused by typhus, referred to as "famine fever."

> The circumstances were ideal for lice and for those micro-organisms, agents of typhus, transmitted by lice. The extent of malnutrition in individuals did not seem to affect the vulnerabilility to typhus, as demonstrated by the large number of voluntary workers – doctors, priests, nuns, government officials and others – who contracted the disease and died of it.

The chronology of Europe's great food crises, often linked to adverse weather, is fairly well known, especially from the sixteenth century on when numerous price and death series become available. There is less information for earlier centuries, but a concentration from the later thirteenth and early fourteenth centuries suggests that the demographic expansion of the Middle Ages had begun to strain resources.

In England, rising prices, indicative of subsistence crises, were only moderately reflected by mortality. This observation holds true for the entire period between 1500 and 1800 and especially after the mid-seventeenth century when periods of famine became fairly rare. The sharp rise in prices during 1647–49 had only a moderate effect on the mortality curve, and in the last decade of the century there were a number of years in which prices were quite high, coinciding with a consistent fall in real wages, while mortality remained in fact below average. Similarly, the very high prices of 1710 following a hard winter and consequently a poor harvest, did not appreciably increase mortality.

The situation in Scotland, the Netherlands, and France was substantially different from that in England. The effects of famine in France during the seventeenth century and the early eighteenth were very serious: the subsistence crisis of 1628–32 combined with plague; the "Fronde" crisis of 1649–54; and the overwhelming crises of 1693–4 and 1709–10 that doubled mortality. Following Louis XIV's reign the crises abated and then disappeared. The general pattern of subsistence crises in Germany – compounded by the devastation of the Thirty Years War – suggests that the economic/demographic old regime ended later there than in France. The German crises of 1693 and 1709 corresponded to those in France, but 1740–1, 1771–4 and 1816–17 were also marked by hunger and increased mortality in Germany. Germany's eighteenth- century record coincides with that of Sweden where 1772–3 was a memorable year of hunger.

Iberia and Italy were both vulnerable to famine, a situation well-documented for the sixteenth and seventeenth centuries, though climatic and geographic differences make it difficult to draw a general picture of events. In the eighteenth century the situation seemed to improve, but 1764–7 was catastrophic in both Spain and Italy (especially in the south), while the Europe-wide crisis of 1816–17 saw greatly increased mortality in Italy.

Comparing these various experiences shows that from the sixteenth century to the beginning of the nineteenth century sharp

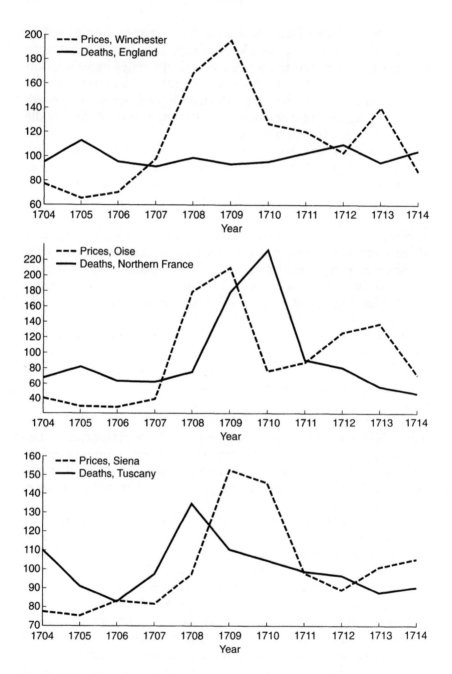

Figure 3.2 Indices (1704–14 = 100) of grain prices and deaths in England, France, and Tuscany

Sources: Tuscany: for prices, G. Parenti, *Prezzi e mercato a Siena*, Carlo Cya,

increases in grain prices, generally associated with limited food availability, generated significantly increased mortality; though the phenomenon is anything but automatic, as we can see from figure 3.2 with regard to the 1709 crisis (marked by a frigid winter) in England, northern France, and Tuscany. While in northern France wheat prices doubled (on the Beauvaisis market) in 1709 and caused a more than doubling of the death rate, a similar price hike in Winchester had little effect on English mortality, which remained below the mean. Meanwhile, in Siena the increase in mortality preceded rather than followed a sharp price hike. Secondly we must keep in mind that increased mortality was almost always directly caused by outbreaks of a clearly defined disease such as typhus, and in many cases the situation was complicated by war or plague. Thirdly, price increases did not have uniform consequences: mortality worsened less in England than in continental Europe; in the French Midi than in the grain-dependent north of France; in areas of mixed cultivation or with a more extensive range of local resources than in regions with one predominant crop; in the eighteenth century than the seventeenth century. And it is impossible to say whether these different reactions to similar price rises imply differing reductions in food availability (due to varying degrees of home consumption, to food relief measures by local authorities, to the presence of substitute foodstuffs, to stored surpluses, to differences in income) or to a different intensity in the onset of an epidemic following the social upheaval of a subsistence crisis. Finally, after the first decades of the nineteenth century, food ceases to be a significant factor of constraint in Europe; though this observation is valid only in the most general of ways, as in many areas, particularly the fringe areas of the continent, the end of old-regime nutrition came much later than in others.

Florence, 1942, pp. 27–8; for deaths, unpublished series of the Department of Statistics, University of Florence. England: for prices, Lord Beveridge, *Prices and Wages in England*, vol. I: *Price Tables: Mercantile Era*, Frank Cass, London, 1965, pp. 81–2; for deaths, Wrigley and Schofield, *The Population History of England*, Arnold, London, 1981, pp. 398–499. France: for prices, P. Goubert, *Beauvais et les Beauvaisis de 1500 à 1730*, SEVPEN, Paris, 1960, pp. 404–5; for deaths, D. Rebaudo, "Le mouvement annuel de la population française rurale de 1670 à 1740," *Population* XXVI, 2, 1979, p. 596

Long-Term Nutrition and Mortality

Does a long-term relationship between mortality and nutrition exist? Were well-nourished populations or times of relative plenty necessarily characterized by low mortality? There are no direct answers to this crucial question though we can follow some indirect signs. The first regards nutritional inequalities: the rich man's table was as varied for its meats, game, fish, spices, sweets, and wine as the poor man's was monotonous and plain, with bread as the undisputed staple, providing that it, too, was not scarce. The comparison, in a number of different contexts, between mortality for a well-fed elite and that of the masses provides some evidence, however indirect, in support of the determinant impact of nutrition on mortality. A second approach is to compare periods during which living standards improved – for example when real wages increased – with periods of decline and analyze survival in order to discover whether the cycles coincide. This coincidence would lend support to the claim that nutrition is one of the major factors in determining demographic growth.

Historical food budgets, reviewed above, confirm that the offerings of the rich man's table were indeed plentiful: the estimated individual daily consumption at the tables of the Bishop of Arles, Cardinal Mazzarino, King Erik of Sweden, the Convent of Marcigny, and the Borromeo College in Pavia was between 4,000 and 8,000 calories. Nor was the fare of the wealthy threatened during times of shortage or poverty; they enjoyed better living conditions, avoiding physical fatigue, and were able to escape contagion or impending war. However, a cursory examination of the available data on mortality among social elites raises serious doubts about the link between wealth and increased chances of survival. The best data we have are for English peers who do not seem to have enjoyed privileged survivorship. Between 1550 and 1750 their life expectancy was roughly the same as that of the rest of the population (and between 1575 and 1675 it was lower): for the elite it ranged between 32 in 1650–75 and 38.1 in 1725–50; for the masses instead it ranged between 32 in 1650–75 and 38 in 1725–50. It was only during the eighteenth century that peers gained an advantage over the rest of the population: 1.1 years in the first quarter of the century, 4.3 in the second, and 9.1 in the third. But for almost two centuries, spanning both the benign Elizabethan era and the catastrophic seventeenth century, life expectancy for the two groups was perfectly equal. This situation of high mortality and minimal advantage for peers seems to date back to previous centuries, as shown by figures which, while perhaps less exact, show that the aristocracy born between 1350 and 1500 suffered a higher mortality than did the less fortunate generations of later centuries (born in the first quarter of the seventeenth century). Nor, if we climb another rung of the social ladder, were the hopes of longevity any better for British ducal families: those born between 1330 and 1479 had a life expectancy at birth of only 22, though that figure does increase to 31 if deaths from violent causes are excluded. Regardless, the leveling effect of the plague in the late Middle Ages would have effectively eliminated any advantage the upper classes may have had, assuming any such privileges existed in the first place.

While we do not have similar data comparing other privileged classes with their corresponding masses, there are indications that the English case was not exceptional: in particular the very low life expectancy of privileged groups who certainly had no nutritional problems (except perhaps overeating). Peller has found that the ruling families of Europe had a life expectancy at birth of 34 in the sixteenth century, 30.9 in the seventeenth, and 37.1 in the eighteenth; and during the late Middle Ages (1100–1500) these levels were lower. Henry has observed that mortality was high among the old families of Geneva between 1550 and 1700, as it was also for French dukes and peers and Danish nobility in the seventeenth century. High mortality combined with low nuptiality and fertility threatened many a ruling dynasty with extinction. High mortality seems to have characterized religious orders as well: for example, Jesuits admitted to the order between 1540 and 1565 and Benedictines of Christ Church, Canterbury in the fifteenth century.

What this all suggests – at least for the sixteenth and seventeenth centuries – is that groups that were certainly privileged with regard to diet and material comforts either had no advantages over the rest of the population (as in England), or suffered in any case a high level of mortality which, though we cannot compare it to that of the population as a whole, seems incompatible with the theory that nutrition was the dominant factor determining mortality in old-regime societies.

A second investigation into the link between nutrition and mortality correlates the course of real wages – which we presume to be related to consumption, primarily of food – and mortality trends, with the idea that they are inversely related. Records of prices and wages for Europe indicate an increase in real wages during the century following the first outbreak of plague, a decrease during the sixteenth century, recovery in the seventeenth, and a gradual decline in the second half of the eighteenth. Altering this basic pattern were of course regional differences in timing and amplitude, reminding us again of the perils of generalization. Periods of population decline caused by plague, as in the fourteenth and fifteenth centuries, combined perhaps with other catastrophes, as in the seventeenth, are periods of low demand for food and falling prices, as well as of labor shortages and so consequently rising wages.

When we compare the Phelps Brown and Hopkins index of real wages for England with the life expectancy trend, using 25 year averages for both, the surprising result is the that the two phenomena are connected by a clearcut *inverse* relationship. Life expectancy was on the rise in the sixteenth century until the first quarter of the seventeenth, while real wages declined; subsequently life expectancy declined, bottoming out in the last quarter of the seventeenth century and the second quarter of the eighteenth, in tandem with steadily increasing real wages; finally, wages declined again between the middle of the eighteenth century and the first quarter of the nineteenth while life expectancy increased significantly. If, then, real wage trends determined changes in nutritional levels, and this certainly held true for the wage-earning population, there is no discernible positive correlation, at least in the aggregate, between those factors and survival. If anything, the exact opposite appears to have been the case.

In the absence of similar data for other European countries we have to settle for indirect indices. A first consideration is that periods of high real wages, and presumably greater food availability, were demographically stagnant ones – like the century after the 1348 plague or the eighteenth century – and were characterized by frequent mortality crises. The great epidemic cycles then did not depend on nutritional levels. In Tuscany the daily wages of a construction laborer allowed him to purchase 0.2 or 0.3 bushels of grain before the 1348 plague. This average rose to 0.6 in the first half of the fifteenth century, only to fall to 0.2 by the second half of the sixteenth. The frequency of great mortality crises peaked in the middle of the fifteenth century (when real wages were at a peak) and declined sharply to a minimum in the second half of the sixteenth century, when real wages were also at a minimum.

To be sure, the plague was devastating and there was little that individual or social defenses – including the type and quality of food – could do in the face of it. Yet in the second part of the seventeenth century and the eighteenth, plague vanished from Italy, and subsequently great mortality crises tended to be linked with periods of famine. And still no significant relationship between real wages and mortality emerges. For example the comparison between real wages for Milanese construction workers (expressed by the kilograms of bread purchased with a day's wages) and the relative frequency of mortality crises in north-central Italy does not reveal uniformity of trend. On the contrary, the period when wages were at their lowest, 1740–1800, coincides with the period of fewest mortality crises. Moreover, real wages declined almost everywhere in the second half of the eighteenth century when life expectancy was beginning to increase.

Paradoxes and Reality

Paradoxically, the preceding discussion seems to absolve European agriculture from the accusation of stinginess and, as a result, from having acted as the primary factor of constraint on the long-term demographic growth of the continent. On the other hand, the short-term link between food availability and mortality has been confirmed. These conclusions need tempering and placement in a larger context.

In the first place, examination of the link between nutrition and mortality reveals that a relationship indeed exists, but primarily in cases of severe malnutrition. Moreover, many diseases that characterized the epidemiological context of old-regime societies – the plague in particular – struck independently of an individual's nutritional levels or wealth, and ultimately affected great mortality cycles in both the short- and long-term. The second point to take into consideration regards "normal" levels of nutrition in non-crisis years, which were moderate but on the whole sufficient for survival. Moreover, a significant chunk of population consistently did not achieve the minimum standards needed to insure normal survival, and this group could swell appreciably in times of economic distress. The third consideration – tied to the first and supportive of the second – underlines the absence of a correlation between socioeconomic status and mortality, and, in the long-term, between standard of living and mortality trends. The fourth argument – which we shall refute in chapter 6 – regards the widely held thesis that the mortality decline enjoyed by most of Europe starting in the second half of the eighteenth century was connected to improved standards of living and nutrition. The fifth and final observation is more general in nature. Nutrition was an essential, indeed primary, component of well-being for an old-regime society. The availability of food not only determined physical well-being (translating into lower mortality, all things being equal) but also the possibility of demographic expansion when the Malthusian "preventive" checks on marriage, reproduction, and mobility were consequently relaxed. A society whose production of resources was severely constrained grew less not only because of higher mortality (if only due to the great frequency of subsistence crises) but also because of the obstacles to marriage, family formation, and mobility. The introduction of new crops in the eighteenth century, especially potatoes and corn, did not so much enrich diet as augment resources and the possibility for population increase. While they did help to decrease the frequency of crises (and so lower mortality), they also favored nuptiality, and so reproduction.

4

Microbes and Disease

Lives on the Brink

While debating the ethical problems created by the plague, the Florentine humanist Coluccio Salutati recalled to his colleagues the surprising number of outbreaks he had witnessed in his travels to Bologna, Florence, Pisa, and Viterbo as a public administrator. Salutati lived to be an old man – born in 1331, he died in 1406 – having survived at least a half dozen virulent attacks of plague in his lifetime. Indeed his destiny was rosier than that of most of his contemporaries, as those born prior to the onset of the Black Death did not, on average, survive past the age of 20. Nonetheless, Renaissance society rose and flourished in spite of the precariousness of life and survival, a precariousness characteristic not only of crisis periods but of normal ones as well.

Life expectancy at birth in old-regime societies was low, usually between 25 and 35 years. Only in those rare periods free of economic difficulties, social unrest, or disease did it reach 40. In England, where the chances of survival were greater than on the continent, during an almost 300-year span from 1541 to 1826 there were only three brief five-year intervals, (two during the fortunate Elizabethan era) in which life expectancy reached 40. The more advanced European countries only achieved a life expectancy of 40 in the early nineteenth century, while the peripheral regions of Europe had to wait until the next century. The life expectancy of old-regime populations was therefore strictly limited. The strongest factor of constraint to demographic growth appears to have been a "syndrome of backwardness" characterized by the combination of a lack of material resources and a scarcity of knowledge. Europe only broke out of this syndrome in the nineteenth century when greater wealth combined with greater knowledge, especially regarding the transmission of disease.

Were it the case that this syndrome of backwardness automatically produced both high and fairly uniform mortality levels, then the historical problem would be fairly easily resolved. But the picture is more complex, as rather than uniformity we find significant mortality cycles which had considerable demographic impact and require explanation. Given a constant birth rate and a life expectancy around 30, an increase (or decrease) of a year in the latter causes the growth rate to increase or decrease by about one per thousand, with significant consequences for the growth trend. In order to better understand the nature of old-regime mortality we should keep in mind that between two-thirds and three-quarters of all deaths were the result of direct transmission of disease from person to person, that is, ultimately, through the agency of microbes: bacteria, viruses, protozoa, and the like. And still, in 1871 England and 1881 Italy (the earliest periods for which we have reasonable cause-of-death statistics), almost two-thirds of deaths were caused by infectious diseases (tuberculosis, scarlet fever, diphtheria, typhus, typhoid fever, respiratory diseases, diarrhea, enteritis, etc.). The dominant role of infectious diseases – though our source is less reliable – finds additional documentation in the London Bills of Mortality for the seventeenth century, and in fact wherever we find an even rudimentary classification of diseases. The impact of infectious diseases may have been less serious for hunting and gathering societies, though it is likely the incidence of violent deaths was much greater.

It is then the microbe that emerges as the primary factor of demographic constraint in old-regime societies, as the cause of disease and the majority of deaths. In order to explain variations in mortality it is important to understand the complex mechanism that determines the transmission of microbes, their virulence, and their deadliness. That mechanism depended upon that very syndrome of backwardness which characterized pre-nineteenth century societies: above all the relative abundance or dearth of assets (food, clothing, shelter, means of production, and so on) and the resulting patterns of production and consumption (and lifestyle) that follow from them; and secondly the level of knowledge, especially regarding the transmission of diseases and how to treat them. Knowledge of this type remained rudimentary at best until the nineteenth century, and the battle against the unknown and invisible enemy – that is, the world of microbes – took place sometimes by sheer chance and sometimes following careful and accurate observations, but almost always guided by incorrect theories.

The universe of microbes is a living and ever-changing one, subject to the laws of biology; it adapts itself to the social and environmental context with which it comes into contact. The adaptive process has special importance for the human species: the severity of virulent diseases decreases over time, while other diseases, initially innocuous, can become progressively more dangerous; some diseases appear for the first time in particular historical moments while still others mysteriously disappear. In the match between microbes and humans – the outcome of which is health or illness, life or death – the playing field (the environment or context), the rules of the game, and the reciprocal knowledge of the players (the adaptations between pathogen and host) are extremely important.

This scheme interprets old-regime mortality as the outcome of the confrontation between the mutating world of microbes and the context of European backwardness. Into that confrontation we need to insert three more elements that had a notable effect on its outcome. The first is geographical; Europe is the western edge of the Eurasian continent and in the modern era has been a crossroads for "microbe migration" between Asia in the east and America in the west . Plague and cholera first appeared in Asia only to retreat back to their origins when they disappeared (a relative notion in Europe). Yellow fever and possibly syphilis instead originated in the New World. In any case, the progressive opening of Europe exposed its peoples more and more to imported microbes and parasites that played an important role in health and illness. The second element is the role of major political upheavals in the spread of infectious diseases. Zinsser has observed regarding typhus: "[w]hen the Thirty Years War ended, no corner of the European Continent was left without its foci of infection." The same could be said of the failed campaign of Charles VIII in Italy or the Napoleonic wars in Europe. The third element is more strictly demographic and concerns the growth of population and cities and, at the same time, the growth and expansion of migration and trade.

The larger and denser a population is, the easier it is to transmit pathogens from person to person. Large populations permit the survival and transmission of pathogens that would not be able to survive in smaller and less dense populations. It is likely then that between the fifteenth-century population nadir following the Black Death and the eve of the age of modern microbiology four centuries later, factors contributing to the intensification of infectious diseases included the growth of European population; the increase in the numbers, size, and density of cities; increased mobility; and greater contact with non-European bearers of new diseases.

A World in Motion

The disease systems that affect human survival, then, are variable, as is the number of lives they claim. To better clarify this observation, we can take a few pointers from epidemiology. Microbes – a general term for bacteria, viruses, protozoa, spirochetes, rickettsia and the like – are the agents responsible for disease and, in past eras, for the majority of deaths. In order for a disease to spread, a microbe (of which of course only a small number are dangerous) must enter the human body, survive, multiply, leave it, survive outside of the body, find a way to enter another organism, and repeat the whole cycle. We can divide the many different methods of transmission and "entrance" into the human body into four general types. The first includes digestive tract disorders and occurs through fecal contamination – usually of a water source – and the subsequent ingestion of contaminated foods. Typhoid and paratyphoid fevers, dysentery, diarrhea, and cholera are the most important of these. The second type includes airborne diseases that enter via the respiratory tract and are passed from person to person when infected particles are emitted through coughing, sneezing, and even talking. These diseases include smallpox, diphtheria, tuberculosis, measles, influenza, and the rarer though more lethal pneumonic form of plague. The third type is sexually transmitted and includes syphilis, other venereal diseases, and AIDS. A fourth type of disease is transmitted not through the natural portals of the human body, but via blood or tissue after the bite or sting of an animal (fleas, lice, mosquitoes, ticks) that transfers microbes from one human to another, or from an animal – which constitutes in this case the reservoir for the microbe (like the rat for the plague) – to a human. This category encompasses such great historical epidemics and endemics as plague, typhus fever, yellow fever, and malaria, and other minor ones as well. It adds a further complication to the disease picture, namely the complex relationship between the animal world – which preserves (reservoir) and transmits (carrier) microbes – and the human one.

This simple classification clearly demonstrates that the transmission of disease is strongly conditioned by the availability of resources as well as lifestyle and behavior. Simply put, the first category (transmission by digestive tract) is dependent on the availability of water, the second (airborne diseases) on human density; the third is influenced by behavior and customs; and the fourth involves hygiene, both public and private. Over the centuries, changes in lifestyle, productive technology, and consumption habits have gradually altered the ways in which single pathologies are transmitted, either increasing or decreasing the risk of contracting them. It would be pointless to study these changes in detail for their development has not been unidirectional. While building houses in brick and stone almost certainly reduced the presence of household rats, the source of the plague, the growth of cities favored instead the existence of rat colonies which made plague endemic. The reclamation of swamps and marshlands undoubtedly reduced the breeding environment of the Anopheles mosquito which carries malaria, but this same advance in agriculture, by increasing the number of water tanks and reservoirs for the purpose of irrigation, introduced new ones. And so to try to weigh the hypothetical consequences of the many changes and innovations over the years would be instructive, though not very useful for understanding overall trends.

A second source of variability in the relationship between microbes and humans is the process of mutual adaptation and the evolutionary mechanisms that it generates. "In general terms," wrote Sir Macfarlane Burnet in 1962,

> where two organisms have developed a host-parasite relationship, the survival of the parasite species is best served, not by the destruction of the host, but by the development of a balanced condition in which sufficient of the substance of the host is consumed to allow the parasite's growth and multiplication, but not sufficient to kill the host. For such a balance to develop, long periods of interactions and selection between the two species must have elapsed, and any protective adaptations on the part of the host must have been stimulated by, and in turn would be likely to provoke aggressive

adaptations on the side of the parasite. A stable balance is only rarely developed; more usually there are rather violent fluctuations, some of which appear as epidemics, but despite these, both species persist.

Thirty years earlier Zinsser had observed that

"[t]hough actually complex in function and metabolism, these supposedly simple things [microbes] display an amazing biologic and chemical flexibility; and since, in them, generations succeed each other with great speed (at least two every hour, under suitable circumstances) the phenomena of infection constitute an accelerated evolution extraordinarily favorable for the observation of adaptive changes. It would be surprising , therefore, if new forms of parasitism – that is, infection – did not constantly arise, and if, among existing forms, modifications in the mutual adjustment of parasites and hosts had not taken place within the centuries of which we have record."

These general principles – excerpted from two eminent biologists interested also in history – are still valid today. According to an official American committee on the subject of dealing with newly emerging diseases:

Because of the relatively small amount of DNA or RNA, or both, that they carry, their rapid growth rate, and large populations, microbial pathogens can evolve and adapt very quickly. These evolutionary mechanisms allow them to adapt to new host cells or host species, produce "new" toxin, bypass or suppress inflammatory or immune responses, and develop resistance to drugs and antibodies. The ability to adapt is required for the successful competition and evolutionary survival of any microbial form, but it is particularly crucial for pathogens, which must cope with host defenses as well as microbial competition.

For the population historian, who knows little about DNA and RNA, immune-defense systems, or genetic mutations and recombinations, it is important to rely on the authority of biologists; the virulence and threat of a disease may change over time, and there is a general trend towards reciprocal adaptation between human and pathogen that favors the less virulent strains of a disease. Moreover, new pathologies may arise as a result of pathogen mutation (as is the case for types of influenza and hepatitis B), of transmigration from other animal species (yellow fever and AIDS, which presumably originated in monkeys), and of zoonosis, the contraction from animals of infections not transmissible between humans (rabies, tularemia, dengue fever, encephalitis).

The complex set of biological and behavioral relationships between microbes, animals (which act as both reservoir and transmitter), and humans then is variable, not only because the human develops materially and socially, but also because evolution changes the nature and complexity of pathogens, and because the interrelationship between the human and animal worlds is constantly changing. In the 1950s and 1960s it was thought that infectious diseases had been conquered once and for all and as a result research institutes and public health agencies lowered their guard. The appearance of HIV and AIDS has abruptly reintroduced the problem of emergent new diseases and reemergent old ones thought to have been defeated, just as it recalls the wise words of Zinsser and Burnet cited above. Dengue fever, tularemia, Lyme disease, Lassa fever, and Ebola are diseases until recently unknown (though they may have already been in existence), while diseases considered under control, such as tuberculosis, malaria, and cholera, have cropped up again. Similar processes certainly occurred in the past, and history offers convincing examples of pathogen variations. An obvious example is plague, which made its first appearance in this millennium in 1347 (of which more below). But modern Europe too offers examples of new or "renewed" diseases that either caused serious epidemics or chronic illness and handicap: typhus fever, syphilis, "sweating sickness', cholera, yellow fever, and the influenza pandemic of 1918.

The origins of syphilis in Europe are still debated: whether it originated in the New World and was imported after 1492 or existed in Europe before then in a nonepidemic and less cruel form. What is clear is that contemporary observers considered it a new disease when it broke out among Charles VIII's soldiers during the occupation of Naples, spreading then to Milanese and Venetian troops, and to German forces under Maximilian I. In the period 1494–6 it reached epidemic proportions throughout Europe as soldiers returning to their native homes carried it with them. Its origins were as unclear then as they are today, an observation borne out by its many different names – *mal français*, sickness of Naples, Spanish pox. More interesting than the origin of the disease was its violence. The military surgeon Marcello Cumano has left us one of the first accurate descriptions of syphilis among Venetian soldiers during the siege of Novara in 1495: pustules that rapidly covered not only the genitals but also the face and entire body; ulcerations;

severe pain in the limbs; pustules that often lasted a year or more, as in leprosy; unsightly tissue loss from the nose, mouth and throat that created a frightful appearance. Fracastoro observed that the ulcerations spread all the way to the bone creating gummy buboes as big as eggs. Many died, and many survivors remained bedridden for years. The very name of the disease comes from a poem, "Syphilis sive de morbo gallico," penned in 1530 by the same Fracastoro, who also observed in his *De Contagione* that the severity of the disease had begun to diminish soon after its onset, as proved by the gradual change in symptoms, such as fewer pustules covering the body.

Syphilis is an important example not so much for its impact on mortality – in mid-seventeenth-century London, out of roughly 10,000 deaths only a few dozen were attributed to the "French pox," although John Graunt thought the figure underestimated – as for the information it gives us about adaptation between microbe and host and the diminished virulence of the disease. Over the centuries it continued to be widespread, though relatively controlled. A disease with a different history was the so-called "sweating sickness" that both appeared and disappeared in less than a century. Most likely viral in nature, it attacked and killed in less than a day, and in some cases in a very few hours. It began either at night or at dawn with violent trembling, followed by a sweaty fever, and chest and head pains. In all there were five epidemics: the first in 1485 just a few weeks after the defeat of Richard III at Bosworth Field; the second in 1507; the third in 1518 – all three limited to England except for an appearance in Calais by the third; the fourth in 1528 starting in England and spreading through half of Europe, first in northern Germany, Denmark, Prussia, Poland, Livonia, Lithuania, and Russia, then to the rest of Germany, the Netherlands, Switzerland, and Austria. The virus miraculously spared France, nor did it cross the Pyrenees or the Alps to Spain and Italy. The final epidemic of 1551 was again confined to England. And that was all. Although theories on the appearance and disappearance of "sweating sickness" are based on conjecture, two things seem clear: that it was a new disease – with precise and distinct symptoms – and that there were no traces of it after 1551.

Instability characterized the great epidemic infections that occupied center stage in the history of epidemiology as well. Take the example of exanthematic or petechial typhus. Caused by the microbe rickettsia, it is transmitted by lice living on humans. In the European or human variety (as compared to the American variety that resides in rats), the infection is perpetuated by human carriers who have the infection but do not display symptoms, and transmit it to other persons by passing lice. Whenever lice infestations became especially severe – for example during periods of war, famine, or other unrest and coupled with poverty, squalor and a high concentration of people (in army barracks, prisons, hospices, hospitals) – transmission of the microbe from person to person increased rapidly and the endemic disease became epidemic. In the first week of the disease an eruption of dark spots occurs; in the second a high fever; and in the third week a heart attack followed by either death or a speedy recovery. Before modern treatment its lethality was about 20 percent. Once again we are less interested in the characteristics of the illness than in the fact that evidence suggests it appeared as a new disease in the sixteenth century. A first indication is purely biological: "There is one feature of typhus which suggests that it is not an old-established human disease; its fatality for the louse. This is one of the few instances in which the insect vector of a human disease is seriously discommoded by the germs it transmits. The likely inference is that typhus of the louse is a relatively recent development, and that the disease has evolved in other hosts than man and the louse." In other words,the mutual adaptation between microbe and host-carrier (the louse) that represents the natural evolution of these diseases has not (yet) evolved. The second feature is instead historical. When typhus fever erupted in Europe, observers believed it to be a new disease with never before seen symptoms. In Spain it was thought that typhus fever, imported by soldiers coming from Cyprus, cropped up among Christian armies fighting the Arabs in Granada in 1489–90. In Italy petechial typhus fever was popularly known as *mal mazzucco* and initially appeared together with an epidemic of plague in 1477–9. In *De Contagione*, Fracastoro reports epidemics of petechial typhus in Italy in 1505 and 1528, and describes them as unknown before then, but also notes that it was known in Cyprus and its neighboring islands as it was to *maioribus nostris* (our ancestors). It may be then that its first appearance in an epidemic and serious form was preceded by sporadic and localized appearances, but there is no doubt that from the beginning of the sixteenth century to the Napoleonic Wars typhus was a major actor in the epidemiological story of Europe.

The three examples we have discussed – syphilis whose virulence quickly declined, sweating sickness that appeared and disappeared into thin air, and typhus that appeared, grew more virulent, and spread – are emblematic of the mutability of diseases within the mechanisms of biological evolution. Other examples of diseases that appear (yellow fever, encephalitis) or vanish (leprosy) can be explained by the combined action of the biological evolution of viruses or bacteria, of the interaction between the animal and human worlds, and of the action of society, whether intentional or not. It should come as no surprise then that over time, and against a background of high mortality – connected to the syndrome of backwardness discussed earlier in this chapter – the conditions of survival for Europe's peoples underwent oscillations and cycles.

The Plague: A Four-handed Game

On June 4, 1529, the Venetian ambassador Campeggio wrote from London that "we continue to wear our winter clothing and keep a fire lit as if it were January. I have never before known such unstable weather. The plague is beginning to rage and there is also some fear of 'sweating sickness.'" Fickle weather went hand in hand with this most lethal microbe, now commonplace two centuries after it first appearance. Of all demographically significant phenomena none is as well known as plague, and it would be pointless to try to summarize in these pages the wealth of texts, images, and scientific analyses that are available.

There were at least one-third fewer Europeans in the mid-fifteenth century than there had been 100 years before, and this was without doubt a result of the numerous waves of plague that followed the initial outbreak of 1347. It was plague again, though not exclusively, that challenged recovery during the late fifteenth and the sixteenth centuries; and steady population growth in the seventeenth century owes much to the disappearance of that disease. Beyond simple mortality and population growth, the transformation of many demographic systems can be traced to long-term adaptations to those great epidemics of plague. I will not discuss here the equally important economic consequences of plague on prices, wages, land systems, and production, nor shall I consider the social, political, religious, and psychological consequences. The plague is a major actor in old-regime demographic systems and needs to be considered from four different points of view: epidemiology; chronology and geography; its disappearance; and, finally, demographic impact.

Let us start with epidemiology. The plague is really a four-handed game, the demographic impact of which depends on the behavior of the players. One of these, the bacillus *Yersinia pestis* (isolated by Yersin in 1894 in Hong Kong), actually never changes its strategy, as its severity – the ability to invade, multiply, and kill a host organism – seems constant in all circumstances. But the other three players – the rat (or other rodent) that serves as the "reservoir" for the bacillus, the flea that transmits it, and man who is its victim – often change their moves. Leaving aside the metaphor for a moment, the simplified epidemiology of plague is the following: the bacillus is endemic in rats (in Europe, the ancient *Mus musculus*, the early modern *Rattus rattus*, and the contemporary *Rattus norvegicus*) and in other rodents (squirrels, marmots, etc.). It is transmitted from rat to rat by the bite of a flea (*Xenopsylla cheopis*) which is the chosen vector of the disease. When the rat population is particularly dense, occasional deadly cases of plague can become epidemic (or more precisely, epizootic). The death of the rat leaves the flea without its favorite environment and if it does not find a host of the same species (increasingly difficult as the epizootic spreads) it is forced to adapt itself to a human host whom it infects in the process of feeding itself. The bite of an infected flea, following an incubation period of a few days, brings on the disease which is characterized by painful swelling of the lymph nodes (buboes), high fever, inflammation of the internal organs, and coma. Between two-thirds and four-fifths of those afflicted die. Bubonic plague may also lead to secondary pneumonia, and through direct contact, give rise to the pneumonic form of plague. This latter disease is still more deadly, and usually causes death within three days. The death of the human host leads to another migration of the infected flea and so to another possible transmission of the disease. Clearly there are many possible variations in the contest: not so much the virulence of the bacillus as (a) the size, density, and mobility of the rat population; (b) the development of immunity by the rats; (c) the parasitic intensity of the fleas – more simply how many per infected rat – and their ability to travel; (d) the distance and relationship between the human and rat populations which naturally affect the mobility of the flea as it travels from rat to man. Research undertaken during the last great pandemic of plague in 1894 in Hong Kong reveals a multitude of elements that help us explain historical plague as well. If the rat population is sparse or lives far from the human population, if the rats are immune having survived a serious epizootic, if humans take precautions to avoid contact with rats, or if the carrier, the flea, is not very mobile or indeed immobile because dormant, then there is less probability of the insurgence of an epidemic. The inverse is equally true and instead leads to conditions that favor an epidemic. In order for an epidemic of plague to break out, a *yersinia* population must be maintained by its host of choice, the rat, or else rats or infected fleas must be reintroduced (by ship, in goods, through migration) and the interaction between rat and man must be close (as it usually is because rats survive best in association with humans). Today, even in the West, there exist sources of plague preserved in species of wild rodents. Every once in a while, as has occurred in the Rocky Mountains, a hunter or hiker is infected, but the infection rarely has the opportunity to spread. In one case, plague can spread without the aid of the flea, in its pneumonic form when transmitted directly through coughing or sneezing, but there has first to be a case of the bubonic variety.

Leaving aside the bacillus, which never varies its behavior, historical records tell us a great deal, even quantitatively, about man, a bit of data about the rat (migrations and the prevalence of various species), and almost nothing about the flea. The outcome of the match is usually known: duration, how many people were struck, how many died, and something about who they were. So we generally know something about the chronology, diffusion, and severity of the infection, which brings us to the second point in our brief discussion of plague: chronology and geography.

It should be pointed out that Europe had been acquainted with plague since the Justininian era. A first pandemic of the disease began in the eastern Mediterranean in 541–4 AD and struck Italy and (especially) southern Europe in a succession of waves that lasted a century. Subsequently, the plague remained in the eastern Mediterranean until the mid-eighth century and continued to trouble Europe, though in a contained fashion. It is the second pandemic, that began in 1347 and only started its retreat from Europe in the mid-sixteenth century that is the subject of our discussion. We should, however also point out that epidemiologists have identified another pandemic beginning with the 1894 outbreak in Hong Kong and Canton and spreading to Manchuria, India, and North America, a pandemic whose most recent episode occurred in India in 1994.

In the fall of 1347, a centuries-long bacteriological peace was broken with the unloading of Genoese merchant ships in Messina, Sicily. The ships had arrived from ports on the Black Sea that had been struck by plague imported from the East. Before the end of 1347 plague had reached the mainland of Italy at Reggio Calabria and maybe Genoa, and had begun a journey that would take it through the whole European continent in the next four or five years. By the end of 1349 the epidemic had spread beyond Italy to Spain, France, England, southern Germany, Switzerland, and Austria. By the end of 1350 it had reached Scotland and the populations around the North and Baltic Seas, and by the end of 1352 Poland and Russia (figure 4.1). This was, however, only the first in a series of rhythmic waves: plague swept through Italy, for example, again in 1360–3, 1371–4, 1381–4, 1388–90, and 1398–1400, and occurred almost simultaneously in Spain as well. The rest of Europe suffered similarly. In Russia plague reoccurred in 1363–5, 1374–7, 1387–90, and 1396; and in England the historical records (with some contradictions) mention a *pestis secunda* in 1361 through to a *pestis quinta* in 1391 (the *tertia* occurring in 1368–9 and the *quarta* in 1375). Plague continued to wind its way

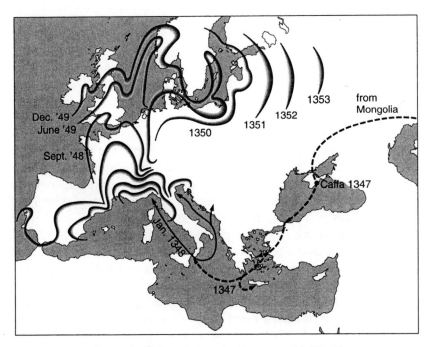

Figure 4.1   Spread of the plague in Europe, 1347–53

Source: C. McEvedy and R. Jones, *Atlas of World Population History*, Penguin, Harmondsworth, 1978, p. 25

through Europe in the following century though the epidemics were on the whole less severe, more localized, and less contemporaneous, so that while a population nadir was reached in the first half of the century, recovery began in the second half . Again, taking the case of Italy, both the sixteenth and seventeenth centuries suffered devastations of plague. There were cycles in 1522–30 (aggravated by the wars that followed the fall of Charles VIII), 1575–7 (especially in the northern Italy), 1630–1 (in the center-north), and 1656–7 (especially in the center-south). Even though these outbreaks were dreadful – Cipolla calculates that more than one-fourth of the population struck by the plague in the center-north was eliminated by the epidemic – the plague was no longer the major catastrophe it had been in the earlier centuries. Nonetheless, its main rival, typhus, would never match its fame. Beginning in the sixteenth century, the plague continued to snake its way throughout Europe along major communication routes, but in fits and starts, with sudden changes in direction, and revisitations upon former sites of devastation. On the continent as a whole plague was widespread during 1520–30, 1575–88, 1597–1604, and 1624–31.

Filling these pages with dates would not be terribly useful, but for a clearer picture we can summarize some data from Biraben, who has sorted out and assessed the location and chronology of plague epidemics in Europe (including Russia but not Ukraine and the Balkans). Between 1347 and 1534 there were 17 identifiable attacks of plague, on average one every 11.1 years. In the period between 1535 and 1683 there were 11 attacks occurring at a slightly less frequent one every 13.4 years. Until the middle of the fifteenth century the epidemics occurred with a simultaneity and timing as if they continued to be introduced from outside; later the plague became endemic and tended to appear locally whenever circumstances permitted, thus losing its synchronicity.

Equally revealing was the plague's disappearance. Excluding eastern Europe and a few other limited episodes, the plague more or less withdrew from the continent in the second half of the seventeenth century. The 1648–52 Spanish crisis occurred in Andalusia, with some incursions into Valencia, Catalonia, and Aragon, but left the interior and northern regions untouched. Its next appearance, between 1676 and 1685, mostly affected the Mediterranean regions of the peninsula. In Italy the last occurrences of plague, with one exception described below, were in 1630–1, in the central and northern regions, and in 1652–7 in the south. The final epidemic cycle in France took place between 1657 and 1670, while the British Isles last saw plague in 1647–8 in Scotland, and in 1665–6 in Ireland, northern and western England, London, and the rest of England. Between 1663 and 1670 the plague reached Amsterdam by sea from Smyrna and spread to England, Belgium, and northern France, making its way also along the Rhine to Switzerland, and reaching northern German ports on the North and Baltic Seas as far as Danzig in 1669–70. By 1670 almost all of western Europe (but not the Baltic region, eastern Europe, or the Balkans) was virtually free of plague.

"Virtually" requires elaboration. The disease remained endemic in Asia and North Africa, and so high-traffic and trade areas remained vulnerable to infection. Consequently plague struck France again in 1720–2, in Marseilles and Provence via a cargo ship from Syria. In 1743, a serious epidemic was imported to Messina and, across the Straits, Reggio Calabria by a Genoese cargo ship coming from the Peloponnese. In 1813 plague came to Malta. Quarantines and *cordons sanitaires* successfully prevented the spread of epidemic so the disease remained contained though still deadly. In eastern Europe, the retreat of plague came on much later as a result of its direct links with Asiatic hotbeds of the disease. The 1709–12 epidemic devastated the Balkans, Austria, Bohemia, eastern Europe, the Baltics, Danzig, Copenhagen, and Stockholm. In Russia, epidemics from the south threatened but did not reach the heart of the country in 1727–8, while the 1770–2 epidemic did instead reach Moscow. The plague remained endemic in the Balkans until 1841 when health measures enacted by the Turkish government successfully arrested it. Only at that point did the era of plague in Europe come to an end.

The Final Match

Why did plague begin to retreat from Europe three centuries after it had first appeared? That is the third point we need to explore, and the most problematic of the four I have proposed. As already noted, the complexity of plague epidemiology makes concrete answers hard to come by and theorizing dangerous. Yet plague was such an important disease for European populations – at once the greatest factor of constraint in population growth, the most symbolically laden, and that which exercised the greatest influence on the organization of early modern societies – that we really must explore the current theories regarding its disappearance, especially the more reasonable ones.

Several explanations are primarily biological. A not very plausible one suggests a progressive natural selection among the population for resistance to the disease. Survivors, though, did not acquire long-term immunity and as they represented a very small portion of the population – about one-fifth of those who contracted the disease survived, a figure little changed before modern cures – they had a modest impact on population, so that even if the disease did provide immunization, the selective process would be very slow. Moreover, there is no proof that the virulence of the infecting agent ever declined.

Another biological explanation concerns not man but the rat. There is some evidence from twentieth-century India that rats acquire immunity, or better a resistance, to plague. Later epizootics then should select rats more resistant to the disease and ultimately their mortality from plague would diminish and become irrelevant, so that the flea-carrier would no longer have to abandon its dead-rat host for a live-human one. In this way the cycle of infection would be broken. This theory may in part explain the disappearance of plague in Europe, but is not likely to be the single cause. And one is forced to ask why this process took place so much later in eastern Europe and the Balkans where, apparently, the selection of resistant rats did not stop the diffusion of the epidemic.

Other theories more appropriately look at the interaction between rat, flea, and human. Any environmental or social change that may have modified this chain of infection is a candidate for the explanation of why plague vanished. For example, some scholars have argued that the migration into Europe of *Rattus norvegicus* (or *decumanus*), originally from Asia, may have been an important factor. We have fairly specific information about this immigration: the species seems to have forded the Volga River *en masse* at the beginning of the eighteenth century and then gradually spread through Europe, reaching the Iberian peninsula around 1800. The predominant house rat, *Rattus rattus*, was the loser in the competition, even though the two species continue to cohabit in special situations. And it is in fact the habitat of *Rattus norvegicus*, and not its characteristics (bigger, and a good swimmer), that is significant: whereas *Rattus rattus* lives in direct contact with humans in their homes, *Rattus norvegicus* lives in ponds, rivers, and sewers. An epizootic among *Rattus norvegicus* presents a lesser risk for humans because when the host rat dies, the flea finds itself relatively far from a potential human host, and, given its sluggish nature, would have to go to great lengths to infect one. Unfortunately for this theory, plague continued to break out in Russia and the Balkans following the invasion of *Rattus norvegicus* and disappeared in western Europe well before its arrival.

Still others have suggested that improvements in living conditions and personal and public hygiene were important factors in eliminating plague. These sorts of improvement should all lead to a diminished infestation of rats and fleas in the human habitat and so make it more difficult to spread the contagion from rat to human. Yet this theory too is problematic. Southwestern Europe could certainly not claim to be in the vanguard of public and private hygiene – though the fact that its homes were mostly made of stone and bricks without any of the wood used in northern European construction and preferred by the rat – may have been an advantage; and yet plague vanished from there very early. Moreover, other infectious diseases that thrive in filth and squalor, such as typhus, showed no signs at all of diminishing in the late seventeenth century and later. If anything, urban growth in much of Europe created still more favorable conditions for the parasitism of insects and rodents. Historical anecdotes provide a measure of proof for this: one has only to think of the famous 20 lice, small and large, that jumped out of Samuel Pepy's wife's hair at the time of the London plague.

We can safely say that there is no simple explanation for the disappearance of plague and that a web of factors were responsible for it. Unfortunately, bacilli, fleas, and rats leave behind no written documents, and so we are destined to continue in our uncertainty. But if indeed there is a web of factors that caused the plague to vanish from Europe, it is still possible that a catalyst existed to activate and sustain it. European societies gradually created policies of defense that in the long term proved to be effective in arresting the contagion. Beginning in the fifteenth century permanent health magistrates were created in Italy, and by the middle of the sixteenth century they existed in all major cities. Their powers included the issuance of bills of health stating where people and goods came from, whether infected or safe areas, and of licenses listing the point of departure of ships, as well as the institution of quarantines and *cordons sanitaires*. During the last two plague epidemics of 1630–1 and 1656–7, there was a constant and accurate stream of information passing between the health offices of the various states, whether infected or not. As one example, let us look at the actions of the health office in Florence during the plague of 1656 which struck the Kingdom of Naples, Rome, and Liguria, but spared Tuscany. The memory of the 1630 plague was still fresh, and it was only natural for health officials to be concerned and follow the progress of the epidemic carefully: on April 5, the City Council of Lucca informed Florence that it had been alerted by the City Council of Genoa that some cases of plague had been confirmed in Cagliari (Sardinia). Lucca then communicated that traffic between Sardinia and the port of Viareggio had been blocked and invited Florence to do the same. On May 6, the Florentine correspondent at Naples announced that some suspicious cases had been reported, that the local authorities had first minimized them and then taken some limited measures. He added ironically that the people of Naples preferred to appeal to the Virgin of Pompeii and Saint Gennaro. On May 20, the Papal State blocked traffic with Naples and informed Florence of this measure. On May 23, Florence banned trade with Piombino and Porto Ercole, two Neapolitan enclaves in Tuscany, and instructed local authorities to check travelers in the coastal Maremma region. On May 25, after consulting the grand duke, the health office issued and published a ban on the Kingdom of Naples (including trade and communication restrictions) and sent copies to Lucca, Venice, Milan, Verona, Modena, Parma, Bologna, Ancona, Cremona, Mantua, and Ferrara. On that same day a series of measures were approved: a quarantine on all ships coming from Naples; bills of health were introduced; deputations were created in the major cities (Pisa, Siena, Livorno, and Volterra) to guarantee that policies were being implemented; Neapolitan goods that had been delayed in customs were sent to the lazzaretto of San Marco Vecchio. On May 27, Genoa issued its own ban on Naples (a futile measure for plague eventually broke out there) and notified Florence. On that same day, Jacopo Felicini of Messina, age 33, average height, brown hair (according to the original bill of health which has been preserved) was given permission by the authorities of plague-free Pisa to go to Florence. Between May 27 and 29, Genoa and Florence exchanged information about suspected outbreaks at Civitavecchia, port of the Papal State. On the 29th, Civitavecchia was banned by Florence and Rome itself. A June 1 circular communicated detailed instructions to 49 cities in the Grand Duchy. On June 6, Florence informed Milan that any merchandise from Germany and Flanders (where plague was suspected) was subject to an additional quarantine in Florence even if it had already been quarantined in Milan or

Verona. Concern about the health status of Rome increased between the 10th and 17th, and on June 18 a ban was declared on Rome, followed some days later by one on Genoa.

This series of events demonstrates the two-pronged strategy carried out by the health magistrates. On the one hand an international health watch entailed a prompt and constant exchange of information; other health magistrates were quickly alerted to actions taken. On the other hand, internal measures were taken: coordinating preventive and repressive measures; controlling the movement of people and goods; issuing bills of health; running lazzarettos; placing ships under quarantine; creating local structures to implement orders and policy.

The case of Florence, and Italy in general, is not unique. The requirement of licenses for maritime transport, listing points of embarkation and call (clean if coming from a contagion-free area and marked if not) and of bills of health spread throughout western Europe in the late sixteenth century. A *cordon sanitaire* surrounded Paris to defend it from plague in 1688, and they were imposed, with more or less urgency, to contain plague in Prussia in 1709–10, Provence and Languedoc in 1720–1, and Messina in 1743. Scotland enacted stricter measures against plague than did England and, apparently for that reason, plague disappeared earlier there. The insularity of England should have afforded it an excellent defense against the disease, but quarantine measures enacted by English authorities were irregular and inadequate prior to 1640. As compared to Barcelona, which began requiring naval licenses in 1558, Russia only introduced this policy to its Baltic ports in 1665, in reaction to the London plague.

The measures I have highlighted here are only those aimed at interrupting the path of infection by blocking the circulation of goods and people. Many others were attempted, often in vain, to slow down the course of the epidemic by quarantining the homes of victims, isolating family members, and confining those with plague or suspected of having it in lazzarettos. But plague began its retreat in Europe most likely in tandem with the measures described above. To be sure, trade embargoes were often violated because of the economic losses they caused merchants; bills of health were faked; *cordon sanitaires* infiltrated; and not all plague victims ended up in the lazzarettos. Just the same, the various measures enacted in the seventeenth and eighteenth centuries had the overall effect of protecting the west by subdividing and compartmentalizing space in case of danger and blocking the free circulation of people and goods, the carriers of lice and infected rats. These measures had the general effect of diminishing the risk of an epidemic and may have acted as a positive catalyst together with other factors which over time contributed to the disappearance of plague: the appearance of *Rattus norvegicus*, the selection of resistant rats, random improvements in public and private hygiene, etc. Naturally this explanation is acceptable only if coupled with the assumption that plague broke out as a result of its "reintroduction" via humans, animals, or parasites. Undoubtedly there were also areas in which the plague was endemic. Take the case of London, for example. According to the London Bills of Mortality described by John Graunt, between 1604 and 1666 there were only three years (1629, 1633, 1635) in which no deaths were attributed to plague, a sign that the infection was kept alive among the rat population. However, London was a large city of several hundred thousand and an active commercial center. Plague presumably did not linger in smaller centers, and in order to reappear had to be reintroduced. The hypothesis described finds further support in the fact that plague lasted much longer in eastern than western Europe. The east was physically closer to the breeding grounds of the infection and administratively less successful in imposing protective or preventive measures. Unlike the west, which could more easily control the risk of contagion by sea, the east had to control the introduction of plague by land, relying on a system of *cordons sanitaires* placed along an endlessly long border.

Demographic Losses

Our fourth and final point concerns the demographic cost of plague. For more than three centuries plague was the strongest obstacle to European population growth and so it would be helpful to our understanding if we could calculate its cost in terms of human life. Strictly speaking this is not possible. For much of the period there are no reliable sources, and epidemics were not always accurately noted, especially in peripheral and outlying rural areas. Where reliable sources do exist, the causes of death may be ambiguous and losses inflated to include emigrants or those fleeing the disease. One can understand why the demographer justifiably avoids answering the simple question: how many people died of plague?

Nonetheless we can attempt an approximate answer to this question by taking into consideration a number of factors. The first, and a decisive one, is the strong decline in European population between the high levels reached at the end of the thirteenth and the beginning of the fourteenth centuries and the minimum reached in the fifteenth century. That the principal cause of the decline was a series of plague cycles is almost universally agreed upon. The estimates given in figure 1.1 (see p. 6) indicate a decline in European population between 1300 and 1450 greater than one third, with as high as 60 percent losses in the north of Europe. There is an abundance of irrefutable evidence – though often only at the local level – of demographic decline. Here are just a few examples: four areas of the Tuscan countryside show demographic losses of 47–80 percent between the fourth decade of the fourteenth century and the third of the fifteenth, and there are similar figures for other parts of Tuscany as well. In a wide range of French regions, from Provence to the Dauphiné, from Normandy to the Ile de France, studies concur in showing a 57–80 percent demographic decline between the period before plague and the mid- to late fifteenth century. In England there is some debate over the size of the pre-plague population (estimates vary between 3.7 and 6.2 million) but none over the low figure for the second half of the fifteenth century: between 2 and 2.5 million. Other indirect indicators gleaned from wills show low reproductivity for close to a century, consistent with a 60 percent decline in population. The population of Norway in 1300 was 350,000 and declined to 125,000 between 1450 and 1500. In Europe overall it took at least two centuries before populations once again reached pre-1348 levels.

Let us look to Tuscany (figure 4.2) once again for even more compelling evidence. Annual mortality series for a number of towns (Florence, Siena, Arezzo, Sansepolcro) peak dramatically in plague years: 1348, 1363, 1374, 1383, 1390, 1400 and so forth. In the period between 1340 and 1450 a crisis (defined as a three-fold or greater increase over the normal number of deaths) occurred roughly every nine years, and the average crisis represented a sixfold increase over the normal number of deaths. A few simple calculations yield the following: a six-fold increase – presuming a normal mortality of 3 percent per year – corresponds to a mortality loss of 18 percent and, assuming a 3 percent birth rate, a net loss of 15 percent. Let us also imagine that a 10 percent recovery occurred in the nine years following each crisis (which implies a natural increase of roughly 1 percent per year, fairly high in an old-regime society) for a net loss during the nine years of 5 percent.

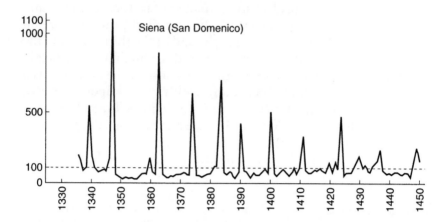

Figure 4.2   Annual deaths in Siena (partial series), fourteenth
and fifteenth centuries (period average = 100)

Source: L. Del Panta, *Le epidemie nella storia demografica italiana*, Loescher,
Turin, 1980

Extending this calculation over the course of a century, the
resulting net loss would be 43 percent, a figure entirely in line with
estimates for the population decline between the zenith and nadir
of the late Middle Ages.

We also have estimates for seventeenth-century plague losses.
Biraben has looked at the four epidemics in France (using today's
borders) during the period 1600–70 and calculated that between
2.2 and 3.4 million people died of plague on top of an estimated
total mortality (without plague) of 44 million. Plague then would
have "added" between 5 and 8 percent to "expected" deaths. In
and of itself this figure seems relatively modest for such a great
calamity, but appearances are deceiving. Assuming that in the
absence of plague the French population would have grown about
3 per 1,000 annually in the 70-year period in question (between
1550 and 1750 population in fact grew at a rate of about one per
1,000) then plague would have eliminated almost all (90 percent)
of the natural increase using Biraben's high estimate, and over half
in the case of his lower one. Plague was clearly a restraining force.

In the Kingdom of Naples (excluding Sicily) the scourge of 1656
presumably cost 900,000 lives out of total population of 4.5
million. Cipolla's detailed estimate for north-central Italy during
the 1630–1 epidemic puts plague mortality at 1.1 million out of a

population of 4 million. Given a hypothetical postepidemic recovery of 1 percent per annum (never achieved over the long term in western Europe, not even in Elizabethan England), then population would have returned to pre-plague numbers after 32 years, or, given a more realistic recovery rate of five per 1,000, after 64.

The preceding calculations refer to large territorial areas. We have more precise data – true statistics for deaths due to plague – for urban centers beginning in the sixteenth century. Here are some examples moving back through time. Moscow in 1771–2 recorded over 50,000 deaths or about 20 percent of the total population; in 1720–1 plague killed half the population of Marseilles and Aix-en-Provence, and roughly one-quarter of Toulon's; the great plague of 1665 in London (which was not its most severe) claimed 69,000 lives, about one sixth of the population while the earlier major outbreaks of the disease (1625, 1603, 1593, 1563) eliminated an average of one-fifth of London's inhabitants. Continuing back in time, those Italian cities hit by the two epidemics of 1630–1 and 1656–7 probably lost an average of 36 percent of their populations. The population of Augusta, struck twice in a short period of time (in 1627–8 and 1632–5) was reduced by 21 and 30 percent respectively, while Barcelona during its five major epidemics in the sixteenth and seventeenth centuries lost a minimum of 12 percent (1507) and a maximum of 45 percent (1653) of its inhabitants. The list could go on and on to further illustrate the devastating effect of plague on cities. London, on its way to becoming the largest city in Europe, suffered, according to the Bills of Mortality reported by Graunt, 150,204 lives lost to plague for the period between 1604 and 1665, or 21 percent of the 714,543 total deaths. Though plague did not necessarily recur in other cities with the same frequency as in London, it is nonetheless the case that almost no city remained plague-free for long periods of time. And the losses, like those cited above, required, in the absence of immigration, decades to recoup.

In the meantime, what was happening in the countryside and more isolated areas? Two competing theories attempt to answer this question. The first depends on the general principle that plague – like other transmittable diseases – is more easily spread in densely populated areas, especially when its outbreak depends upon reintroduction of the contagion from outside the community. Clearly the density of human population is important (especially in the case of pneumonic plague which is transmitted from person to person), but so is the density of rat and flea communities, which are not necessarily in direct correlation with human ones. The second theory instead suggests that in cities (like London) where plague was endemic and the rat population represented a constant reservoir for the disease, the rats themselves would quickly develop resistance to the disease through natural selection and ultimately give rise to a population which might carry *yersinia* but be resistant to it. In this way, the flea would not need to migrate to humans and bring about the well-known outcome. In rural areas instead this selection would not take place; rats would remain vulnerable to plague – usually reintroduced from cities; and so they would transmit the disease more easily to humans. Specialists will have to evaluate the merits of these two not necessarily opposed theories and their overall effects. The history of plague, however, does not point to a decided difference between city and the countryside. So while it is true that during the 1720–1 epidemic in Provence-Languedoc, there is a discernible inverse relationship between mortality and the demographic size of towns, it is also true that in sparsely populated Norway, with no large urban centers at all, the plague caused more damage than in more urban areas. During the first century of plague in Europe, the losses sustained in the countryside – revealed by the decline in number of hearths and the disappearance of villages – were so great that it is hard to believe that plague was more devastating in urban areas. In any case, the majority of the massive population decline experienced by the continent as a whole – in which less than one person in ten lived in centers of any notable size – took place in rural areas.

Other Factors and the Road to Normality

The disappearance of plague from Europe did not mean that the continent was free of dangerous diseases. As I have already mentioned, new diseases emerged in the modern period, for example exanthematic or petechial typhus, inextricably linked to the migration, poverty, and malnutrition that accompanied war and famine. It is difficult to properly evaluate the contribution of typhus to old-regime mortality because of its confusion with other epidemic forms having similar symptoms and because of the scarcity of relevant data. Two facts however shed some light on this subject. The first is a series of outbreaks in Europe in the sixteenth century of a disease which, if not new, was certainly more aggressive. Zinsser suggests that typhus was well established in the

Orient and that it was generally thought to have exploded during the assault on Granada, brought by soldiers from Cyprus where the contagion was endemic. From Spain it spread to Italy, France, and central Europe, accelerated by war. Typhus also entered Europe on its eastern border: the imperial armies in 1542 were struck by a great epidemic of typhus while fighting against the Turks in Hungary. Zinsser further maintains that typhus devastated the ranks of the imperial armies – Germans and Italians – but not those of the Turks or Hungarians who had in part developed an immunity to it as a result of a long-term and endemic presence of the disease. This would be indirect proof of the relative novelty of typhus west of the Balkan peninsula. The subsistence problems of the late sixteenth century created by slow demographic recovery on the continent, together with a constant state of conflict culminating in the Thirty Years War, gave typhus many opportunities to develop into an epidemic.

The second point to emphasize is that typhus spreads when general events create serious problems of production and subsistence. Sudden increases in mortality during famines were not so much the result of malnutrition as of the social upheaval that led to the rise and spread of deadly epidemics; there were more poor, hungry, and homeless people, and the public institutions that might receive them – the poorhouse, hospital, prison – suffered overcrowding. In other words, the factors that contributed to the spread of the disease multiplied. Famines and the consequent mortality crises were often largely the result of weather conditions that affected large geographical areas. In Italy the subsistence crises of 1591–2, 1648–50, 1764–7, and 1816–17 went hand in hand with epidemics of typhus and significant increases in mortality for almost the whole country. Moreover, when war, poverty, and hunger are woven together into a long-term syndrome of death dominated by typhus fever and plague, the results can be truly devastating. Figure 4.3 shows population fluctuations for Germany during the Thirty Years War and provides a dramatic illustration of the syndrome.

Smallpox is another disease that seems to have emerged in the seventeenth and eighteenth centuries. Though not a new disease – there are written descriptions of it going back centuries before – it did not produce serious crises until the sixteenth century. It is likely that urban growth and increased population density in general favored its rise and spread. Smallpox is viral and harbored by humans; it is transmitted directly, person to person, and so does

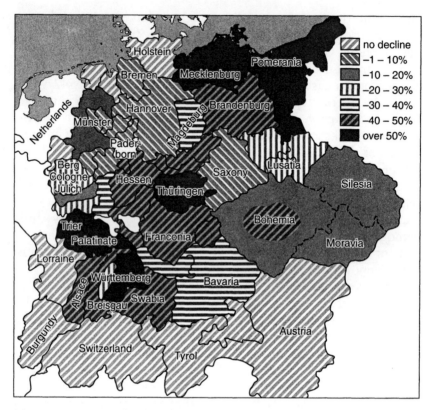

Figure 4.3 Population change in the Holy Roman Empire during the Thirty Years War

Source: G. Franz, *Der Dreissigjährige Krieg und das Deutsche Volk*, Jena, 1943

not require a carrier. Because survivors of smallpox develop immunity, in those areas where it is endemic it breaks out periodically (every three, five, 10 years or so), namely once it finds a sufficient population of children who are not immune. According to Creighton, smallpox emerged gradually in England and became prominent during the reign of James I (1603–25). Similarly, in Italy, historical records before the mid-sixteenth century mention smallpox only occasionally, while epidemics became frequent in the last half of the century, rare during the seventeenth, and again numerous during the eighteenth century.

In areas where smallpox is endemic, mortality is highest among children because much of the adult population, having survived previous epidemics, is immune. On the other hand, where the virus is normally absent – in an isolated or sparsely inhabited area – its occasional reintroduction leads to high mortality among all age groups. Smallpox like other childhood diseases, including fatal ones, did not get the same attention as the adult illnesses: the upper classes seemed almost to fear the physical disfiguration it brought more than the risk of death for children. Yet over the long term, the negative effects of smallpox, concentrated among the very young, were much greater than those of other diseases of equal intensity but more equally distributed among age groups. Daniel Bernoulli, who in 1788 estimated that three years would have been added to life expectancy if smallpox had been controlled through inoculation (not as effective as the vaccination discovered by Jenner in 1798), grossly underestimated by not taking into account the concentration of the disease among very young children.

Table 4.1 lists smallpox episodes in various parts of Europe – Ireland, Great Britain, Scandinavia, Italy – in the eighteenth century. In most cases, death due to smallpox accounted for 6 to 20 percent of total deaths. And rural areas seem to have been as vulnerable to the disease as urban ones.

Our initial premise, that old-regime societies were subject to high mortality systems as a result of backwardness regarding material resources and knowledge, is substantiated by the examples of plague, typhus fever, and smallpox (in addition to those of syphilis and "sweating sickness'). However, these systems were also highly variable because of changes in complex circumstances – in part biological, in part social – that determined the spread, intensity, and deadliness of communicable diseases. While it is impossible to synthesize these circumstances into a single model for the various pathologies, it does seem generally to be the case that the intro-duction of a new pathology into a "virgin" population has an initially devastating effect that is then weakened by subsequent biological adaptations, immunities and resistance, and social defense mechanisms. Finally, there are different reasons for the attenuation or disappearance of a pathology from the continent: in the case of sweating sickness the causes are unknown (or unknow-able); in the case of plague, they are predominantly tied to a coherent social policy of "compartmentalizing" space and blocking the spread of the contagion; for smallpox they depend on a discovery (Jenner's vaccine); and in the case of typhus fever they are linked to economic and social progress (reducing food short-ages). Nonetheless, we remain in the dark or uncertain about many aspects of epidemiology in the modern era. For example, there is

Table 4.1   Percentage of deaths from smallpox, selected European populations, eighteenth century

Population	Years	% of deaths from smallpox
Kilmarnock	1728–62	13.8
London	1710–39	8.2
Boston, Lincolnshire	1749–57	15.3
Maidstone	1752–61	17.2
Whitehaven	1752–80	19.2
Northamapton	1740–74	10.7
Edinburgh	1744–63	10
Dublin	1661–90	21.1
Dublin	1715–46	18.4
Copenhagen	1750–69	8.8
Sweden	1749–73	12.4
Finland	1749–73	14.4
Finland	1749–73	13.2
Berlin	1782–91	9.1
Stuttgart	1782–1801	8.6–16.4
Königsberg	1782–1801	6.2–8.3
Vienna	1752–53	10.2
Verona	1774–1806	6.3
Livorno	1767–1806	7.1

Sources: For Great Britain, Ireland, and Scandinavia: A. Mercer, *Disease, Mobility and Population in Transition*, Leicester University Press, Leicester 1990, p. 232; for Berlin, Stuttgart, and Königsberg: E. François, *La mortalité urbaine en Allemagne au XVIIIe siècle*, in "Annales de Démographie Historique," 1978, p. 157; for Verona and Livorno, L. Del Panta, *Le epidermie nella storia demografica italiana*, Turin, Loescher, 1980, p. 222

much to be learned about the historical course of malaria, a disease that affected mortality both directly and also indirectly as a pre-disposing cause of other illnesses. The case of malaria is complex because of the interrelationship between vector (Anopholes mosquito), an environment that favors its breeding, and human settlements. Agricultural development itself has widely differing effects, and land reclamation projects have not always produced the desired outcome. As with other diseases we have discussed, instability, crisis, and social upheaval certainly favored its spread. And in much of Europe – the whole of the Mediterranean as well as the Balkans, Russia and other parts of north-central Europe – malaria conditioned both mortality trends and the geography of settlement. The cycles of the disease are not clear, though it seems that malaria became a serious problem in the Mediterranean world in the first and second centuries AD, and that the beginning of its remission in the late nineteenth century was preceded by many centuries during which it was widespread.

A few more words on long-term mortality trends. As pointed out at the beginning of this chapter, if we assume a hypothetically constant birthrate, then every year either gained or lost from a similarly hypothetical life-expectancy at birth of 30 years is roughly equivalent to an increase or decrease of one per 1,000 per year in the growth rate. Since this figure was under three per 1,000 throughout Europe between 1550 and 1800 one can readily see how significant even modest variations in mortality are to population growth. Unfortunately, it is difficult to reconstruct long mortality series for large populations and so historical demographers cannot offer a wealth of examples. A sample or two, though, confirms the existence of important mortality trends. For England,

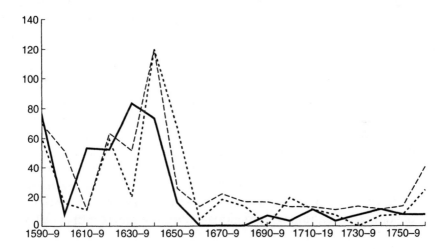

Figure 4.4   Intensity of mortality crises in northern Italy, central-southern Italy (*Mezzogiorno*), and Tuscany, 1590–1769

Note: The intensity or frequency of crises, based on multiple series, is defined as the number of observation-years (per 1,000) in which mortality is at least double the underlying trend. *Mezzorgiorno* here includes all Italian regions south of Tuscany

Sources: M. Breschi and L. Del Panta. "I meccanismi dell'evoluzione demografica nel Seicento: mortalità e fecondità." Paper presented to the *Convegno della Società italiana di demografia storica*, "La popolazione italiana nel Seicento," Florence, November 1996

life expectancy in the 50 years between 1566 and 1616 was roughly 39 years as compared to 34 years one century later (1666–1716). In France, life expectancy fluctuated between 25 and 31 (ten-year averages) between 1740 and 1800. The fluctuation was still greater in Sweden between 1750 and 1820, from 30 to 40 years of age.

More examples of the five to 10 year swings are also found in pre-Unification Italy – in Lombardy, Venetia, Tuscany, and the Kingdom of Naples from the mid-eighteenth to mid-nineteenth centuries (before the modern transition) – as well as in the rest of Scandinavia. These ranges are even greater for smaller areas. The clenching grip of mortality – basically death from transmittable diseases – tightened and relaxed throughout the old regime and strongly influenced the pace of demographic growth.

The eighteenth century ushered in a period of fewer crises throughout most of Europe. In a study of 23 central European localities, Flinn demonstrates a strong decline in the frequency of crises during the last quarter of the seventeenth century and further decline during the eighteenth. Crisis frequency in the Iberian peninsula and Italy remained at a higher level, though even then it was lower than in earlier periods. Figure 4.4 considers three areas of Italy – north, Tuscany, and south-central – and looks at the frequency of truly catastrophic crises. The indicator of frequency or intensity reflects the number of years in which the number of deaths is at least twice the normal level. A strong decline in catastrophic crises is evident beginning in the last third of the seventeenth century, though they do not disappear during the whole of the next century. In other areas, like England, the incidence of crises had already been low for some time, while instability and with it the continuance of crisis mortality continued to characterize most of the outlying areas of the continent – the Mediterranean, Atlantic, Balkan, and Scandinavian regions – until the nineteenth century.

5

Systems

Demographic Systems

In the first four chapters I have attempted to describe the primary forces of constraint in old demographic regimes and how they worked. Land, space, resources, food, microbes, and disease defined the rather narrow path along which preindustrial European populations grew. These populations established demographic systems that, while often very different from one another, shared, at least by contemporary standards, a low growth rate. By "system" I mean the combination of demographic behaviors governed by fairly stable rules and relationships. Biologists, for example, identify two systems that govern the survival and growth of animal species. In one, typical of large mammals, relatively few offspring are produced but parental investment is high and so is the rate of survivorship. A very different strategy operates in the second system, typical of smaller mammals: many offspring are produced, parental investment is low, and survival precarious. The result is that combinations of completely different behaviors can each produce long-term equilibrium. The biological example is useful, but hazardous to apply in the human case where social factors dominate. We can easily see how very different "combinations" of behavior can produce similar population increases: population A is marked by high mortality, early marriage, and high fertility and grows at the same rate as population B, marked by low mortality, late marriage, and moderate fertility. It may strike the reader as odd to describe mortality, an essentially biological event, as a behavioral phenomenon, but it will simplify our discussion to do so. The various demographic behaviors, or phenomena, that together determine demographic growth are relatively few: mortality, nuptiality, fertility, and migration.

The various mechanisms that underlie demographic change do not interact randomly. They follow the logical interdependencies that constitute a demographic "system," the nature, rules, and operation of which are the topic of this chapter. The most obvious interrelationship derives from the examples described above for the animal world; namely the incompatibility in the long run of high fertility combined with low mortality. Not only does that combination lead to excessive population growth, but lower mortality generally implies high parental investment in each offspring, conduct hardly compatible with a large number of offspring. The reverse is also true. High mortality is incompatible in the long term with low fertility not only because it leads to extinction of the species, but also because it creates a generational imbalance as the elderly become increasingly vulnerable when inadequately supported by the young.

European society is complex, and so describing the predominant "systems" and how they change over time is difficult without the help of a model. The measure of *reproductivity* is at the heart of a demographic system, and this can be simply expressed as the relative number of offspring a given generation produces. Demographers calculate reproductivity – for reasons of simplicity and because the data is generally available – by comparing the number of female offspring born to a given generation of women (born in the same year or other specific period) to the size of that generation of mothers. If, for example, there are twice as many daughters born as there are women in the mothers' generation, and if that behavior is extended to the population as a whole, then that population will double each generation (approximately every 30 years) with an intrinsic annual growth rate of more than 2 percent. If instead there were 10 percent more daughters than (potential) mothers, the growth rate would be around three per thousand per annum (a normal rate of increase in old-regime societies). A simplified system might work as follows (using convenient but not unrealistic values; see also table 5.1): take a given number of female offspring (say 1,000) born in a single year "t" and multiply that number by a coefficient (here 0.5) that expresses the probability of survival to adulthood (for example, 30 years of age) to get 500. If 80 percent of these women marry, we have a group of 400. If during an average year of marriage (in the childbearing years) 15 percent of these women give birth to a female, 60 female offspring will be born. Finally, if each married woman remains so for 20 of her childbearing years during each of which an average of 60 daughters are born, then in 20 years there will be 1,200 female births and, and assuming that no unmarried women have children, we conclude that the original generation of 1,000 females has produced 1,200 daughters in all, accounting for a 20 percent increase in a 30 year period (or six per 1,000 per year). This simple model predicts that the initial generation multiplied by its probability of survival, intensity of migration (a factor excluded from the preceding description for simplicity's sake), nuptiality, fertility, and average length of marriage results in the number of births (expressed notationally as Initial Generation (G) x Survival (S) x Migration (E) x Nuptiality (M) x Fertility (F) x Length of Marriage (D) = Births resulting from Initial Generation). It is a model that combines the primary "behaviors" that generate a population's growth rate, rates we know to have been fairly low in old-regime societies. Nonetheless, similar growth rates could be achieved by substantially different combinations (or systems), or again, similar systems with a single slightly different element could produce different rates of increase and in the long run, very different total populations.

Of course, none of the variables in the model are entirely independent of one another. For example, lower legitimate fertility (due to longer birth intervals caused by prolonged breastfeeding) allows more parental investment in offspring and increased survival. Increased survival reduces widowing and so signifies a longer life with a marriage partner which in turn leads to higher legitimate fertility. A sharp decline in infant mortality may lead to longer birth intervals and so lower fertility. Similar examples abound.

Finally, the variables in the model can be broken down into subcomponents more directly related to living conditions and social behavior. Survival can be divided into two categories: infant (influenced by childrearing techniques) and youth/adult, which is linked to labor regimes and hygiene. Nuptiality relies on relative access to marriage (represented by average age at marriage) and the percentage of the marriageable population which never marries. Both variables are sensitive to cultural and legal norms that regulate choice of spouse, systems of succession, land entitlement, and family strategies. Legitimate fertility is connected to length of breast-feeding, frequency of sexual intercourse, fetal mortality, and birth control (generally considered low or non-existent in historical societies): each demographically quantifiable component has clear social and cultural correlates. The average length of child-bearing unions depends on several factors: age at marriage, age at the end of the fecund period (ammenorrea) , and the premature termination of unions because of the death of either partner. The first factor depends on cultural norms, the second on biological variations, and the third on survivorship.

Table 5.1   England, Germany, and France: a comparison of systems

	Population	Period	G (f) Initial generation born in the year "t"	Survival = S Proportion of the initial generation surviving to adulthood
			(1)	*(2)*
(1)	England	1650–75	1000	0.532
(2)	England	1775–99	1000	0.577
(2) / (1) × 100	Eng 2 / Eng 1			108
(3)	France	XVIII	1000	0.418
(4)	Rouen	XVIII	1000	0.405
(5)	Crulai	XVII–XVIII	1000	0.438
(4) / (3) × 100	Rouen / France			98
(5) / (3) × 100	Crulai / France			105
(6)	Germany	1750–99	1000	0.52
(3) / (2) × 100	France / Eng 2			72
(6) / (2) × 100	Germany / Eng 2			90
(6) / (3) × 100	Germany / France			124

Note: The values in lines 1–6 should be understood as follows (with reference to the data for England, 1650–75). 1,000 births in year "t" (col. 1) are multiplied: by the proportion surviving to adulthood (approximately the average age of childbearing), equal to 53.2% (col. 2); by the proportion added or subtracted by migration before adulthood (col. 3; in the example 0.987 means that 1.3% is the net loss from migration); by the proportion who marry (col. 4, equal to 68.9%) before the average age of childbearing; by the average number of legitimate births per woman in an average year of marriage (col. 5, equal to 14.5%;

England, France, and Germany

The "system" model described above is a useful tool for interpreting old-regime demography. We can apply it especially to the seventeenth and eighteenth centuries, a period rich in population records, primarily parochial registers, that allow reconstruction of the major demographic phenomena. A look at three well-known and representative reconstructions, for England, Germany, and France, allows us to compare the general characteristics of each

Migration = E Proportion added to or subtracted from initial generation because of migration	Marriage = M Proportion of the initial generation that marries	Fertility = F Legitimate fertility: births per woman in an average year of fecund marriage	Cohabitation = D Average length of fecund marriage	Births = N (f) Total births to initial generation $(1)\times(2)\times(3)\times(4)\times$ $(5)\times(6) = (7)$	Generational ratio: daughters/ initial generation of mothers N(f) / G(f) $(7) / (1) = (8)$
3)	(4)	(5)	(6)	(7)	(8)
0.987	0.689	0.145	18.8	996	0.996
0.997	0.785	0.160	20.5	1,484	1.484
101	114	110	109	149	149
1	0.807	0.185	16.7	1,042	1.042
1.251	0.690	0.200	16.5	1,153	1.153
0.847	0.805	0.188	18.2	1,021	1.021
125	86	108	99	111	111
85	100	102	109	98	98
0.968	0.769	0.19	17	1,250	1.25
100	103	116	81	70	70
97	98	119	91	92	92
97	95	103	102	120	120

this percentage is equal to the percentage of women who have a child in a given year); and finally by the average length of fecund marriage (col. 7, equal to 18.8 years). The result then is the total number of daughters born to the initial generation (the 1,000 births of col. 1), equal to 996 (col. 7). The ratio between daughters born and the number of potential mothers is less than 1 (0.996 in col. 8), indicating a slight reproductive deficit. In line 2 instead, for eighteenth-century England, col. 8 gives a ratio of 1.484, a notable reproductive surplus (48.4% more daughters than potential mothers).

system (table 5.1) and draw conclusions which can help us better understand other lesser-studied historical populations.

The case of England is well known thanks to the pioneering work of a group led by Tony Wrigley at Cambridge University beginning in the late 1960s. Using both aggregate methods and family reconstitution they have succeeded in a complete reconstruction of population growth mechanisms. Historical reconstruction for England benefited from the considerable "homogeneity" of its population with respect to both social factors and demographic behavior, a situation not characteristic of other more heterogeneous European societies. We have already reviewed some of the Cambridge group's results in chapter 1: between the mid-sixteenth century and 1800 the English population almost tripled (from 3 to 8.6 million inhabitants); in the same period the population of Europe doubled, while that of France grew by a mere 50 percent. The most rapid periods of English growth were the Elizabethan period and then the eighteenth century, while the second half of the seventeenth century was marked by crisis. Comparing the late seventeenth and the late eighteenth centuries (table 5.1, lines 1 and 2), we find a surge in population and the previously negative growth rate (inferable from the model) turns positive and reaches about 1.3 percent per annum. This growth spurt was due primarily to an increase in nuptiality (reflected by the two components M and D) and secondarily to increased life expectancy and legitimate fertility. Lower net migration to North America also made a modest contribution. The system underwent a change not only because chances of survival improved (life expectancy increased from 36.3 to 39.5 years), but especially because the average age at marriage declined (from 25.8 to 24.1 years). The entire reproductive cycle shifted earlier, and the percentage of women "excluded" from marriage (unmarried for life) declined. The pace of reproduction in marriage (that is, legitimate fertility) also significantly increased. This analysis basically solves the mystery of rapid demographic increase in England, often attributed to positive developments in mortality, but in fact the result of changes in marriage practices which show flexibility in adapting to economic and social changes.

The case of France is more complex than England's because it is less homogeneous. Customs in the southwest, for example, were quite different from those in the north, so that it is really not appropriate to refer to a French demographic "system." But we are working along general lines and so can justify some conscious generalizations. Following the lead of Louis Henry, the father of modern historical demography, family reconstitutions for a sample of about 40 French villages, representative of the old regime (not including Paris) have been carried out. The French system, unlike the English, in the late eighteenth century (table 5.1, line 3) was not under much demographic pressure in the sense that its growth potential was relatively modest. Two specific cases present marked contrasts to the French average: Crulai (line 5), a village in Normandy, and Rouen (line 4). Crulai was characterized by strong growth spurts tempered by substantial emigration and Rouen by a modest natural growth potential but strong immigration. The greater potential for natural growth of Crulai was mostly due to more and earlier marriages.

Compared to late eighteenth-century England, population growth in France was modest: England's considerably lower legitimate fertility was more than compensated for by higher nuptiality (average age at marriage was 24 years for English women and 26 years for the French), longer duration of marriage, and higher life expectancy (39.5 years in England and 30.0 years in France). Migration seems to play only a minor role: neutral for France and slightly negative for England.

Our German example (table 5.1, line 6) is drawn from Knodel's family reconstitution based on *Ortsippenbücher,* or local genealogies, for fourteen villages in the eighteenth and nineteenth centuries. The sample is not representative of the German population as a whole, though it is taken from a wide geographical area (eastern Friesland, Waldeck, Württemberg, Baden, and Bavaria), and is half Catholic and half Protestant. The indices given here (for the second half of the eighteenth century) refer to the villages taken as a whole, and the emigration estimate is not local but for all Germany. Growth falls somewhere between that of England and of France and differs from the former for its higher marital fertility and from the latter for higher life expectancy.

The three cases of England, France, and Germany offer a schematic representation (with some forcing of data) of demographic systems in three important European societies. They highlight the factors that create different potentials for growth: the strong influence of survivorship and nuptiality in creating the differences between systems, and their potentially dynamic natures, as in the case of England in the seventeenth and eighteenth centuries; and the internal diversity of situations when city and country are compared, as in the case of France. In sum, we have a representative model, meant to help us navigate a complex and changing subject matter.

And elsewhere? At the extreme ends of the continent two very different systems were at work that produced strikingly similar overall results. Russian population during the eighteenth and nineteenth centuries (still a century of old-regime systems in eastern Europe) developed within a system of low survival, high nuptiality, and high fertility: a classic "high pressure" demographic system. On the Atlantic coast instead, England grew (at least from the second half of the eighteenth century) at the same pace as Russia but in a "low pressure" system characterized by high survival, moderate nuptiality, and moderate fertility. Population growth was also strong in Ireland, but under worse circumstances due to low survival and barely controlled nuptiality. In England, the situation as a whole did not conceal great regional differences, whereas in Russia extremely varied situations coexisted which ultimately verged on a distinctly Asian system (early and universal marriage) as one traveled across the empire southeastward from the Baltic. It is unusual for large populations to be as homogenous as the English; in fact, the majority of major European countries incorporate internal differences. France can be more or less divided into the southwest, with moderate fertility and fair chances for survival, and the northeast, with higher fertility and lower survival. Nor is it prudent to make generalizations based on the experiences of only a few small villages; the 14 studied by Knodel reveal strong contrasts between eastern Friesland (low age at marriage, low infant mortality, moderate legitimate fertility) and Bavaria (high mortality, high age at marriage, high legitimate fertility); here too there seem to be two distinct systems at work, the first "low" pressure and the second "high."

The Mediterranean world is perhaps even more complex. The Iberian peninsula is characterized by an Atlantic system of strong marriage controls as opposed to the Mediterranean system of early marriage and low percentage unmarried. The situation in Italy is fairly complicated, and its subdivisions do not always match the usual historical/geographical divisions. We can identify an Alpine system of low nuptiality and continuous emigration, while in parts of the south controls to growth are less vigorous. In Italy, like other parts of the Mediterranean, the spread of malaria, especially in coastal areas, produced specialized demographic regimes characterized by high mortality, a compensatory high birth rate, and strong immigration. Within the Grand Duchy of Tuscany there were contrasts between the north-central area – low demographic pressure – and the malarial south (Maremma) where population renewal was faster paced. There was also a divergence among Jews in Europe; western Sephardic Jews and eastern Ashkenazi adapted to very different models of development. "Around 1900," writes Della Pergola, "the Jewish communities of Eastern Europe plus their kin abroad numbered about 7.5 million inhabitants, while there were 43,000 Jews in Italy. This is rather extraordinary considering that at the end of the fifteenth century these two groups had equivalent populations (20,000–50,000 people)." Behind this incredible development differential lie two very different demographic systems: in eighteenth-century Italy, there was a balance between births and deaths and an absence of growth, whereas the east combined high mortality and very high fertility, the latter in turn the product of social norms favoring high fertility and family cohesion.

Groupings at the national and regional level often conceal and level out strong local differences, but they also "confuse" groups or classes that follow different strategies and demographic models: the aristocracy and elite who limit their reproduction in order to preserve their property and wealth; small landowners who try to balance resources, work, and family size; and the peasantry who must deal with completely different limitations.

Marriage

Marriage was at the heart of old-regime demographic systems. In most of Europe, with some important exceptions, marriage sanctioned the right to reproduce; births outside of marriage generally represented only a few percent of total births. Naturally one should not imagine that sexual relations between men and women were limited exclusively to the sphere of matrimony; demographic studies reveal in fact that a considerable number of marriages were celebrated concurrently with, and as a result of, pregnancy. Nevertheless, the unmarried state was almost universally an insurmountable barrier to procreation, hence the role of marriage as the primary regulator of fertility in societies that had not yet discovered or adopted voluntary birth-control strategies. Malthus considered marriage (and its postponement) as a prudent and preventive check against growth and observed "either that a considerable number of persons of a marriageable age never marry, or that they marry comparatively late, and that their marriages are consequently less prolific than if they had married earlier." In fact, the nuptiality of a population breaks down into two main factors: how quickly the members of a generation – once past the minimum age required by biology (the onset of puberty was later then, around 15 or 16 years of age) – enter into a procreational union, as a function of custom, law, or religion; and the percentage that do not enter into such a union (i.e. marry) during their reproductive lifetime. The first factor can be expressed by the average or median age at first marriage, and the second by spinsterhood or bachelorhood, the percentage of people who have not married by age 50. At least two other phenomena influence nuptiality. One is mortality, as it severs unions and creates widows and widowers, and the other is nuptiality among the widowed which moderates the effects of mortality.

As Malthus pointed out, normal variations in nuptiality could have a considerable effect on both fertility and the growth rate. Two years more or less added to the average age at first marriage could translate into one more or one fewer birth, and so an acceleration or slowing down of generational renewal and considerable consequences for the natural growth rate of a population. Similarly, a level of spinsterhood (the proportion of women never married at age 50) that varied by 10 percent more or less with respect to a hypothetical level of 15 percent implied an equivalent (or slightly greater) change in the birth trend, if all other factors in the system remained constant.

The quantitative study of nuptiality requires the existence of censuses or counts (like the *status animarum* or the list of parishioners taken at Easter) that give age and marital status, or else family reconstitutions – which link birth certificates to marriage certificates – as the ages of brides and grooms were rarely specified in the marriage registers. Studies in historical demography have defined a fairly detailed European "geography" of nuptiality, at least for the seventeenth and eighteenth centuries. There is less certainty for earlier periods. As complex as these quantitative studies are, their interpretation is still more so as nuptiality was strongly linked to family systems, land-ownership systems, inheritance laws and customs, and economic and professional activities. Rarely do we find simple explanations for the differences in nuptiality between geographical areas or social classes. Cantillon has observed that workers and peasants married late because "they waited to accumulate savings in order to begin a *ménage*, or else to find a woman who could bring with her some wealth to this end." In much of rural Europe, a neolocal residence system required that couples establish a separate household from that of their parents, and so the accumulation of sufficient resources was a prerequisite for starting a family. Access to marriage for land-owning farmers was often conditioned by the inheritance of property, by accession to a tenant farming arrangement, or by acquisition of land on the open market. Among property-owning classes, the system of inheritance – whether partitive or indivisible – had a great bearing on nuptiality. When property could not be divided, the inheritance of the family resources by only one of the children meant emigration or celibacy for the others; in the case of a partitive inheritance no one was excluded from marriage, though the meagerness of available resources might present limitations. Nevertheless, the eventual repercussions of the inheritance system were never revealed in their "pure" form but were diluted through other mechanisms. In the case of indivisible estates, it was not a given that younger sons had to emigrate or remain unwed; high mortality might in fact eliminate the first-born son before the death of the father, or else new lands might be acquired on the open market or through land reclamation, or even be leased. In patrilocal systems, where newlyweds lived with the parents of the groom (or in rare cases the parents of the bride) rather than estab-lish a home of their own, the accumulation of resources was not so weighty a problem and age-at-marriage could be lower. The socioeconomic level of a given society naturally determined what was considered essential to family formation; when the standard of living was only slightly above subsistence the question of resources required for a new family was different from what it was for the more well-off. The material prerequisites for marriage for southern Italian or Andalusian agricultural wage-laborers were probably rather modest and perhaps explain their low age at marriage. Although not an ironclad rule, there was a close relationship between age at marriage and percentage never mar-ried; populations with a higher average age at marriage also had more bachelors and spinsters and the factors that influenced the former also did the latter. Clearly it is difficult to pinpoint the complex factors that determined the geographic profile of European nuptiality. Moreover, within each region, differences in occupation, land ownership, and family structures imply a diver-sity of specific nuptial behaviors and traditions.

We know a fair amount about the geography of nuptiality before the nineteenth century and also something about temporal dynamics and territorial or social differences. Research findings over the last few decades substantially support John Hajnal's 1965 assessment of the European situation. In the nineteenth century, Europe was more or less divided by a line that ran from St. Petersburg to Trieste. The dominant features west of the line were low nuptiality, high age at first marriage (generally above 24 years for women and 26 years for men), and high percentage never married (greater than 10 percent). This system was typical and unique for Europe and does not match that of any other population in the world at any point in history (figure 5.1). The dominant system east of the line consisted of early and more or less universal marriage, average age at first marriage below 22 years for women

Figure 5.1   Low nuptiality Europe, high nuptiality Europe, and Hajnal's line, end of eighteenth century

and 24 years for men, and a percentage never married less than 5 percent.

These differences, as we have already pointed out, had great demographic implications and explain the higher birth rate in eastern Europe, which during the eighteenth and nineteenth centuries exceeded 40 per thousand, 10 points higher than the prevailing figure in the west. Later research has confirmed this distinction though it is less clearcut for the Mediterranean region and some fringe areas. Within the low nuptiality zone there is a clear gradient that runs approximately northwest to southeast. Great Britain, Scandinavia, Germanic central Europe and France lie solidly in the low nuptiality area (Ireland is the exception, with an age at marriage of 20–22 years), while in the rest of the area low-nuptiality systems like those of north-central Italy, Sardinia, and the Atlantic region of the Iberian peninsula commingled with population behavior that Malthus would have termed less "prudent," though these systems did not match the high nuptiality typical of societies east of the St. Petersburg–Trieste line. Available data support this scheme in its broad outline: during 1740–89 the age at marriage for women in France was 25.7 (26.6 in the north and 24.8 in the south), and for men it was 27.9; in England between 1610 and 1760 women tended to marry at 25 to 26 years of age and men at 26 to 28; the average for 14 German villages in the eighteenth century was 25.5 for women and 28 for men. Both Scandinavia (with the exception of Finland which we shall discuss below) and the Netherlands followed similar patterns. Hajnal's dividing line clearly distinguishes between two systems: Austrian and Czech peoples to the west of the line tended to marry between 23 and 24 years of age, while to the east Hungarians (an average for 10 parishes during the period 1730–1820) married earlier, at 20 to 21 years of age. According to Andorka, Russian and Balkan women married still earlier. Naturally this line may be interpreted ethnically or linguistically and not just geographically: to the east Slavs (excluding Hungarians) and to the west Scandinavians, Czechs, and Germanic peoples (while the Finnish belonged to the eastern model till the nineteenth century).

The situation in the Mediterranean, as already noted, was more complex. In Spain, according to the 1787 census, the highest average age at first marriage was on the Atlantic coast (over 26 for Basque women, and 25 in the Asturias and Galicia) and the lowest was in Estremadura, Andalusia, and Murcia (22 years). Northern Portugal, Beira and especially Minho (a detailed study of a village there reveals a constant average age at marriage between 27 and 28 years for the entire eighteenth century) differs substantially from the south; Alentejo and Algarve for example belong to an early-marriage model. The case of Italy is even more complex and splintered, and lacks a clearcut north-south gradient. Later marriage was the norm in Alpine regions (on the northern, non-Italian slope as well), Sardinia (in particular among males), and the part of central Italy characterized by sharecropping. Earlier marriage was more common instead in the south, especially in Puglia, Basilicata, Calabria, and Sicily, but intermediate situations could be found in both the north and south.

I have concentrated on age at marriage, at the expense of percent unmarried because of the lack of data. Where there is information however (for Spain in 1787 for example) a strong inverse relationship is found: the earlier the age at marriage, the fewer unmarried and vice versa, allowing of course for the inevitable deviations from the norm.

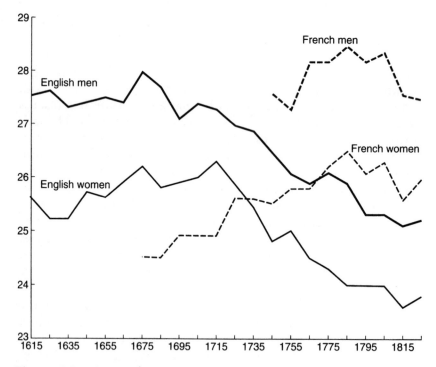

Figure 5.2 Age at first marriage, England and France, seventeenth to nineteenth century

A second important topic is temporal trends. Hajnal first suggested, though others have agreed (perhaps too readily), that the low-nuptiality system in western Europe that appeared at the end of the early modern era was the end point of a long process of change that gradually transformed an early-marriage system dating back to the Middle Ages and also ancient times. Various factors are cited to explain this transformation, including growing individualism promoted by the Protestant Reformation, the birth of capitalism, or the sense of "prudence" produced by demographic growth that outpaced available resources. Summarizing the temporal evolution of nuptiality is no easy task: long and sufficiently representative series exist only for England and France (figure 5.2); for other situations, the data are much more fragmentary. Overall though, it would seem that with some exceptions there was a widespread trend towards increasing age-at-first-marriage between the sixteenth and eighteenth centuries.

The most obvious exception was England where age at marriage was stable (25 to 26 years) between the early seventeenth century and 1720 and then declined by roughly two years over the rest of the eighteenth century. Elsewhere the situation was different; in France there were cases of increase between the sixteenth and seventeenth centuries (from 19 to 22 in Athis and Bourg-en-Bresse), while an INED survey shows a rise from 24.5 (1670–89) to over 26 in the late eighteenth century. Lebrun asks whether this increase, apparently general in the first half of the seventeenth century, was a new phenomenon or a return to traditional behavior dating from the thirteenth century; his query remains unanswered. In Spain, local studies seem to concur on an increase of one to two years in age at marriage between the seventeenth century and the end of the eighteenth century (according to estimates based on Floridablanca's 1787 census). In Flanders and Germany compatible series exist only for the eighteenth century and are proof of a high age at marriage, but they do not help us understand the trend leading to that point. The data for Italy, though fragmentary, is considerable, though the scarcity of long historical series prevents us from discovering whether northern and central Italy adapted to the northern European model of late marriage as the result of a long evolution or as an expression of deeply rooted behaviors. There is no shortage of examples illustrating an increase in age at marriage during the seventeenth and eighteenth centuries – for example, in the predominantly sharecropping Prato countryside – in response to declining standards of living; while in some areas of the south,

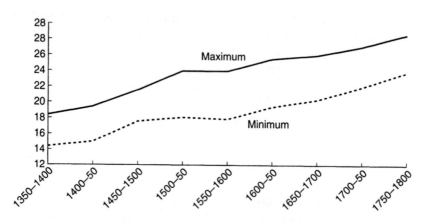

Figure 5.3   Age at first marriage for women in Tuscany, 1350–1800

Source: Based on M. Breschi and R. Rettaroli, *La nuzialità in Toscana. Secoli XIV–XIX*, in *Le Italie demografiche. Saggi di demografia storica*, Udine, 1995

especially those characterized by extensive farming like Puglia, age at marriage was quite low, even below 20 and showed no significant change between the sixteenth and eighteenth centuries. In the north, Finns adopted northern European ways only in the second half of the eighteenth century, while the low Irish age at marriage did not change from the early seventeenth century through to the nineteenth. We may then, with some hesitation, conclude that low nuptiality at the end of the eighteenth century in many parts of Europe was the culmination of a process initiated in the sixteenth century.

Again according to Hajnal, the European system was completely different during the plague-dominated late Middle Ages. Working with the Florentine cadastre of 1427, Herlihy and Klapisch have derived an average age at marriage of 17.6 years for Florentine women (the average for men was roughly ten years higher) that increased to 20.8 around 1480. The young women of Prato instead married at 16.8 years in 1372 and at 21.1 in 1470. The trend in the countryside was similar, though with a smaller difference in age between newlyweds. The situation in France, in Toulouse, Périgueux, and Tours, was similar. Christiane Klapisch, who has perhaps studied the subject in more depth than anyone, concludes that "throughout Europe, adolescents between 14 and 18 years old became the brides of men six to ten years older." Russell and Hajnal also claim to have proof of early marriage and low percentage unmarried in England, according to the 1377 Poll Tax, but their work has provoked a still unresolved controversy. What is certain is that the English peerage – for whom there exist long genealogies – in the 350 years before 1680 followed a pattern of early marriage (well under an average 20 years for women) and low percentage unmarried. It is only after this date that a low-nuptiality system is established. The Scandinavian system also seems to have been characterized by high nuptiality.

At the end of the old regime, much of Europe had developed a low-nuptiality system with late access to marriage and a significant percentage of the population permanently unmarried. The area in question included all of Europe north of the Alps and Pyrenees and west of the St. Petersburg–Trieste line, ideally extended by the Adriatic Sea. The Atlantic coast of the Iberian peninsula and the Alpine and Apennine regions of Italy also belonged to this group, whereas other more typically Mediterranean areas behaved in significantly different ways. On the other hand, high-nuptiality systems seem to have dominated the late Middle Ages. The transition then must have taken place in the intervening centuries, at different times and in different ways, and perhaps even suddenly. Thirty years after Hajnal's initial analysis, we still remain cautious. Perhaps, a high-nuptiality system prevailed in the late fourteenth and fifteenth centuries in reaction to devastating plague losses and a breaking-down of the economic obstacles that restricted access to marriage. Historically marriage customs have revealed, from the late Middle Ages to the beginning of the contemporary era, a wide range in average age-at-marriage; ranging from 16–17 years of age to 27–8 (a variation reinforced by corresponding differences in percentage unmarried). We can conclude then that nuptiality played a crucial role in population growth in historical demographic systems.

Fertility

A majority of births took place, as one might expect, within marriage. In England during the period 1600–1800, illegitimate births represented between 2 and 4 percent of total births; in eighteenth-century Sweden and Finland the figure was 3 percent, while in France, Italy, and Spain in the eighteenth century it was closer to 1 percent. These are very low figures, and only become notably higher in some parts of central Europe. Hence the increase in births, and so the birth rate, was almost entirely dependent on legitimate fertility – that within marriage – and on the number of women who married (determined by nuptiality: age at marriage, proportion of women who married, duration of marriage).

As we have already noted, sexual relations outside of marriage (and not including prostitution) were not so rare as the low figures for illegitimate births suggest. Family reconstitutions from parochial registers attest to the fact that a fair number of firstborns were conceived before the parents married: during the eighteenth century, figures for Germany, France, and England indicate that the incidence of premarital conceptions was somewhere between 10 and 30 percent. Naturally this affected nuptiality, hurrying along a considerable number of marriages.

Before the end of the eighteenth century, European populations, with some rare exceptions, were characterized by "natural" fertility, and voluntary birth control was practically nonexistent. The concept of natural fertility was proposed by Louis Henry in 1961 to describe procreative behavior that is not influenced by the number of children a couple already has, as opposed to situations in which family size is instead a determining factor for the planning of births. In other words, fertility is "natural" when couples of every age behave identically whether they have zero children, or one, two, five or more. Where natural fertility has been abandoned, the behavior of a couple is influenced instead by the number of children already born, because the couple is working towards a certain goal; reproduction slows down or stops following the birth of a certain number of children. Natural-fertility populations are subject to two categories of factors that affect their rate of reproduction. The first are purely biophysical and have to do primarily with age: a woman's ability to conceive diminishes after a certain age, and comes to a definitive end before the onset of menopause. In addition, the frequency of sexual relations tends to naturally drop off as a function of the age of partners and the duration of marriage. Finally, there are of course the added components of primary or acquired sterility, and diseases that decrease reproductive capacity, etc. The second category of factors are behavioral (even when they are biological in nature and effect), such as the length of breastfeeding which, while practiced, inhibits conception, or the abstention from sexual relations during particular times or at important milestones (such as becoming grandparents). The effects on fertility of these two sets of factors can be considerable, but they are independent of behavior deliberately based on the number of children a couple has already borne: one breastfeeds, when possible, a lastborn child the same amount of time as a firstborn.

These are important considerations because natural fertility in different populations varied considerably – by as much as 50 percent – according to the combined impact of the different determining factors (length of breastfeeding, frequency of sexual relations, sanitary conditions, etc.). Because we are more concerned in these pages with how demographic systems worked than in a sophisticated behavioral analysis, let us examine the (natural) fertility levels of old-world regimes and their variability.

Table 5.2 gives the legitimate fertility rate by age of women for Sweden, England, France, Flanders, Germany, and Italy in the seventeenth and eighteenth centuries. The data for Sweden are derived from complete and official reports; for England, France, and Germany from the already mentioned samples of villages and parishes; and for Flanders and Italy they represent the average of a geographically and chronologically varied group of parishes (though all still in the seventeenth and eighteenth centuries). The age-group values are then added together beginning at ages 20 and 25 to get sums which, with some equivocation, we can consider to be the hypothetical number of legitimate children born to women who marry at 20 (or 25) and remain in that marital union till the end of their reproductive years.

The figures in the table allow us to make two important observations. First, fertility varies considerably: of the six populations included, two – England's and Sweden's – seem to have had considerably lower than average numbers of offspring, while Flemish fertility was much higher than that of the three middle groups – France, Italy, and Germany. The differences are significant, as Flemish fertility was roughly one-third greater than English fertility: given an age at marriage of 25, the Flemish mother bore on average 7.1 offspring as compared to the Englishwoman's 5.4, and with marriage at 20, the difference was 9.6 as compared to 7.4. The bigger the population studied, the less noticeable the fertility differences as local variations tend to balance out. In the French reconstruction, for example, a geographical combination masks the characteristic properties of French society. So, for example, the northeast (Aisne, Ardennes, Côte d'Or, Marne, Haute Marne,

Table 5.2 Legitimate fertility rates (per 1,000) in selected European countries, seventeenth and eighteenth centuries

Country	Age							Theoretical number of offspring for women married at age:	
	15–19	20–4	25–9	30–4	35–9	40–4	45–9	20	25
Sweden	–	458	380	326	228	123	30	7.725	5.435
Italy	430	430	410	375	310	160	15	8.500	6.350
England	383	407	364	313	245	128	21	7.390	5.355
Germany	380	447	426	375	302	164	26	8.700	6.465
France	–	462	413	361	286	153	13	8.440	6.130
Flanders	442	494	453	413	338	196	24	9.590	7.120
				Indices (England = 100)					
Sweden	–	113	104	104	93	96	143	105	101
Italy	112	106	113	120	127	125	71	115	119
England	100	100	100	100	100	100	100	100	100
Germany	99	110	117	120	123	128	124	118	121
France	–	114	113	115	117	120	62	114	114
Flanders	115	121	124	132	138	153	114	130	133

Meurthe-et-Moselle, Moselle, Seine-et-Marne, Yonne, Territoire-de-Belfort) seems to have enjoyed a natural fertility considerably greater than the southwest (the area between the Loire and the Pyrenees): the theoretical number of offspring for a woman married at 25 was 6.6 in the northeast and 5.4 in the southwest. Similar differences are evident among German villages: the highest legitimate fertility was in Bavaria while the lowest was in eastern Friesland. The English sample was more homogenous; indices were fairly similar among villages and no distinct regional profile emerges. There are no regional subdivisions available for Swedish legitimate fertility before 1870, when the northernmost counties revealed fertility well above the average. For Italy, relatively few family reconstitutions have been carried out, and so it has not been possible to trace substantial differentiations; nonetheless, there do not appear to have been cases of either particularly high or low fertility. For the countries not included in table 5.2 we know even less. Reher makes the observation that in Spain the areas of lowest marital fertility were concentrated along the Mediterranean coast, in the south, and in some parts of the northwest. The highest fertility was found in Old Castile and some parts of the northern Atlantic coast. Other inferences can be drawn from the levels of legitimate fertility that prevailed before the historical onset of fertility decline in the late nineteenth century. In Germany, higher than average fertility levels were found in western Prussia, Silesia, part of Bavaria, the Rhineland, and Westphalia; in Austria the highest levels prevailed in the Tyrol and the Voralberg; and in Russia in the northeast.

The second observation concerns the fact that natural fertility levels are not stable over time. We must of course approach this point with caution, as there are few long historical series reliable enough for making comparisons and ascribable to large groups. Nonetheless, in England fertility appears to have been notably lower in the second half of the seventeenth century than in the first; and in France fertility between 1690 and 1710 was much lower than either before or after that time. We can be sure, in any case, that the frequency of mortality crises – along with political and economic upheavals – affected the demographic system as a whole, and it is unlikely that a single important component – fertility within marriage – would have remained unaffected.

Before leaving the topic of natural fertility, it is worth exploring its interaction with other components of the demographic system. In addition to the factors we have already discussed (breastfeeding, frequency of intercourse, infertility, etc.), the level of natural fertility also depended on infant mortality levels. The case of the German villages illustrates this point: the villages in eastern Friesland had low natural fertility and low infant mortality, while the Bavarian villages experienced high natural fertility and high infant mortality. This direct correlation between natural fertility and infant mortality is found in other contexts as well, in France for example, and can be explained. In the course of a couple's child-bearing life, the death of a newborn directly affected fertility; once breastfeeding ceased the potential for conception increased, and so conceptions occurred much sooner than if the infant had survived. In addition, the birth and survival of a child could alter the sexual behavior of a couple, reducing the frequency of intercourse and temporarily inhibiting it. Finally, the pressure on a mother to care for children born at very close intervals could, in and of itself, have contributed to higher infant mortality. These mechanisms explain the interrelationship between the levels of infant mortality and natural fertility. In the case of the Bavarian villages cited above, the practice of breastfeeding was virtually nonexistent for cultural reasons. The result was high vulnerability and mortality of children, a reduction in the birth interval, and high legitimate fertility.

More on Infant Mortality

The effect of infant mortality on general mortality levels – discussed in chapter 4 – deserves its own discussion. Those familiar with research in historical demography are aware that infant mortality levels in traditional societies were extremely variable, given that between one-fifth and one-third of children generally died in the first year of life. However, local studies are not entirely reliable because of both the frequent omission of newborns from death registers and the frequent use in family reconstitution of integration, correction, and estimation made necessary by the limitations of data. In order to establish a general frame of reference, we can examine some national groupings and their mortality levels for infants and children during the second half of the eighteenth century (table 5.3).

Although these figures come from the end of the old regime when mortality had begun to decline, they are of considerable interest nonetheless and reveal a wide range of infant mortality; the probability of a newborn's dying before his first birthday ranged from

165 per 1,000 in England to 273 per 1,000 in France, with Sweden and Denmark somewhere in between. According to a recent study, Moscow at this time had an infant mortality of 334 per 1,000. The difference in infant mortality between France and England by itself (assuming identical mortality after the first year of life) is roughly equal to four years of life expectancy at birth.

The same table shows clear differences in mortality in subsequent years up to age 15. Variations at the national level are both confirmed and strengthened by looking at cases at the subnational level (and without resorting to special or extreme cases, but relying on representative areas rich in reliable data). For example, the French regions in the INED sample for 1750–79 demonstrate the lowest infant mortality in the southwest (191 per 1,000) and the highest in the northeast (292 per 1,000); eighteenth-century English villages vary between the very small villages in Devon

Table 5.3 Infant and young mortality in selected European countries, second half of the eighteenth century

Probability of death $(1000\ q_x)$	France (1750–99)	England (1750–99)	Sweden (1750–90)	Denmark (1780–1800)
$_1q_0$	273	165	200	191
$_4q_1$	215	104	155	156
$_5q_5$	91	33	63	42
$_5q_{10}$	42	21	34	–
l_{15}	491	736	612	641

Note: The symbols in the first column indicate, in order, how many babies out of 1,000 births die before their first birthday ($^1q^0$); how many, of 1,000 who celebrate their first birthday, die before their fifth ($^4q^1$); how many, of 1,000 who celebrate their fifth birthday, die before their tenth ($^5q^5$); how many, of 1,000 who celebrate their tenth birthday, die before their fifteenth ($^5q^{10}$). The symbol l^{15} corresponds to the number of survivors to age 15 from an original group of 1,000 births

Sources: France: Y. Blayo, "La mortalité en France de 1740 à 1829." *Population*, special issue, November 1975, pp. 138–9. England: A. E. Wrigley and R. Schofield, "English Population History from Family Reconstruction: Summary Results 1600–1799," *Population Studies*, XXXVII, 1983, p. 177. Sweden: *Historisk Statistik för Sverige*. Stockholm, National Central Bureau of Statistics, 1969. Denmark: O. Andersen, "The Decline in Danish Mortality before 1850 and its Economic and Social Background." In T. Bengtsson, G. Fridlizius, R. Ohlsson eds., *Pre-Industrial Population Change*, Almquist & Wiksell, Stockholm, 1984, pp. 124–5

(below 100 per 1,000) and bigger centers such as Banbury and Gainsborough (between 200 and 300 per 1,000). The literature abounds on the subject; of 51 Finnish parishes in the late eighteenth century, three had a very low level of infant mortality (under 100 per 1,000), two a very high one (above 300 per 1,000), while the rest were scattered in between. Similar differences can be found in Sweden, Belgium, Germany, Italy, Spain, and more or less all the populations that have been carefully studied.

We can conclude then that mortality during the first year of life in old-regime demographic systems could differ by as much as 200 points per 1,000, corresponding to roughly 7–8 years of life expectancy at birth. The explanation for such differences is one of the most interesting subjects in historical demography and involves: the epidemiological events discussed in chapter 4; background conditions – especially environmental ones – linked to economic well-being; nutritional levels for mothers and children; and traditions and culture and how they affect the practice of child-rearing.

In all likelihood, the health and survival of children depends in part on the health and nutritional condition of mothers, which in turn depends on how well-fed the population in general is. Women who breastfeed need more calories than women who do not, and insufficient nutrition reduces milk supply and probably reduces its fat and vitamin content. Nevertheless, the breastfeeding mechanism appears to be extraordinarily adaptable insofar as it allows the child to be at least partially shielded from the nutritional stress that the mother may be suffering. In fact, except in cases of extreme malnutrition, undernourished mothers are normally able to breast-feed their children. Malnourishment, especially in remote areas or during periods of famine or drought, undoubtedly has a negative impact on mothers, as it does on the rest of the population, yet maternal intermediation diminishes and minimizes its effects both on the fetus during pregnancy and on the newborn while it is being breastfed.

The influence of breastfeeding – up until weaning – on infant survival is considerable. An infant's immune system is very weak at birth, but maternal nursing provides scientifically verified protection. Unlike other baby foods, both colostrum and breast milk contain biologically active substances that protect the child from infection. Some scholars believe that in the Middle Ages, following the teachings of Soranus, it became the practice to delay breastfeeding by a few days in order to avoid administering colostrum, thought to be harmful. The custom is echoed in sixteenth-century treatises as well: "lac enim eo in tempore indigestibile, crassum et vitiosum est, quod Latini vocant colostrum." The substitution of artificial foods was recommended – and even laxatives to encourage the expulsion of the meconium – to give the mother time to mature her milk. Two hundred years later, eighteenth-century medical practitioners and pediatricians espoused a different philosophy: not only did they believe there to be no substitute for mother's milk, but women were encouraged to begin breastfeeding immediately in order for the infant to enjoy the nutritional and protective benefits of colostrum. Clearly there is no necessary link between people's behavior and medical opinion, but various authors have claimed that changes in breastfeeding custom impacted significantly on mortality in the first months of life.

Independently of how early or late breastfeeding is begun, its duration and age at weaning play a primary role in infant survival. The immune system of a non-breastfed baby is deficient and highly vulnerable to gastrointestinal and viral respiratory infections. Those infants run greater risks of death than breastfed babies, a fact amply demonstrated by the tragic fate of infants left in foundling homes and the very high mortality in those rare areas where breastfeeding was discredited. The protective effect of breastfeeding lasts, more or less, all through the first year of life and eventually decreases as milk supply diminishes. Age at weaning is therefore an important variable in infant survival. If it occurs too early the infant is vulnerable to infection, the risk of which increases (whatever the age at weaning) as a function of the handling of foods and their possible contamination. Eighteenth-century treatises unanimously favored breastfeeding, and various authors associated improvements in infant mortality at the end of the eighteenth century with both immediate postnatal breast-feeding and the prolonging of its duration, especially in areas where early weaning had prevailed. There is, however, no documentary evidence, and we should add that in order to be significant, changes in customs during the first year of life surely must have affected the first six months of an infant's life, during which 70 to 90 percent of first-year deaths occurred. And since breastfeeding customs (except for the moment at which it began) could not have varied much in the early months, other factors must be sought out to more fully explain variations in mortality.

These factors, often of primary importance, were linked to environmental conditions, climate, childrearing techniques and practices, and the care exercised in watching over infants. There is a great deal of evidence that factors of this sort largely determined variations in infant mortality, except in those areas or among those groups in which breastfeeding was discouraged. Otherwise it would be impossible to explain the great differences in mortality between infants born in the winter and those born in the summer that are recorded for some areas, but not for others that share an identical climate. Strategies for fending off cold temperatures – efficient in some areas and disastrous in others – came into play. In some cases, high infant mortality can be explained, for example, by unsatisfactory childcare in cases in which the mother is employed outside the home. Finally, notable differences in infant mortality in urban areas among different social classes were mostly attributable to environmental factors, crowded living conditions, and the easier transmission of infection.

Migration

It is not possible to fully understand the workings of any demographic system without taking into consideration the essentially stabilizing effect of human mobility. The process of settling continental Europe, discussed in chapter 2, is also the history of mobility, whether of short-range movements – the founding of a new village, urban expansion, the settlement or cultivation of new rural areas – or medium- or long-range ones – Germanic emigration to the east, the southern spread of settlement in the Iberian peninsula, and emigration outside of Europe. I shall consider here several aspects of long-range mobility, namely at the level of states or large regions, in keeping with the scale of our analysis thus far. This choice greatly simplifies the task at hand, because short- or medium-range migration took many forms: newlyweds; domestics and apprentices moving between families; those engaged in seasonal work, transhumance, or agriculture. People moved from country to town for a wide variety of reasons; and the very poor moved out of necessity, their ranks swelling especially in times of economic disaster, famine, or political instability, and shrinking again when conditions improved. Movements of this sort, in an otherwise relatively static society, could be large: at the end of the eighteenth century in western Europe, clearly defined areas of occupational mobility emerged – especially for seasonal or periodic labor. These migrants were often small farmers and landowners looking for ways to supplement their incomes or simply attracted by economic opportunities: the North Sea (figure 5.4), and especially the Netherlands, attracted a constant flow from Westphalia for fishing and dike construction; the Irish in particular flocked to London and East Anglia for public works and farming; and the area around Paris attracted workers for the same reasons, primarily from the Massif Central and the Alps. Other magnets of migration could be found further south: Madrid and Castile mainly attracted workers at harvest time; the coastlines of Catalonia and Provence attracted migrants

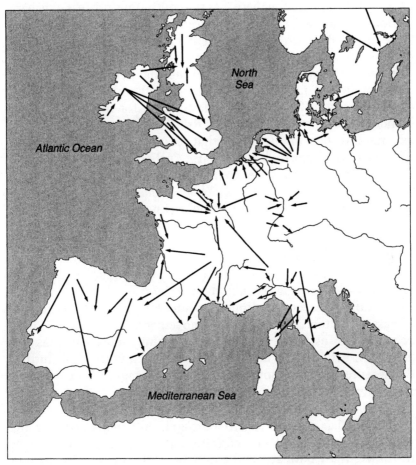

Figure 5.4 Temporary migration systems in western Europe, end of the eighteenth century

Source: J. Lucassen, *Migrant Labour in Europe 1600–1900: The Drift to the North*, Croom Helm, London, 1987

from the Alps, the Pyrenees, and the Massif Central; the Po Valley drew laborers from the Alps and the Apennines; southern Tuscany together with Latium and Rome were immigration regions, as was Corsica which drew workers from the Apennines. The sum total of these migrations – not counting more minor ones – moved several hundreds of thousands of workers every year, and supplemented the incomes of as many families, thus contributing to the demographic equilibrium of vast areas in Europe.

In addition to these short-range and periodic migrations, there were long-range definitive ones between states or large regional areas. Important among these was the continuous process of urbanization encouraged by the demographic deficits of medium and large cities. Between 1650 and 1750 London grew by 250,000 inhabitants, despite an equivalent excess of deaths over births, so that the net flow of immigrants during that century was around half a million. Amsterdam grew from 30,000 inhabitants in 1550 to 200,000 in 1700 and was a destination for immigrants from Flanders, Germany, and Norway. Rome in the eighteenth century experienced net immigration that exceeded 130,000. Similar dynamics characterized other large urban centers and many medium and small ones too, so that simply maintaining the dimensions of the urban network – which as we have seen accounted for about 10 percent of the population of Europe at the start of the modern era – required considerable movement from country to town.

Definitive migration strongly affected the operation of demographic systems, as there was nothing immobile about early modern European society. Germanic migration did not end with the Middle Ages but continued at intervals, as we have already discussed. Other international movements were, in reality, processes of osmosis between neighboring areas, such as the migration between the late fifteenth century and the first third of the seventeenth from southern France to Aragon, Valencia, and especially Catalonia; in the late sixteenth century probably one Catalonian in five was born across the border. Similar movements include Galician migration to Portugal, Albanians crossing the Adriatic to Italy, and Swiss migration after the Thirty Years War to Alsace, the Palatinate, and southern Germany. Finally, further north, there was migration into the Netherlands from Germany, Flanders, and Norway, and Scottish migration to Ireland and England. These migrations were strongly motivated by economic inequalities, aided by the absence of political/legal obstacles, and encouraged by the voids created by war and high mortality. In addition to these movements spurred by what we today call market forces, others were motivated by political events and, in particular, religious intolerance. The voids created by the expulsion of Jews, and especially *moriscos*, in Iberia had grave consequences for the social and productive tissue of the peninsula, and there were serious demographic repercussions as well. The 1492 expulsion of Jews involved more than 90,000 people, and that of the *moriscos* – the descendants of indigenous converts to Islam who were ethnically (but not culturally) indistinguishable from the Spanish population – involved roughly 310,000 people in 1609 and 1610; this was the equivalent of 5 percent of the whole population, and represented one out of eight inhabitants of Murcia, one out of five in Aragon, and one out of four in Valencia. Yet another loss, though less devastating demographically, was the departure of 140,000–160,000 Huguenots from France between 1685 and 1690, following the revocation of the Edict of Nantes, out of a population four times the size of Spain's. There were, of course, many religiously motivated migrations in modern European history, and an estimation of their magnitude is no easy task.

Last, but not least, was extra-European migration to empires in Asia and, especially, America. While the data regarding these migrations is largely conjectural, it is not conjecture that at the end of the eighteenth century North America was populated by about 4.5 million inhabitants of European origin, and there were only slightly fewer – 4 million – in Latin America. These settlements – mostly the fruit of British and Iberian emigration, with smaller contributions from the Dutch, Germans, and French – were modest in terms of the sheer physical dimensions of the continent but significant in relative terms, representing approximately one-third of the total population of the Americas and about 6 percent of the population of Europe, excluding Russia (figure 5.5).

There were hundreds of thousands of European emigrants, particularly in the sixteenth and seventeenth centuries, whose numerous offspring would contribute to the demographic expansion of centuries to come. An estimated 440,000 people emigrated from Spain prior to 1650; an average of about 3,000 per year (while some argue reasonably for a figure closer to 5,000). The majority of these emigrants came from the Kingdom of Castile (a little more than one third from Andalusia, about the same from Castile y León, and one sixth from Estremadura) which had a population of slightly more than 5.5 million at the end of the sixteenth century.

The outflow amounted to almost one per 1,000 per year and was considerable for an old-regime society whose potential for growth, as we have already discussed, was fairly limited. In neighboring Portugal, emigration was even more intense; about 4,000 people left annually during the sixteenth and seventeenth centuries, and the discovery of minerals in Brazil in the eighteenth century increased that number to 9,000 per year. Portuguese emigration drew off about 2–4 per 1,000 per year, concentrated in the northern regions of Minho and Beira; it was partially compensated for by immigration from Galicia.

Emigration from the British Isles, particularly to America, was

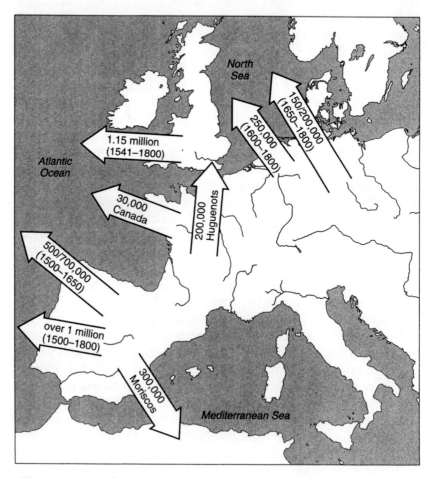

Figure 5.5   Selected extra-European emigrations in the modern era

on a similar scale: about 378,000 people between 1630 and 1700. The total figure for English emigration alone (to all destinations) is thought to have been around 1–1.5 per 1,000 per year between the middle of the sixteenth century and the end of the eighteenth, the trend declining over time and with a peak in the middle of the seventeenth century. According to Wrigley and Schofield, this would imply a negative balance of 270,000 people between 1541 and 1599; 713,000 in the seventeenth century; and 517,000 in the eighteenth. The Netherlands too contributed to extra-European migration: during the seventeenth and eighteenth centuries net emigration was roughly one-quarter of a million, the majority directed to Asian destinations, with lesser incursions into Latin America and the Caribbean (15,000) and the United States (10,000). For the Netherlands, however, immigration from neighboring areas greatly exceeded emigration and so the net balance over two centuries was strongly positive.

Of the great colonial empires, only France experienced relatively modest emigration. Between 1600 and 1730, barely 27,000 people migrated to Canada, a low figure from a population that at the end of the seventeenth century was four to five times greater than that of England and triple that of Spain. Departures for the Antilles were not much greater. We still do not know why the French – unlike other European colonialists – did not choose to emigrate in the face of the strong Malthusian pressure they faced. Dupâquier suggests that the key may lie in the distribution of small landholdings and in an attachment to the land, although similar explanations do not hold in other contexts. Among the non-imperialist powers, Germany experienced significant emigration to America (125,000–200,000) over the course of the eighteenth century, though far more Germans emigrated to other areas in Europe, especially Hungary.

Transoceanic emigration in this period, though overall quite modest, opened the way to the great migrations of the nineteenth century, made possible the vast expansion of European space abroad, and had important long-term demographic consequences. Meanwhile, in eastern Europe, settlement in the southern part of the Russian Empire (New Russia) and the stabilization of the southern border (see chapter 2) led to settlement beyond the Urals, which a century later would take on massive proportions.

All told, though the people of Europe were essentially bound to the land, they were not an entirely immobile people; nor was their mobility exclusively of a short-range or small-scale nature. Areas in need of labor existed and periodically caused hundreds of thousands of workers to move. Exchanges between states developed, particularly between neighboring regions. The movement of people from the country to towns attracted not only those from immediately surrounding areas, but also from more remote ones to help compensate for urban demographic deficits and support city growth. Finally, the seventeenth century witnessed an extracontinental migration of millions of emigrants, mostly originating from the great imperial states. Together these movements represented an important component of old-regime demographic systems, sometimes at the national level, more often at the regional level, and almost always at the local level.

Equilibrium and Transformations

European populations operated within a narrow path of growth but using a variety of systems. These systems were elastic – for example they compensated for crises and absorbed temporary shocks – and could also change. The action of Malthusian checks characterized much of Europe. For England, Wrigley and Schofield have found a direct correlation between real wage cycles and reproduction trends: when standards of living improved, reproductivity increased and the population grew, and the opposite was true when real wages declined. This relationship between nuptiality and variations in living standards (measured by real wages) was reflected in the number of births. Overall, the English showed themselves capable of modifying their own growth in relative harmony with economic events, employing the virtuous preventive check of marriage rather than the catastrophic and repressive check of mortality.

Though the structure of other systems changed in the demographic old regime, the scarcity of historical sources and the difficulties of research do not allow us to reconstruct demographic events with enough precision to pinpoint the ways in which they changed. Connell studied the case of Ireland almost half a century ago, and his conclusions have been confirmed by later findings. He found that the "natural" tendency of the Irish to marry early was inhibited by the difficulty of acquiring the land to support a family. This obstacle disappeared in the late eighteenth century as the result of a series of complex factors (among which was the great spread of the potato) that allowed the expansion of farmland and subdivision of landholdings. The result was an increase in nuptiality which, combined with a high natural fertility and an average level of mortality, caused population growth to greatly accelerate. According to Connell's estimates, population grew from 2.2 million in 1687 to 3.2 million in 1754, at a considerable rate for the period of 0.6 percent annually. By 1841 – four years before the Great Potato Famine that overturned the Irish system once and for all – the population had grown to 8.2 million (with a rate of increase of 1.1 percent). Scholars who have since worked on Ireland agree that there was rapid population growth throughout the eighteenth century (some claim that growth was even more explosive), but disagree over the demographic causes; the theory of increased nuptiality remains to be confirmed. "In the late eighteenth and early nineteenth centuries," writes Connell, "it is clear that the Irish were insistently urged and tempted to marry early: the wretchedness and hopelessness of their living conditions, their improvident temperament, the unattractiveness of remaining single, perhaps the persuasion of their spiritual leaders, all acted in this direction." The notion of postponing marriage in order to accumulate some capital and improve one's standard of living – an idea common to large groups of European peoples – carried little weight given the miserable conditions of the island. Large landowners managed to keep their tenants at a level of bare economic subsistence; rents were high, and improvements in the standard of living difficult. Moreover, the cost of marriage was low: houses were little more than huts and could be built in a day or two with the aid of friends and family; furnishings were likewise simple and rudimentary. The real problem in a society of tenant farmers was that of finding a plot on which to establish the new family. As long as this was difficult (unless inherited upon the death of one's father), marriage was discouraged. During the late eighteenth century, the situation changed. The conversion of pasture and the opening of new farmlands through the reclamation of marshlands and mountainous areas, supported by the reforms of the Irish Parliament, eased these restraints. The division and parceling was furthered by the introduction and spread of the potato as the primary, and often only, food of the Irish. The potato was a high-productivity crop and allowed for the subdivision of plots that previously had been barely sufficient to support a single family. Moreover, the potato, when eaten in great quantities (according to Arthur Young, 8 lbs. daily, or 3.6 kgs., per capita), provided adequate nutrition. So the availability of new lands together with the fragmentation of existing ones – now more productive thanks to the potato – made possible the early age-at-marriage and high nuptiality of the Irish, which, together with a high natural fertility and normal old-regime mortality, supported the high rate of increase in the century preceding the Great Famine.

Connell's theory implies that the demographic system that dominated eighteenth- and nineteenth-century Ireland derived from a transformation which took place still in the context of the demographic old regime. Such a system could not hold up for long, and already in the third and fourth decades of the nineteenth century emigration had begun to increase and age at marriage to rise, although not enough to prevent the Great Famine of 1845–6 and its disastrous demographic consequences (see chapter 6).

The contrast to the Irish case is that of the Netherlands. Within the present-day borders, there lived 1.9 million inhabitants in 1650, roughly twice as many as in 1500. In the following century and a half population stagnated and only reached 2.1 million at the end of the eighteenth century. The reasons for this are ably explained by de Vries and van der Woude and lie in the complex equilibrium of an extremely urban society in which deaths exceeded births; great immigration from rural areas and outside the Netherlands compensated for the urban natural deficit, supporting growth; demand for manpower was high to support trade and colonization first in the Orient and later in America; and changes in the marriage market pushed up age at marriage. In the seventeenth and eighteenth centuries, Dutch cities, like most European cities, suffered an excess of deaths in relation to births. In addition, many city dwellers who sailed with the Dutch East India Company never returned to their homes. De Vries and van der Woude estimate that this combination forced Dutch cities to make up a deficit of about 1 million people over the two centuries, achieved about half-and-half through foreign and domestic immigration. For most of the seventeenth century, immigration from abroad originated in Scandinavia and the German coast of the North Sea, and much of it consisted of sailors. Towards the end of the century this particular type of movement declined and was replaced by a primarily female immigration from the neighboring German countryside. As the sea absorbed men, the cities absorbed women. The results were a large surplus of women, an increase in the age at marriage (in Amsterdam age at marriage for women rose from 24.5 in 1626–7 to 27.8 in 1776–7), and a decrease in births.

For nearly two centuries, The Netherlands had maintained a labor market of international dimensions, which imposed unique burdens on the domestic, especially the urban, population. The demographic behavior of the Netherlands in that period is inexplicable except in the context of the migratory patterns required to support an economy that had extended, as it were, far beyond the boundaries of the nation.

Ireland and the Netherlands are examples of systems that changed in response to economic and social transformations. If more historical data were available we would be able to probe other ambiguous situations. The populations of central and southern Spain during the seventeenth and early eighteenth centuries behaved differently from those of the Atlantic or Mediterranean regions; fertility in northern Italy between 1690 and 1770 seems to have been lower than elsewhere. Differentiations in levels and dynamics – the fruit of systems in transition – are visible throughout Europe.

Meanwhile, in the eighteenth century, conditions were ripening that one century later would bring about the onset of a great and irreversible transformation of European systems into the low-fertility, low-mortality, and high-mobility systems of today. With regard to survival, Europe – especially in the central and western areas – had begun to extricate itself from the grip of those unpredictable, irregular, and severe crises that were the great traditional constraints to growth. Not only was plague beginning to disappear, but other pathological manifestations may have been in decline as well, and the productive capacities of the continent were increasing as new markets opened up. A decisive decline in normal mortality had still not occurred, but survival had ceased to depend on exceptional circumstances. With regard to reproduction, low-nuptiality areas were emerging that pointed to a willingness to place limits on the pace of reproduction, a prelude to the process of voluntary birth control that would mark the next century. Finally, the urban network grew denser and more robust; migratory systems expanded; and overseas colonies gained autonomy and prepared to receive new waves of immigrants.

6

The Great Transformation (1800–1914)

A Frame of Reference

The "long" nineteenth century – from 1800 to the outbreak of the First World War – witnessed the end of an old-regime demographic system in Europe and the beginning of a rapid transition to the system that dominates today; one tending towards stability and characterized by long life expectancy and low fertility. Between 1800 and 1914 the population of Europe more than doubled, swelling from 188 to 458 million. The prospect of living to a ripe old age became the destiny of many rather than the privilege of few. The inevitability of women devoting all their childbearing years to pregnancy, breastfeeding, and the rearing of small children came to an end. And the tens of millions of people that departed from Europe for old and new lands turned emigration into a mass phenomenon. These changes had as profound an impact on the demography of the continent as did the Industrial Revolution on the production of wealth, or the French Revolution on political systems. Indeed these processes all acted together to bring about the social transformation of Europe. My goal in this chapter is to outline the course of European demography in a succinct and orderly way. Thanks to the establishment of national statistical systems in the nineteenth century and the abundance of data they produced, the course is a well-documented, if complicated, one. Change occurred in fits and starts, across geographical and social gradients, and with extremely different rhythms. In fact, on the eve of the Great War traditional systems, virtually untouched by change, existed side-by-side with well-evolved "modern" systems. We need to outline the main causes for this transformation and, in particular, identify the specific forces that brought the old-regime systems to an end and accelerated, or slowed down, the transition to present-day systems. Finally, we need to outline the impact this demographic transformation had on European society.

From one point of view – the one I have used throughout this book – the demographic dynamics of the long nineteenth century can be interpreted as the result of weakened constraints and greater choices. More resources, the availability of new lands, and changes in the epidemiological context combined to loosen up the rigid framework of the old regime. Improved health, controlled fertility, greater individual choice regarding marriage, and increased mobility all expanded the scope of individual choices. Fewer restraints and more choices allowed the potential for growth to increase and the demographic processes to become more fluid.

The system of constraints began to relax, though it was a gradual and uneven process. The advances in technology and production that made up the Industrial Revolution led to rapid changes in the way people lived. The conversion of inanimate material into harnessable mechanical energy meant an end to depending on land availability for the production of energy, as till that time land was needed both to sustain draught animals and to provide fuel. It is estimated that world production (Europe and North America for the most part) of coal grew tenfold between 1820 and 1860 and by as much again in the following 60 years; the increase in the production of energy from all inanimate sources grew similarly. This multiplication of per-capita energy, once almost exclusively limited to human or animal muscle power, allowed for a proportional diversification of activities and expansion in the production and trade of goods. In this way – very generally speaking – the rise and spread of the Industrial Revolution had a similar effect on the potential for population growth as did the Neolithic Revolution and the transition from a hunting and gathering system to one of settled agriculture. While the latter freed people from their dependence on fixed resources spontaneously produced by the ecosystem, the former allowed the production of energy and resources to be independent of the availability of land.

Two points related to this general process require further consideration. The first is the general improvement in the standard of living that took place. For our purposes, standard of living is expressed by per-capita income, which measures the real flow of goods and services per person. In table 6.1, the economist Maddison meticulously documents the trend in per-capita gross domestic product in dollars for 14 European countries between 1820 and 1913.

Already in the decades before 1870, per-capita income in the leading country – England – had risen considerably (20 percent between 1785 and 1820 despite war and international instability). Then, in less than a century, the per-capita income of Europe as a whole almost tripled; growth was slowest in Russia where GDP doubled, and fastest in Germany where it grew by 3.5 per cent . The most dynamic continental growth occurred in central Europe – Germany, Denmark, Belgium – and the slowest on the periphery – Russia and Spain. Considering the large countries, and setting the level for the UK at 100, in 1820 France ranked second (69),

Table 6.1 Per-capita gross domestic product in selected European countries, 1820–1913 (1990 dollars)

Country	1820	1870	1900	1913	Ratio 1913/1820	Ratio 1913/1870
United Kingdom	1,756	3,263	4,593	5,032	2.9	1.5
Netherlands	1,561	2,640	3,533	3,950	2.5	1.5
Norway	1,004	1,303	1,762	2,275	2.3	1.7
Sweden	1,198	1,664	2,561	3,096	2.6	1.9
Finland	759	1,107	1,620	2,050	2.7	1.9
Denmark	1,225	1,927	2,902	3,764	3.1	2
Germany	1,112	1,913	3,134	3,833	3.4	2
Belgium	1,291	2,640	3,652	4,130	3.2	1.6
France	1,218	1,858	2,849	3,452	2.8	1.9
Spain	1,063	1,376	2,040	2,255	2.1	1.6
Italy	1,092	1,467	1,746	2,507	2.3	1.7
Austria	1,295	1,875	2,901	3,488	2.7	1.9
Czechoslovakia	849	1,164	1,729	2,096	2.5	1.8
Russia	751	1,023	1,218	1,488	2	1.5
Average	1,155	1,801	2,589	3,101	2.7	1.7

Source: A. Maddison, *Monitoring the World Economy 1820–1992*, OECD, Paris, 1995

Germany third (63), Italy fourth (62), and Russia fifth (43). In 1913 instead Germany was second (76), France third (69), Italy fourth (50), and Russia again last (30). In 1913 the most prosperous area in Europe was the United Kingdom and the nearby geographic cluster of Benelux, Germany, and Denmark (plus Switzerland), while the most backward areas were all located on the periphery of the continent: the Balkans, Scandinavia (Finland and Norway), and the Mediterranean. This geography of economic development, as we shall discover, only partly coincided with the geography of demographic development, the course of which took some very interesting turns.

Other indices might be more useful than income – levels of education or urbanization, for example – but income – especially in the early stages of modern development – is fairly closely linked to the basic living conditions of a society and its survivorship. In an essentially rural society with a low standard of living, a dollar-equivalent increase in available wealth meant better diet and clothing, and a cleaner, sturdier, and better-heated home: though rudimentary, these advances are closely associated with increased life expectancy. Of course, culture, knowledge, environment, climate, and social and family structure are equally important factors in bringing about a decline in mortality. Using Maddison's guide, it is doubtful however that a per-capita income less than $1,000–$1,200 (1990 dollars) could have been compatible with a sustained improvement in survival (not attributable to variations in the epidemiological cycle caused by exogenous factors). Old-regime mortality levels continued to persist in impoverished areas with incomes below that level: Ireland, Finland, and Russia, for example, where at the end of the nineteenth century life expectancy at birth only barely exceeded 32 years of age.

The other important point in our discussion is the transition from a rural society to one in which agriculture is important, but secondary in the production of wealth and the organization of labor, and in which the hallmarks of rural lifestyle steadily decline. This fundamental transformation is important demographically for a number of reasons. First, increased productivity, in part predating the Industrial Revolution, permitted the gradual attenuation of subsistence crises. Second, limited available land combined with a rapidly growing rural population and growing productivity resulted in great numbers moving to cities or emigrating. Third, and directly related to emigration, was the opening of new "European" lands, overseas and beyond the Urals, and the expansion of the food trade. Fourth, the greater availability and variety of foods, together with rising incomes, allowed for improved nutrition. Finally, a shrinking rural population and rural culture permitted demographic behaviors to change more quickly (take, for example, the spread of birth control or different childrearing methods). These five points, to some of which we shall return below, require some clarification.

There is relatively little information available on the breakdown by occupation of the working population. Censuses only began to provide reliable data on occupation around the middle of the nineteenth century when, in much of Europe, the Industrial Revolution had already altered modes of production. Nevertheless, it is generally believed that in preindustrial Europe, between 60 and 80 percent of the working population was employed in agriculture, and that an even greater percentage of the population lived in the countryside. According to Bairoch, approximately 80 percent of the population was traditionally dependent on agricultural work: about 75 percent in England (the birthplace of industrialization) in 1688, and 80–85 percent in France around 1700. Data for the period between 1840 and 1870 give lower percentages of people engaged in farming in more developed countries (England, 26 percent in 1841; Belgium, 51 percent in 1846; France, 54 percent in 1856; Denmark, 60 percent in 1850) but higher ones for those societies still in the early stages of industrialization (Italy, 64 percent in 1871; Sweden, 67 percent in 1860; Austria, 68 percent in 1869; Spain, 72 percent in 1860). On the eve of the First World War, the proportion employed in agriculture in the largest European countries had dropped to 41 percent for France, 37 percent for Germany, and 9 percent for the United Kingdom, while it was still about 54 percent in Italy and over 60 percent in Russia. Beginning in the middle of the nineteenth century, the agricultural population, which had continued to grow in the early part of the century, began its decline in total number (and declined even more abruptly in relative terms).

These figures reveal the rapidly diminishing importance of agriculture in the development process and, indirectly, the marginalization of those demographic behaviors most deeply rooted in the rural character of a society (the last of the five points listed above). In terms of the logical "sequence" of change in the European system, according to which mortality decline provided the initial and powerful catalyst, the most significant feature was the increased productivity of labor (an "agricultural revolution" that was slower and less spectacular than its industrial counter-part); that increase amounted to around 1 percent annually in western Europe after 1800. According to Bairoch, whose analysis I follow, before the agricultural revolution a worker produced an average surplus of no more than 20–30 percent over family require-ments, a surplus needed both to supply workers in nonagricultural sectors and to guard against poor harvests. Fluctuations in yield were often dramatic, easily as much as 25 percent from one year to the next, and so preindustrial populations were victim to those frequent subsistence crises, accompanied by mortality crises. Greater productivity permitted greater surpluses and so reduced the risk of subsistence crises, which during the nineteenth century dwindled in frequency and were often confined to outlying areas. In general terms, the agricultural revolution took place at the begin-ning of the eighteenth century (or even before) in England, and after mid-century in France, Switzerland, Germany, and Denmark; around 1820–30 in Austria, Sweden, and Italy; and around 1860–70 in Russia and Spain. Naturally the reasons for increased productivity are many: shorter fallow periods; land reclamation; new crops; better tools; selection of seeds and livestock; and the introduction and widespread use of machinery. The spread of new crops – while also the cause of widespread nutritional deficiencies (an almost exclusive reliance on corn, for example, caused pellagra) and greater exposure to risk (for instance, because the Irish diet was almost exclusively based on the potato, the failure of that crop led to the Great Famine) – did in the long run lead to improvements in diet. On the eve of the First World War, nutritional levels in western Europe had improved considerably, as shown by the smaller percentage of the family budget spent on food.

Increased productivity of labor together with limited propri-etorship also led to surplus labor in the countryside. This situation was promoted by declining mortality and so natural increase; only later on would fertility decline in the countryside. In Denmark, between 1850 and 1880, the number of people engaged in agriculture grew by 46 percent; in Sweden between 1860 and 1890 by 66 percent. These are two countries in which mortality declined substantially and birth control did not spread to the countryside before the end of the century. These population surpluses became a reservoir which fed the abundant demand for labor in urban and industrialized areas, and so contributed to waves of internal and transoceanic migration. Finally, the open-ing of new spaces across the Atlantic to the west and beyond the

Urals to the east meant the addition of immense expanses of cultivable land and a significant importation of foodstuffs in the last third of the nineteenth century.

This agricultural transformation influenced demographic evolution during the nineteenth century in many ways. Together with rising wages (in themselves propelled by the changes in agriculture), the "revolution" loosened the tight grip that the factors of constraint had on population growth in Europe, and allowed European population to expand.

Demographic Expansion: Numbers and Interpretations

The uneven demographic development of Europe is best understood when put in historical context: it was a time when deeply rooted structures and behaviors came under pressure, and the divisions between populations and social groups widened. Europe in 1914 represented the moment of greatest demographic variety; a

Table 6.2   Population of major European countries and average annual rate of growth, 1800–1913

Country	Population (× 1000)				
	1800	*1850*	*1870*	*1900*	*1913*
United Kingdom	10,834	20,976	26,249	37,334	41,440
Germany	24,500	35,397	40,818	56,367	67,362
Russia	39,000	60,000	73,000	109,700	132,610
Austria-Hungary	24,000	32,604	37,495	47,143	52,578
France	26,900	34,907	36,765	38,962	39,853
Italy	18,124	23,900	26,650	32,475	35,531
Spain	10,745	14,700	16,500	18,618	20,357
Total for 7 countries	154,103	222,484	257,477	340,599	389,731
Europe	187,693	264,591	305,399	400,577	457,515
7 countries as % of Europe	82.1	84.1	84.3	85.0	85.2

Sources: G. Sundbärg, *Aperçus statistiques internationaux*, Imprimerie Royale, Stockholm, 1908. For 1900 and 1910 corrected and additional figures from I. Svennilson, *Growth and Stagnation in the European Economy*, United Nations, Geneva, 1954.

time in which distinctly old-regime societies coexisted with others near the end of their transition. And then, at the height of its demographic vitality, Europe was leveled by the unifying destruction of the First World War.

Consider the seven major European countries, which account for roughly five-sixths of the total population (table 6.2): between 1800 and 1913 the population of the United Kingdom quadrupled and Russia's more than tripled; the population of France, on the other hand, increased by barely 50 percent, while those of Italy and Spain did not quite double.

A hypothetical NW/SE line that joins Dublin – skirting around England – to Trieste clearly divides Europe into a dynamic and quickly growing half and a sluggish and slow-growing one. Though one should not overlook that the slower growing part of Europe – Ireland, Italy, Portugal, and Spain – were major contributors to mass emigration, and in those cases rates of increase fail to accurately reflect the growth potential. Moreover, a rate of increase that exceeded 10 per 1,000 between 1900 and 1913 was three to four

1913 index	*Average annual rate of growth (per 1000)*			
(1800=100)	*1800–50*	*1850–70*	*1870–1900*	*1900–13*
382	13.2	11.2	11.7	8.0
275	7.4	7.1	10.8	13.7
340	8.6	9.8	13.6	14.6
219	6.1	7.0	7.6	8.4
148	5.2	2.6	1.9	1.7
196	5.5	5.4	6.6	6.9
189	6.3	5.8	4.0	6.9
253	7.3	7.3	9.3	10.4
244	6.9	7.2	9.0	10.2

times greater than it had been during 1500–1800, proof of an
entirely transformed system.

Table 6.3 gives the rate of natural increase, as well as birth and
death rates, for the six largest countries and Sweden during particular years of the transformation phase. Three points are especially
worth mentioning. The first point is that all the countries experienced, to varying degrees, a considerable decrease in both birth and

Table 6.3   Demographic indices for selected European countries, 1800–1913
(per 1,000 inhabitants)

Country	c.1800	c.1850	c.1870	c.1900	1913
		Birth rate			
Sweden	31.4	31.8	30.7	26.1	23.2
England	37.7	34.0	35.5	28.1	24.1
Germany	40.3	34.6	38.8	34.3	27.5
Russia	–	50.7	50.8	47.8	43.1
France	33.1	25.8	25.5	21.2	18.8
Austria	40.5	36.5	39.3	36.4	29.7
Italy	–	38.6	36.8	32.6	31.7
		Death rate			
Sweden	24.4	21.7	18.3	15.5	13.7
England	27.1	22.5	22.0	16.1	13.8
Germany	25.8	27.1	27.8	19.5	15.0
Russia	–	36.5	37.1	31.0	27.4
France	30.1	23.8	24.9	19.6	17.7
Austria	26.7	32.0	32.6	24.3	20.3
Italy	–	29.9	30.4	22.0	18.7
		Natural increase			
Sweden	7.0	10.1	12.4	10.6	9.5
England	10.6	11.5	13.5	12.0	10.3
Germany	14.5	7.5	11.0	14.8	12.5
Russia	–	14.2	13.7	16.8	15.7
France	3.0	2.0	0.6	1.6	1.1
Austria	13.8	4.5	6.7	12.1	9.4
Italy	–	8.7	6.4	10.6	13.0

Note: Russia: 1861–5 for *c.*1850; Italy: 1862–6 for *c.*1850; Germany: 1913
territory including Lorraine and Holstein, 1817–21 for *c.* 1800; Austria:
Cisleithanien not including Lombardy and Venetia, 1820–40 for *c.*1800
Source: Sundbärg, *Aperçus statistiques internationaux*, Imprimerie Royale,
Stockholm, 1908

death rates. The second point is that potential increase, expressed by the difference between births and deaths, was for the most part in excess of 10 per 1,000 per year, and came near 15 per 1,000 in more than one case. The third point is that as a result of variations in timing and trajectory for declining births and deaths, marked differences emerge between the several countries: for example, the Russian birth rate is more than double the French on the eve of the First World War, while mortality in Russia is twice that of Sweden or England.

Other synthetic, but more precise, measurements of births and deaths – the rates of which are determined by the age structure of a population – add to our understanding. Tables 6.4 and 6.5 illustrate – again for a select group of countries – two useful and comprehensible measures: life expectancy at birth and average number of children per woman. Again, one must keep in mind that modern statistical methods only became established in the latter part of the century, so many of those figures are estimates.

Table 6.4 Life expectancy at birth in selected European countries, 1750–1915

Country	1750–9	1800–1909[1]	1850–9[2]	1880[3]	1900[4]	1910[5]
Sweden	37.3	36.5	43.3	48.5	54.0	57.9
England	36.9	37.3	40.0	43.3	48.2	53.4
Netherlands	–	32.2	36.8	41.7	49.9	54.1
Germany	–	–	–	37.9	44.4	49.0
Russia	(24.2)	–	(24.4)	27.7	32.4	–
France	27.9	33.9	39.8	42.1	47.4	50.5
Italy	(32)	(30)	(32)	35.4	42.8	47.0
Spain	–	28.0	29.8	31.0	34.8	42.3

Notes: [1]Netherlands, 1816–25; Spain, 1787–97. [2]Netherlands: 1841–50 and 1851–60 average; Spain, 1863–70. [3]Sweden, Germany, and Netherlands, 1871–80 and 1881–90 average; England, 1876–80. [4]England, Sweden, Germany, and Netherlands, 1891–1900 and 1901–10 average; Russia, 1896–7. [5]Netherlands, 1900–9 and 1910–19 average; Sweden, 1911–15
Sources: L. I. Dublin, A. J. Lotka, and M. Spiegelman, *Length of Life*, Ronald Press, New York, 1949. Data for Spain are taken from D. Reher, *La familia en España. Pasado y presente*, Aleanza Editorial, Madrid, 1996, pp. 169–71. For Italy, averages for Lombardy, Venetia, and Tuscany for 1750, 1800, 1850 taken from M. Breschi, L. Pozzi, R. Retaroli, "Analogie e differenze nella crescita della popolazione italiana, 1750–1911," *Bollettino di Demografia Storica*, XX (1994); for Russia, the data refer to Moscow, 1745–63 and 1851–8, and are taken from A. Blum and I. Troitskaja, "La mortalité en Russie au XVIIIe et XIXe siècles: estimations locales à partir des Revizie," *Population*, LI, 2 (1996)

Table 6.5 Average number of children per woman (total fertility rate) in selected European countries, 1800–1910

	1800	1850	1870	1900	1910
Sweden	4.27	4.27	4.49	3.91	3.31
Finland	5.07	4.91	4.95	4.80	4.36
England	5.55	4.95	4.94	3.40	2.84
Netherlands		4.60	5.23	4.48	3.32
Germany	–	–	5.29	4.77	3.52
Switzerland	–	–	4.03	3.32	3.01
France	–	3.38	3.42	2.79	2.25
Italy	–	–	4.88	4.43	4.28

Sources: J.-C. Chesnais, *La transition démographique*, PUF, Paris 1985 and national sources

The life expectancy figures confirm that progress had already been made in several countries before the mid-nineteenth century. Other countries – Italy, Spain, Germany – made strides only later in the century, while Russia continued seriously to lag behind. Between 1800 and 1900, most of the countries had experienced a 15- to 20-year increase in life expectancy at birth.

Fertility began its decline after 1870 in all countries save France, a pioneer in the use of birth control; France's fertility was already significantly lower than that of other countries by mid-century. In fact, on the eve of the First World War, French fertility had dropped below replacement (that is below the level at which offspring numerically just replace the parents' generation). Between 1870 and 1910 fertility dropped in the countries under consideration, from between a minimum of slightly more than 10 percent (in Finland and Italy) and a maximum of over 40 (in Great Britain).

Emigration also became quantitatively relevant in this period, particularly after 1840. It is estimated that throughout western Europe (that is, excluding Russia, Hungary, the Balkans, and Greece), net population loss due to emigration amounted to nearly 35 million people between 1841 and 1914, the equivalent of about half a million per year, or roughly 2.5 emigrants per 1,000 inhabitants. This net loss amounted to between 25 and 30 percent of natural increase (the excess of births over deaths) for that period. Emigration varied a great deal of course depending on time and place, a variation which these figures tend to obscure; they do however tell us that for much of the century emigration was an important outlet for surplus population. Emigration in eastern

Europe was not quite so great; total net population loss for the period 1840–1915 was about 10 million, less than 10 percent of the natural growth of the period. However, one must keep in mind that the 5 million Russians who went to Siberia (a true intercontinental migration) are not included in these figures, and that at the same time Russia was busy settling its southern territories.

The sober data presented in tables 6.2–6.5 summarize the elements of the great demographic revolution that occurred in the nineteenth century. This transformation is generally referred to as the "demographic transition," a term that has entered into common usage much as has Industrial Revolution, and refers to the complex process of passage from the old regime to that of the present day: the former characterized by high fertility and mortality, and the latter by low.

The great transformation of the long nineteenth century presents a series of interpretative problems which multiply in number as we move away from broad generalizations. There is a well-established model of demographic transition, which at its most general identifies declining mortality as the first agent of this change. This mortality is ascribed partly to exogenous causes – the disappearance of plague and natural changes in epidemic cycles – but primarily to factors endogenous to the social and demographic system including: increased agricultural productivity and better economic organization which reduced famine; growing per-capita resources; and changes in sociocultural practices which helped to reduce the spread of infectious diseases. Mortality decline spurred demographic growth; while increased pressure on available resources stimulated the equalizing mechanisms of the system and led to fertility decline by restricting marriage and, especially, by spreading the practice of voluntary birth control. This sequence – mortality decline/accelerated growth/fertility decline- is self-propelled until equilibrium is reestablished when first mortality and then fertility reach low levels. The duration of the entire transition cycle varied according to the economic progress that accompanied it. The above is an adaptation of the Malthusian model that implies an adjustment of population to available resources by means of a check on reproduction – reproduction being less and less conditioned by biological factors and more and more dependent on individual fertility control.

The transition model can also be applied at the micro level, for individuals, or families. Assuming that mortality decline is a prerequisite for the transition process, families found themselves –

assuming constant fertility – with an increasing number of surviving offspring and therefore sought to balance family size by reducing fertility, the simplest and least painful remedy. At the same time, economic development influenced reproductive behavior: the growth of urban industrial society increased the relative "cost" of raising children. This increase came about as children themselves became autonomous wage earners and producers at a later age than in agricultural societies; they also required greater investments in terms of health, education, and welfare, thus increasing financial and parental obligations. In particular their presence prevented mothers from returning to the workplace, which was by now distinct from the domestic sphere. The increased cost of children (a cost that was increasing relative to rising incomes) appears to have been the spur behind fertility control, a behavioral change made easier by the relaxation of social controls exercised by tradition, religion, or institutions. Improved communication aided the spread of these practices from city to country, from the upper classes to the lower, and from centers of development to more peripheral regions.

This model is based on several major postulates: (a) that mortality decline sets off the process; (b) that diminished fertility follows as a consequence; (c) that economic and social progress lead to demographic change; (d) that other demographic factors are of secondary importance. These four postulates, however, have not always held, and, as we shall discover, there have been many significant exceptions in the demographic history of Europe. Declining mortality, for example, has not always preceded declining fertility; demographic transition has not always taken place at the pace dictated by economic development; the other demographic factors have not always been of secondary importance; nor, as it turns out, is there a simple dependent relationship between demography and economics, but, as we shall see, the two interact in important ways.

It is this mutual dependence that we should emphasize when revisiting the transition model. Earlier we discussed the interaction between the factors of constraint and the factors of choice. For many centuries the relationship between the two was fairly static and demographic structures remained relatively fixed, cemented in the similarly relative stability of the old regime, a stability which, it goes without saying, was constantly jeopardized by major crises. However, when the system of constraints relaxed – as it did in the eighteenth century for reasons tied to technological progress, biological and pathological change, or the settlement of new lands

– then the system of choices was affected as well. The reactions varied in their nature and timing. For example, accelerated demographic growth may follow a Malthusian path whereby an increase in population (caused by a decline in mortality or increased nuptiality following the relaxing of constraints) leads to the re-establishment of equilibrium through an increase, or even an explosion, of mortality levels. This was the case for some of the more backward European populations which made the transition from an old-regime to a contemporary system relatively late. Or else adjustment may occur by means of different combinations of restricting factors – lower nuptiality, lower fertility within marriage, higher emigration – according to particular natural, historical, or cultural factors. So, for example, the reaction of France was a precocious and widespread control of fertility, whereas the Scandinavian countries reacted through emigration and delayed marriage. Yet another reaction was to adjust to rapid population growth by relaxing the factors of constraint even further and creating, for example, new resources to support demographic growth. This happened in England where fertility began to decline almost a century later than in France because the greater human resources in the presence of capital stimulated economic development, and for a long period population growth was regulated – insofar as it was regulated at all – through migration.

We need then to consider the demographic transition as a collection of reactions to rapid population increase following the weakening of the traditional system of obstacles and constraints. In this light, the fact that fertility declined later in England, home of modern industrial development, than in France, which remained very rural until well into the last century, is no longer incomprehensible. Nor for that matter, is the case of Ireland, where emigration and delayed marriage helped to re-establish demographic equilibrium, and where fertility within marriage declined later than in Sicily; in Sicily instead migration was an available option but not changes in nuptiality, the patterns of which were profoundly rooted in tradition. In other words, the paths that various societies followed towards low-fertility/low-mortality regimes differed from one another and did not necessarily follow the procedural logic and order of events prescribed by the transition model.

Two Months Per Year: Increasing Life Expectancy

The causes of the great increase in life expectancy during the nineteenth century are at the same time both extremely simple and extremely complex. On the eve of the Great War, Koch, Pasteur, and a legion of microbiologists had discovered and isolated the origins of the major infectious diseases; public health and medicine had organized and spread; the broad dissemination of scientific knowledge had an ever greater impact on human behavior, in particular in the area of childrearing; nutrition had improved considerably; and per-capita economic resources had roughly tripled since the beginning of the long century. Little surprise then that life expectancy was increasing at the pace of two or three months every calendar year.

What is difficult, however, to sort out are the causes of mortality decline: how much was due to improvements in the standard of living and better nutrition, and how much instead to medical discoveries and their applications, the role of public health, and changes in individual behaviors? That the causal web is tightly woven has not prevented scholars from trying to isolate, as much as possible, the role of the dominant factors of decline; moreover, this historical experience can help us to understand the problems that high-mortality populations face in today's world.

"The enjoyment of old age preceded medical progress," writes Ariès, and the changed view that Europeans in the eighteenth and early nineteenth centuries took of death was an important factor in the progress of European society: "Given the growing complexity of social life, intelligence and organizational capability, as opposed to physical strength, became increasingly important, and so continued economic activity at older ages." Still we need to ask what made this changed attitude possible? How did the prospect of a longer life become no longer a chimera but a reasonable certainty? Four elements can help us better understand the mortality transition.

The decline of subsistence crises

A decline of subsistence crises was the outcome, as we have already discussed, of an agricultural revolution; increased agricultural productivity mitigated the impact of annually fluctuating crop yields. Those crop yields – and consequently grain prices – did continue to fluctuate for most of the century (also affecting mortality), but they did so to a lesser extent than in preceding ones. The integration of economic markets also played a role, while a greater variety of foodstuffs freed many (though certainly not all) from the traditional heavy dependence on grain. As an example of the new importance trade assumed: in 1878–9 Russia exported 20.6 million tons of wheat, more than half of Italy's total production for the same period, while Germany during 1875–9 imported the equivalent of more than one-fifth of its entire production. The last great European subsistence crisis occurred in 1816–17 – caused by severe weather and rising prices, and accompanied by an outbreak of typhus – and led to a widespread rise in mortality. Later crises were increasingly local and confined to those areas which had yet to experience the agricultural revolution.

Ireland provides an example of a classic old-regime, Malthusian-type crisis. Its population, 8.6 million according to the census of 1841, had tripled since the beginning of the eighteenth century; and most of that population consumed a diet based almost exclusively on the potato. In the decade prior to the crisis, indications of overpopulation were already evident: delayed marriage and increased emigration. These developments did not, however, avert catastrophe: in 1845 a fungus badly damaged the potato harvest; in 1846 it destroyed it entirely. The winter of 1846–7 brought famine, poverty, desperate and massive emigration, and typhus. It has been estimated that the Great Famine together with associated epidemics caused between 1.1 and 1.5 million more deaths than normal. Emigration became an exodus, and 200,000 people per year left Ireland between 1847 and 1854. The long-term repercussions of this catastrophe – perhaps the most intense in the history of Europe – were profound. Not only did people emigrate *en masse*, but the demographic regime itself was transformed into a system characterized by later marriage and a high percentage never married. By 1901 the population had fallen to 4.5 million, just over half that registered on the eve of the Great Famine.

There were other subsistence crises over the course of the century. The 1860s in Finland were marked by a series of famines; first in 1862, then 1865, and the most severe in 1867. The impact of the first shortage in 1862 was minimal as it followed many years of plenty, but the effects of the other two were tragic. Mortality in 1868 was three times greater than normal, and the population of Finland declined 9 percent between 1866 and 1868. Once again, high mortality was accompanied by an outbreak of typhus. In Russia, the severe shortages of 1891 in the black earth wheat-producing regions cost many lives; a crisis which even showed up in statistics for the whole of that vast country. In fact mortality was 20–5 percent higher in 1892 as cholera also ravaged the population. Such events nevertheless were the exception, and in general subsistence crises – even in rural and backward parts of Europe – became rarer and less devastating in demographic terms.

Improved nutrition

General nutritional levels tended to improve not only because of the absence of subsistence crises, but also because day-to-day diets improved. By 1914 the nutritional situation in almost all of Europe was certainly better than at the beginning of the long century. There is both direct and indirect evidence to support this claim. For instance, family incomes had increased and less of the family budget was being spent on food, a sure sign of improved living standards (as incomes rise, food expenditures increase by a smaller percentage). Diets became richer and more varied. Fewer total calories came from grains, and meat consumption increased. Moreover, sound nutrition is a necessary condition – if not a sufficient one – for longer life expectancy. In this regard, we should consider an "intuitive" explanation for mortality decline that has gained favor in recent years: the "nutritional" theory championed by McKeown, according to which demographic acceleration starting in the eighteenth century was due to mortality decline. That mortality decline, however, can be explained neither by medical advances, which had no impact for the whole of the nineteenth century and beyond (except for Jenner's smallpox vaccine discovered in 1798), nor by changes in public or private hygiene (which in some cases, for example the large cities, probably deteriorated), nor by other causes. The true cause, according to McKeown, was the improvement of the population's nutritional level, which increased organic "resistance" to infection, and so led to increased life expectancy.

This theory is contradicted by a number of factors which force us look to other causes. First, there is the complex relationship between nutrition and resistance to infection which we have discussed at length in chapter 3. The link holds in cases of severe malnutrition or undernourishment, but is less certain when basic nutritional levels are adequate, as was the case for most of the population of nineteenth-century Europe. Second, mortality had already begun to decline in the latter half of the eighteenth century and the first decades of the nineteenth (in northern Europe and France; see table 6.4). However, that period did not witness great improvements in diet. In France – to use the example of a country which experienced a notable decline in mortality – in 1870 about 70 percent of total calories were supplied by grain and carbohydrates and few came from animal proteins. This diet scarcely differed from that of the late eighteenth century. And in fact meat consumption in all of Europe had reached an all-time low at the beginning of the nineteenth century. The introduction of new more productive crops such as buckwheat, potatoes, and corn, while they increased the supply of foodstuffs, actually contributed to qualitative deterioration. In addition, the decline in real wages in most of Europe between the middle of the eighteenth century and the early nineteenth is well documented, and almost four-fifths of those wages were spent on food. Yet another indicator of nutritional levels is average height, which seems in this period to have stagnated or even declined, certainly not a sign of dietary improvements. There are, then, strong arguments against the nutritional theory of mortality decline, at least until the middle of the nineteenth century, after which improved nutrition certainly did play a positive role in increasing life expectancy.

Changes in epidemiology

The definitive retreat of plague from eastern and western Europe, the control of smallpox by the spread of the vaccine, the gradually diminishing frequency of outbreaks of typhus, in part because of the attenuation of subsistence crises, all played a role in removing the threat of irregular – though frequent and intense – mortality crises. Cholera, on the other hand, was a new disease, contracted by ingesting a bacillus transmitted directly by contact between people or indirectly through contaminated water. The epidemic originated in India, reached Russia in 1829, and had crossed the whole of Europe by 1837. In general, only one person in ten of those infected with cholera actually develops the disease, but it tends to be highly lethal. The pandemic of the 1830s was followed by others in every decade of the century save the 1870s, though public health measures – Koch had identified the cholera vibrio in 1883–4 – helped to contain the later outbreaks. While cholera devastated Hamburg, Germany, in 1892, causing 9,000 deaths, in nearby Bremen – where a system of water purification had been installed – it claimed only six lives, an illustration of the impact of medical discoveries by that time. In Italy, the most severe epidemic occurred in 1865–7 and caused 128,000 deaths, about 5 percent of total deaths for the three-year period. In France the 1854–5 epidemic claimed 150,000 lives, just under 10 percent of total deaths for those two years. Cholera did not, however, raise mortality on the scale of old-regime crises: despite the tragic events of 1867, Italy experienced only an 18 percent increase over normal mortality for the time, a relatively mild outcome compared to earlier crises. In any case, the epidemiological events that most strongly marked the century were the return of old diseases, such as tuberculosis and malaria, and the continued spread of more recent ones, such as pellagra, rather than the introduction of new diseases (though one of the latter was yellow fever, which arrived in Mediterranean Europe from the Americas).

The frequency and severity of tuberculosis depends on many factors, perhaps the most significant of which are levels of immunity and resistance, and the virulence of infection. These factors, however, evolve over very long periods of time and so cannot explain how the disease changed over the course of the nineteenth century. More and more evidence points to the fact that tuberculosis mortality peaked early in the century and began to decline in the latter half. Though statistics on causes of death only document the declining phase of the disease's cycle, recent research on mid-eighteenth century Sweden and Finland support this basic claim. This distinct epidemiological cycle was strongly influenced by living standards: nutritional levels and their relation to resistance to infection; population density; conditions of the home and workplace; personal hygiene, and so forth. Those above factors influence the risk of exposure to disease, and are in turn associated with growing urbanization. We can characterize the early nineteenth century then as an era in which industrialization and urbanization contributed to rising mortality and the latter part of the century as one in which improved living standards began to have a positive effect. In England in 1871 one out of every seven deaths was from tuberculosis, and the situation was similar in Sweden and Finland around the middle of the century. In Stockholm one death in five was from tuberculosis between 1750 and 1830, with significant differences by social class. By contrast, at the end of the 1880s, in those European countries for which we have reliable data, death from tuberculosis was between 2 and 3 per 1,000 at a time when total mortality was between 20 and 30 per 1,000. The cyclical history of tuberculosis indeed confirms the observation that the effect of nineteenth-century economic development on mortality was both positive and negative.

Malaria is also an old disease in Europe, found especially but not exclusively in the Mediterranean and in both coastal and swampy areas. Bonelli has described the impact of malaria in the context of Italy: "each occurrence [of malaria] caused people to flee to the healthier hillsides or mountains, and so led to the exploitation and deforestation of those areas. The subsequent deterioration of the water system and the flight of inhabitants slowly created more extensive swamplands and caused malaria to continue to spread." It was widely held in late nineteenth-century Italy that malaria was spreading geographically, spurred by random deforestation, public building projects (in particular the extension of the railway system which created pools of stagnant water), expansion of rice cultivation, and the greater mobility of seasonal laborers, a factor which increased the population exposed to infection. In 1887, the first year for which cause of death statistics were published, there were 21,000 deaths from malaria (slightly less than one per 1,000), but the effects of malaria are multiplied because those infected are more vulnerable to other diseases as well. It was for this reason that mortality levels were higher in malarial regions than could be explained in terms of deaths ascribed to the disease. Malaria, without a doubt, contributed to the high mortality levels in Iberia, Italy, Greece, and the Balkans, but it also spread (and not always in a benign form) to the Atlantic coast of France, England, the Netherlands, northern Germany, parts of the Danube basin, and large areas of central and southern Russia. In southern Tuscany, where malaria was endemic, life expectancy between 1810 and 1850 was five to six years shorter than in the nonmalarial parts of the region. Examples of this sort abound. A recent study has shown that sharp differences were registered even in northern climes: in early nineteenth-century Essex, Kent, and East Sussex, the infant mortality rate in ten inland and hilly parishes was between 62 and 149 per1,000, while in nine parishes located in malarial coastal areas or in the Thames estuary it was between 240 and 377. Some interesting figures for the prewar period give a good idea of the incidence of the phenomenon: in Greece in 1905, 38 percent of the population was infected by malaria, and deaths were equivalent to 2.3 per 1,000; in Romania it is estimated that between one- and two-thirds of the population in malarial zones (along the Danube River and on the coast) was infected; in the Soviet Union, 9 million cases were recorded in both 1934 and 1935, primarily in the Volga basin and Black Sea regions.

Pellagra, a more recent disease, is connected to the cultivation and consumption of corn, as a diet consisting almost exclusively of that grain creates severe vitamin deficiencies. A chronic and season-ally acute disease, it could cause death. Pellagra appeared in Spain, where it was described by the Asturian physician Gaspar Casal, then spread to southern France, northeastern Italy, and the Balkans. Although it caused fewer deaths than malaria, pellagra nevertheless afflicted a high percentage of the population and was seriously debilitating.

I have discussed tuberculosis, malaria, and pellagra – in descending order of effect and diffusion – because these diseases were recognized in their time as veritable social scourges, requiring the mobilization of great resources. They are also relevant because their decline began before the discovery of the responsible pathogens and the mechanisms for the infection and transmission of the diseases, and before the introduction of medicines for their treatment. Because contemporaries recognized the factors associ-ated with their outbreaks – poor hygiene, poor and crowded living conditions, and insufficient diet in the case of tuberculosis; swampy conditions in the case of malaria; a corn-based diet for pellagra – they were able to combat them even in the absence of effective treat-ment. In addition, death from these diseases was – presumably – on the rise in the early part of the century, encouraged by deterio-rating living conditions for certain social and professional classes (the urban proletariat, the peasantry) or deteriorating environ-mental conditions caused by hydrogeological upheaval. Public measures, and in particular an improved standard of living, served to attenuate their impact already in the pre-World War I period.

The impact of medicine

This topic is a highly controversial one because the pronounced decline in nineteenth-century mortality has long and widely been attributed to advances in medicine. Nevertheless, the prevailing opinion is that, with the obvious exception of smallpox, immu-nization and effective therapeutic treatments had little effect on mortality decline before the twentieth century. For example, the incidence of typhus had already declined dramatically when in 1909 it was discovered that lice transmitted the disease; and similarly that of malaria before Ross proved in 1897 that a mosquito bite was responsible for the infection. As for tuberculosis, Koch isolated its agent in 1882, but effective treatments only became available in the early decades of the twentieth century. It is true, however, that although not providing specific cures, biology and medicine by the end of the nineteenth century had developed a series of defensive strategies for the control of infectious diseases. It was possible, for example, to almost completely repress infections by interrupting their transmission: uncontaminated food and water prevented cholera and typhoid fever; good hygiene and the elimination of parasites and carrier animals contained the risk of plague, malaria, or typhus; and the isolation of patients helped to control acute infections such as diphtheria, scarlet fever, and measles. Bacteriological discoveries subsequently provided the scientific foundation for these strategies, and encouraged successful public measures and more prudent individual behavior. This complex line of defense was further reinforced with the discovery of vaccines and immunizing serums, and, when prevention of the infection proved impossible, therapeutic cures.

In conclusion, we can make the following observations: the abatement of subsistence crises was a first important advance made in the early decades of the nineteenth century; overall improvement of nutrition, however, only became significant at the end of the century; industrialization, urbanization, and environmental change jeopardized the health and survival of many people, while benefiting others, and caused a slowing (or inversion) of the general trend towards declining mortality; the specific curative or immunizing role of medicine was weak or nonexistent before the twentieth century, though accumulated scientific knowledge did permit the organization of a rational defense against many diseases.

Infant Mortality Yet Again

In chapter 5 we traced a general outline of infant mortality in the old-regime demographic systems of Europe, with a particular emphasis on the variability associated with breastfeeding customs, childrearing practices, and a series of complex social factors that influenced the spread of infectious disease and therefore the survival of small children. Very distinct differences persisted among national groups in the middle of the nineteenth century. Infant mortality rates were twice as high in Austria, for example, as in Denmark; and twice as high in Bavaria as in France. Even sharper differences can be found between villages, among families living in the same neighborhood, between streets in the same city, or among different professional groups. A closer look at infant mortality is interesting not only because it helps us understand how mortality declined in the nineteenth century – life expectancy increases only when infant and child mortality levels drop – but also for the three fundamental reasons relating to a changing demographic system. First, a greater number of surviving offspring – fertility being equal – increases the burden of childrearing and favors the limitation of family size. Second, the higher infant mortality, the shorter the intervals between births, in the absence of voluntary birth control: the death of an infant in the early months of life interrupts breast-feeding and increases the chances of another pregnancy. Third, fewer children per family allow for greater investment in each surviving child and is therefore in and of itself a reason behind improved survivivorship. Infant mortality and fertility are interrelated, and variations in one are never independent of variations in the other. The processes of production and destruction of human capital, so intense in old-regime societies, are inextricably linked.

In some European countries – France, England, Sweden – infant mortality was already declining between the middle of the eighteenth century and the early decades of the nineteenth, while in almost all, levels dropped sharply by the end of the century. For much of the continent, though we lack national series for the period, there is a wealth of local data indicating that infant mortality levels for much of the nineteenth century differed little from levels in previous centuries, and that the experience of the northern countries and France, while not unique (similar trends were registered in northern Italy), did not apply to the majority of European populations. We also find that for those countries in which mortality began to decline early, there was a period of stagnation or regression in the trend starting in the third or fourth decade of the century. Comparing the periods 1840–5 and 1895–9, infant mortality was 150 and 158 per 1,000 (respectively) in England, 160 and 162 per 1,000 in France, 156 and 158 in Belgium, and 137 and 134 in Denmark. For the countries which had already made considerable progress (or in any case had achieved moderate levels for the times) and were forerunners of economic development, this slump can be interpreted as the price paid for industrial and urban development, and for a relative deterioration in living standards. The high mortality of cities such as London, Manchester, Birmingham, Liverpool, Sheffield, and other northern industrial centers, well above the national average, was well known to the nineteenth-century public, from the Farr reports for example, and was openly debated. The growing percentage of urban population, with a shorter life expectancy than its rural counterpart, is one of the reasons for the stagnation, or increase, in infant mortality in England. In other industrialized areas, such as Belgium and Germany, where more and more people were residing in cities, there was a direct link between level of urbanization and infant mortality rates. Indeed throughout Europe – in Stockholm, Madrid, Rome, Paris – urban survivorship was poor. On the other hand, the reason behind the mid-century stagnation of infant mortality rates in strongly rural countries such as France remains something of a mystery (a decrease in duration of breastfeeding or heavier workloads for women are possible explanations).

It seems reasonable to maintain that general levels of knowledge prior to the discovery of bacteria would not have allowed – except in particular social and environmental situations – infant mortality to decline below about 150 per 1,000. Subsequently, beginning in the 1890s, a significant drop in infant mortality was registered almost everywhere: in the brief period between 1895 and 1899 and 1910 and 1914 infant mortality declined 20 to 30 percent: from 100 to 72 per 1,000 in Sweden, from 158 to 109 in England, from 162 to 119 in France, from 171 to 139 in Italy, and from 217 to 163 in Germany. In the meantime, almost all the agents of the principal infectious diseases had been identified; pasteurization of milk had made artificial feeding for children safe; water purification reduced the risk of intestinal infections; a number of effective treatments had been introduced (for diphtheria, for example). According to Catherine Rollet, there are three phases in the history of social commitment to the problem of infant survival. Between 1860 and 1880, the public awoke to the social problem of high infant mortality, viewing it as the destruction of a precious family and societal resource. The 1871 English parliamentary hearing on the subject, and the 1874 introduction in France of the Roussel law to control wet-nursing are two examples of this growing public sensitivity. In this period public activism sought to improve environmental and living conditions associated with high mortality. The second phase, between 1880 and 1900, followed the bacteriological discoveries of the day; and questions of correct infant nutrition became central to battling against digestive diseases. The third phase began in the twentieth century and addressed the problem of reducing infant mortality by safeguarding the health of mothers in order to better protect infants. These phases can also be seen as a process of gradually substituting the "quality" of children for their "quantity," a sign of the increasing importance of human investment to families and society.

Another relevant, if ambiguous, indicator was the practice of infant abandonment in the first days and weeks of life, an ancient practice that underwent a dramatic increase between the eighteenth and nineteenth centuries. Abandonment characterized Catholic countries in particular, though it was not unknown in Protestant areas as well – London, Germany, Scandinavia; in the latter it was, however, dealt with differently, often involving intervention at the level of the parish. Catholic countries, instead, had institutions specifically designed for the receipt of foundlings, some of which were quite old; the Spedale degli Innocenti in Florence, for example, was founded in 1445. The growth of infant abandonment in the second half of the eighteenth century seems to have been widespread, and can be attributed to a variety of factors, not the least of which were the creation of foundling homes themselves, their large capacity and territorial spread, and their easy acceptance policies. Still, what we might today refer to as the increased "supply" of services was not the only, or even the major, reason for increased abandonment; instead, more and more mothers and couples felt pressure to free themselves of the burden of their newborns; at an extremely general level of explanation, this phenomenon can be interpreted as an adaptation to changing circumstances (the higher cost – absolute or relative – of offspring) which, in the second half of the nineteenth century, took on the less traumatic form of fertility control. This interpretation finds confirmation in the fact that the abandonment of legitimate children rose (in some cases more numerous than the abandonment of illegitimate children) and much of the abandoning was done by nondestitute segments of society (workers, artisans). As to the scale of abandonment, 4.3 percent of children born in the Kingdom of Naples were abandoned in 1836; 2.3 percent in Tuscany in 1843–52; 4.8 percent in Lombardy in 1842; 2.7 percent in France in 1846, but over 10 percent in districts of major cities such as Paris, Naples, and Milan. With regard to mortality, the precariousness of the circumstances surrounding abandonment, inadequate breastfeeding, and the ease of transmitting infectious diseases combined to insure that a minority of abandoned infants survived to their first birthday. Infant abandonment is a complex phenomenon; more than simply a crude surrogate for birth control, and rarely an indirect form of infanticide, it certainly was a sign of widespread hardship.

The Advent of Birth Control

Birth rates in much of Europe by about 1910 had already begun to decline. More precise measures like the number of children per woman (technically speaking, the Total Fertility Rate) reveal an average decline between 1870 and 1910 (for the countries listed in table 6.5 on p. 136) from 4.7 to 3.4. As we know, it was the beginning of an irreversible decline that has brought us to the extremely low levels of the past 25 years. For precisely this reason, it is important to understand what prompted this great change. We know that the primary immediate cause of fertility decline was the spread of voluntary birth control; other related causes (nuptiality variations, among others) had a relatively minor impact.

In order to better understand this process we must keep in mind this important fact: as a mass phenomenon, voluntary birth control was something new, but among select groups of people it had been practiced for some time. Moreover, individuals have had recourse to it in the simple form of coitus interruptus ever since people first became aware of the consequences of sexual intercourse. Family reconstitutions and genealogies, for example, have shown in the eighteenth century, and in some cases, even a century earlier, fertility limitation was relatively diffuse among the privileged classes of Europe: royal families, French dukes and peers, English peers, the aristocracies of Belgium, Milan, Genoa, and Florence, the bourgeoisie of Geneva, and the prominent families of Ghent. Proof is found not only in the lower rates of legitimate fertility for these groups, but also in other unequivocal signs of "control," for example the lowering of the average age at the birth of the last child, which is about 40 years old in a natural fertility regime and approaches 30 as fertility declines. Other select groups, such as Jewish communities in Italy (Florence, Livorno, Modena) and outside of Italy (Bayonne), had already reduced their fertility in the eighteenth century; and there is increasing evidence for similar behavior among certain urban groups. In other words, the "precursors" for voluntary birth control existed, but their behavior did not extend beyond the strict limits of family strategies practiced by privileged classes or religious communities, small groups that did not transmit their behavior to outsiders. Then, during the first Restoration, the French clergy came to realize that an apparent decline in births – evident from their parish birth registers – was the outcome of new marital behavior; no longer limited to certain well-defined groups, the practice of "onanism" (this term was also used for coitus interruptus) had become widespread (and the Penitentiary tribunal in Rome received no end of queries about whether it was permissible behavior). Voluntary birth control was developing into a mass phenomenon.

By that time, the effectiveness of the marital check – the traditional method of reproductive control in old-regime societies – had been largely exhausted in almost all of western Europe. At the beginning of the nineteenth century, average age at marriage west of the St. Petersburg–Trieste line was high – 25–27 years for women – and a considerable percentage of the population did not marry at all, a model already discussed in chapter 5. In the face of declining mortality, especially in the second half of the century, the ultimate Malthusian preventive check (reduced nuptiality) was no longer sufficient to moderate growth; a more powerful one was needed.

Measures for marital fertility, which are not affected by nuptiality, allow us to follow, though indirectly, the trend in voluntary birth control. Table 6.6 gives figures for 1910 and an earlier period (in most cases between 1850 and 1880) during which uncontrolled natural fertility was the rule, except in France where fertility had already begun to decline.

The measure used is standardized by age and marital status (eliminating the influence which different age structures and marital structures can have on less sophisticated measures); it is expressed in parts of 1,000, where 1,000 (a measure no European society achieved or even came close to) represents the highest empirical level of legitimate fertility. Values greater than 650 usually correspond to unchecked fertility (which could vary from country to country according to factors such as the duration of breastfeeding, intrauterine mortality, etc.); values lower than 600 were almost surely the result of deliberate measures to increase the interval between births or stop procreation.

With the exception of France and Hungary, all the countries in the table registered levels between 650 and 800 in the period between 1850 and 1880; on the eve of the Great War, legitimate fertility had dropped below 600 in nine countries, representing declines of 10–40 percent; in still others (Scandinavia, Italy, Spain) the drop was less than 10 percent and the average remained above 600, but there were indications in those countries as well that fertility had begun to decline.

Figure 6.1 reflects table 6.6, giving the distribution of over 700 subnational European areas (provinces, departments, districts) according to the presumed date of the onset of "irreversible" fertility decline: this date is taken to be when marital fertility declines by 10 percent with respect to a preceding period of stability (and without subsequent increases). Applying this criterion to national groups, the earliest date is 1827 for France and the latest 1922 for European Russia and Ireland. The rest date their decline some time after 1880. At the disaggregated level of figure 6.1, two distinct distributions emerge: the French departments (clearly preceding the rest of Europe) began their fertility decline between 1780 and 1850 and occupy the left side of the figure, while the rest of Europe is on the right. In 60 percent of the cases the date of the onset of decline falls between 1890 and 1920; and the most crowded decade is 1900–10. The last areas only began decisive decline in the 1940s.

The geography of fertility decline reveals a process that began in France and spread to the more developed parts of Europe, including Catalonia, Piedmont, Liguria, and Tuscany in the south, and England, Belgium, Germany, and parts of Scandinavia in the center-north. The more peripheral areas (in the Mediterranean, southern Italy and much of Spain; on the Atlantic, in Portugal and Ireland; the Balkans; Russia) and areas geographically central but culturally traditional (the Alps) were the last strongholds of high fertility, gradually conquered in the course of the twentieth century.

Two other factors must be added to this description of the fertility transition. As expected, fertility appears to have declined first, and more quickly, in urban areas as compared to rural. In Italy, for example, marital fertility in large towns (over 100,000 inhabitants) in 1871 was 15 percent lower than in small, mostly rural, towns (fewer than 30,000 inhabitants). Between 1871 and 1901 fertility in the former declined by 16 percent and in the latter by only five, widening the gap even further. However, this contrast, which can be applied to much of mid-nineteenth century Europe, needs to be understood in relation to both peculiarities inherent to urban areas and their close ties to rural ones, complicating the interpretation of data, especially during phases of intense urbanization. In particular, city-dwellers included a high percentage of people for whom marriage and reproduction were unlikely (those

Table 6.6   Marital fertility in European countries

Austria			Ireland		
1880	677		1871		708
1910	588		1911		708
Index	87		Index		100
Belgium			Italy		
1846	757		1864		677
1910	444		1911		616
Index	59		Index		91
Denmark			Netherlands		
1852	671		1859		816
1911	522		1909		652
Index	78		Index		80
England			Norway		
1851	675		1875		752
1911	467		1900		701
Index	69		Index		93
Finland			Portugal		
1880	698		1864		682
1910	647		1911		636
Index	93		Index		93
France			Russia		
1831	537		1897		755
1911	315		1926		665
Index	59		Index		88
Germany			Scotland		
1867	760		1861		742
1910	542		1911		565
Index	71		Index		76
Hungary			Spain		
1880	589		1887		650
1910	529		1910		623
Index	90		Index		96
Switzerland			Sweden		
1860	724		1880		700
1910	513		1900		652
Index	71		Index		93

Note: The index gives the more recent value as a percentage of the earlier one.
Marital fertility (Ig) is standardized for age and marital status
Source: A. J. Coale and S. Cotts Watkins, eds., *The Decline of Fertility in Europe*, Princeton, Princeton University Press, 1986

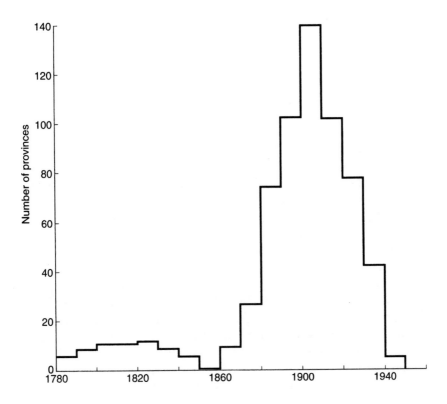

Figure 6.1 Distribution of European provinces by date of onset of fertility decline

Source: Coale and Cotts Watkins, eds., *The Decline of Fertility in Europe*, Princeton University Press, Princeton, 1986

belonging to the military or to religious orders, those living in institutions, domestic servants); there was a large proportion of recently arrived inhabitants who had left behind their families; in the case of France especially, there were many families who sent their children to wet nurses in the countryside (shortening the breastfeeding period this way made for briefer intervals between births, in the absence of birth control); and finally, the ratio between men and women was often out of balance. These factors skew statistics and make them difficult to interpret. Nevertheless, over the course of the nineteenth century fertility seemed to come under control earlier and more quickly in cities than in the country. Once again France presents an important exception: voluntary birth control seems to have taken hold in cities beginning in the early eighteenth century (this was certainly true in the case of Rouen), but early on its effect was barely sufficient to counterbalance the higher fertility that resulted from sending children out to wet nurses (as described above). The second point to take into consideration is that fertility decline occurred first among the higher social classes (by income, profession, or education), and took its time to spread to other social groups.

The French exception has been, and continues to be, a subject of great debate and research. There is no doubt that French couples in cities and the countryside alike practiced contraception some 50 to 100 years before the rest of Europe, and that urban, industrialized England discovered birth control much later than did rural France. The beginning of the birth control movement coincided with the French Revolution, and fertility decline, coincided more or less with mortality decline. Two not necessarily mutually exclusive lines of reasoning exist to explain this. The first is a cultural explanation and based on the widespread influence of revolutionary ideology, the sudden termination of religious and moral control, and the suspension of individual and collective religious practices. These factors would have accelerated transition where it had already begun, and produced new behaviors where it had not, supported by greater mobility, new social contacts, and the unifying experiences of the revolutionary and imperial armies. Of course everything cannot be attributed to the Revolution: fertility decline was already evident in Normandy and Vexin in the decades preceding 1789, but cultural or social changes of this magnitude do not take place from one day to the next. The other explanation is more economic than social or cultural. France remained for a long time a rural society and could not have absorbed over the long term the demographic pressure caused by declining mortality without, for example, having to excessively fragment land holdings. Moreover, the nuptiality check in the form of late marriage together with a high percentage unmarried in the old regime was already well developed and could not have offset resultant demographic increase. According to Bardet: "We can hypothesize that in general the adoption of contraceptive practices helped avoid what would have been excessive delays in marriage within the traditional system of land tenancy". He adds moreover, that the decline in births between 1790 and 1850, "did not truly constitute a modern demographic transition but the continuation by other means of the usual agrarian Malthusian practices." Meanwhile, industrialization in England created new "niches" in cities and in new sectors that absorbed surplus population (both the rural surplus and that created by lower mortality) and made mass migration possible, all without modifying reproductive behavior. In France, again, the persistence of traditional economic structures and the relative lack of the migration option led to adjustments in the system through fertility control, more easily practiced in the "revolutionary" environment of relaxed religious and moral controls. The cultural component then also plays a role in the economic argument, and helps to explain the much later adoption of voluntary birth control in other rural societies like France.

The transition paradigm is challenged by more than just the French exception. The map of economic development in western Europe corresponds only very roughly to that of fertility decline, and the France/England contrast is by no means unique. For instance, Lombardy in Italy and the Basque provinces of Spain, though leaders in economic growth, were not in the avant garde of fertility control; the more economically developed north of Portugal controlled fertility later than did the less developed south; in 1890 fertility began to decline simultaneously in Hungary, where three-quarters of the workforce was employed in agriculture, and in highly-industrialized Germany. There seems to be no end of evidence for and against the transition model, but ultimately the debate fails to suggest an explicative model which incorporates the many variables and produces convincing results, either because the evidence itself is ambiguous or because what it must explain is not only differences in fertility but the whole complex process of demographic transition that involves the other demographic variables as well.

A final important observation is that by the early twentieth century declining mortality had made traditional fertility levels unfeasible almost everywhere, because of the subsequent accelerating population growth. The nuptiality check had reached a limit and controls were being placed on emigration by the receiving countries who were finding it difficult to absorb the surpluses, so fertility control emerged as really the only way to reign in demographic expansion. The process of fertility decline, for the most part, followed the geographical path of economic development and declining mortality, but with many deviations and exceptions attributable to culture and tradition, religions and institutions, permanence and change, all of which can only be understood at local and specific levels of analysis.

Outside of Europe

What would Europe have been like without America, and America without Europe? While no scholar should ever pose such a question, the temptation is great, given the enormous importance of emigration in linking together the two continents in the nineteenth century. We have already discussed the importance of prenineteenth-century transoceanic emigration, which though scant in absolute terms was demographically relevant (not to mention politically and socially influential); it constituted an important outlet for some societies (Great Britain, Spain, and Portugal), had an important "founding" effect (relatively few families generated many descendants), and even laid a receptive foundation for later emigration, based on linguistic and cultural affinities and similarities in family and social structures.

During the nineteenth century, but especially after 1840, European emigration developed into a mass phenomenon. The following are estimates for gross European transoceanic migration between 1840 and 1932 from the major countries of departure: 18 million from Great Britain and Ireland, 11.1 million from Italy, 6.5 million from Spain and Portugal, 5.2 million from Austria-Hungary, 4.9 million from Germany, 2.9 million from Poland and Russia, and 2.1 million from Sweden and Norway. This flood of emigration, which was of course balanced to some degree by a countercurrent of return migration, went primarily to the United States (34.2 million), Argentina and Uruguay (7.1 million), Canada (5.2 million), Brazil (4.4 million), Australia and New Zealand (3.5 million), and Cuba (0.9 million). In the first 15 years of the twentieth century the annual rate of European emigration exceeded 3 per 1,000 equal to about one-third of natural increase. Figure 6.2 shows emigration reaching a peak in the early part of the century; the First World War and later restrictions on emigration imposed by the United States, the principal destination of emigrants, dramatically reduced the numbers. The composition of emigrants to North America, whose number was about triple that for the rest of the continent, changed in the last two decades of the nineteenth century: from predominantly British, Germanic, and Scandinavian origins to Mediterranean, mostly Italian, eastern European, and Balkan. This was a "new" immigration, geographically and socially remote from the "old," and the new immigration laws of the 1920s were surely prompted by this change in composition as much as by the changes in the economy and American society in general.

How do we explain the genesis and development of this mass emigration? All phenomena of this type commonly begin with a supply of potential migrants in a continent rich in human resources but lacking in capital (land scarcity, for example), and a demand for labor in a continent scarce in human resources but rich in capital (land availability). In order to understand how this came about let us concentrate on supply, and once more choose synthesis and the identification of macromechanisms over analysis and micro-explanations. Three fundamental elements stand out: the purely demographic factor of accelerated growth of the labor force; increased agricultural productivity and the creation of surplus labor; and the demand for labor by the industrial and urban sector.

In terms of population growth, as we already know, natural increase was well above 15 per 1,000 many parts of Europe (United Kingdom, Germany) and was everywhere increasing significantly compared to old-regime levels. Over the course of the nineteenth

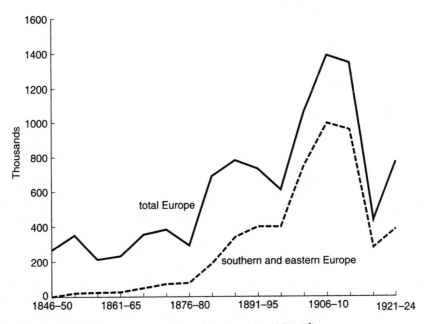

Figure 6.2   European emigration 1846–1924 (five-year averages)

Source: I. Ferenczi and W. F. Wilcox, *International migrations*, 2 vols., NBER, New York, 1929–31, vol. I, pp. 230–1

century this acceleration was on average greater in rural areas where birth rates remained high and fertility control was introduced later relative to mortality decline. There is a striking relationship between growth rates (the difference between births and deaths) and the intensity of emigration about 25 years later (more or less the average age of the emigrants); emigration served to lower demographic pressure caused by the influx of larger cohorts of workers into the labor market. The significance of changes in natural growth from year to year or between countries of emigration finds confirmation in econometric studies that have also taken other variables into consideration, such as wage differences between sending and receiving countries. Johnson recounts a telling example of the effects of demographic pressure:

> A case in point was furnished by Rum in the Hebrides. The proprietor of the island found, in 1825, that his rents were £300 in arrears. A visit to the locality conclusively showed him that the indebtedness of the people was not due to any lack of industry on their part, but that the overcrowded numbers precluded any of them from gaining an adequate livelihood. Recognizing that matters would never improve of themselves, he canceled their debts, shared a sum of £600 amongst them, gave them cattle, and paid their passage out to Canada. Later on, it is recorded that this proprietor had repeopled his island on a less crowded basis and was deriving £800 per annum as a rent for it.

This example – peculiar for both the proprietor's shrewdness and its location in the far north of Europe – sounds like a Malthusian parable, but one runs into mechanisms of this type throughout the continent.

Earlier in this chapter I discussed the second factor: the increase in agricultural productivity and the resulting creation of surplus manpower. According to Bairoch, productivity of labor in Europe (excluding Russia) increased 0.6 percent annually between 1800 and 1850, 0.9 percent between 1850 and 1880, and 1.2 percent between 1880 and 1910. These substantial increases were entirely consistent with the growing importance of emigration during this period. The combined pressure on the demographic system of rapid population growth and increased productivity had complex consequences, from declining real wages to the breaking up of landholdings, the impoverishment of small landowners, and the rising number of landless families. Outside of Russia, no new lands were available in Europe for cultivation: Grigg has calculated that arable land in Europe grew slowly, from 140 to 147 million hectares between 1860 and 1910. So the pressure to emigrate grew, encouraged by improved means of communication and lower shipping costs; in other words, by the "shrinking" of the world.

Though pressure to leave the countryside grew considerably over the course of the century, it did not necessarily translate into international or intercontinental emigration. The process of industrialization absorbed a significant percentage of the rural population surplus. Indeed, the very same forces that stimulated agricultural growth and increased productivity contributed to the Industrial Revolution. Industrialization and urban growth, accompanied by the growth of the service sector, created new opportunities for rural surplus labor. About three-quarters of the European workforce (again not including Russia) were employed in agriculture at the beginning of the nineteenth century, but by 1850 only about one-half were, and by the beginning of the twentieth century the proportion had dropped to one-third. The size of the agricultural workforce had grown steadily up until 1850, after which it stabilized and began to decrease. Europe was steadily becoming less rural while manufacturing, mining, building, and what we now call the "tertiary" sector expanded. The urbanization process was intense; the total population of the 39 European cities with more than 100,000 inhabitants in 1850 grew from 6.1 million in 1800 to 11.2 in 1850, 29.5 in 1900, and 34.4 in 1910, an almost sixfold increase. Medium and small cities were also growing, and so the number of jobs available in administration, shipping, trade, and services.

As industry developed and the demand for labor in manufacturing grew, the pressure to emigrate diminished. Between the late nineteenth century and the early twentieth there was a clear inverse relationship between industrialization levels and emigration; when the number employed in industry approached the number employed in agriculture the level of transoceanic emigration declined. There were more people employed in industry than agriculture in Great Britain in the last decades of the nineteenth century, and emigration had long ceased to be a mass phenomenon. Prior to the First World War, there were more people employed in industry in Belgium, where mass emigration had never taken hold, and in Germany and Switzerland, where it had ceased. In Mediterranean countries such as Italy and Spain, where industrialization took hold generally only in the two decades after the Second World war, large-scale emigration ended at the same time. In other countries (the Netherlands, Sweden, Norway) where manufacturing industries came to dominate the national economy in the period between the World Wars, emigration had already been halted by restrictions relating to the economic crisis.

In discussing emigration, we have emphasized certain macro-level aspects while ignoring others; a few of these merit mention. The first is the "political" aspect of emigration, ranging from religious persecution (relevant not only in old-regime societies but in the nineteenth century as well; consider the emigration of Russian Jews) to domestic politics, both liberal and protectionist, including price and tax policies that encouraged or discouraged emigration, policies regulating or hindering emigration and so on. The case of France, again an exception in Europe for the absence of migratory pressure (even though it was a politically influential colonial power), can be analyzed from a number of perspectives. Demographically speaking, for instance, low fertility created less demographic pressure and made emigration "superfluous". From the economic and social point of view, one has to consider the multitude of small landowners who were strongly attached to the land, and so not attracted by emigration. Culturally and politically, France rejected the subordinate status that went with mass emigration. Another factor often neglected in explaining the phenomenon of emigration is the self-feeding nature of the migration process; once an initial group of select and adventurous pioneers departs, their conationals are more willing to go as well because the "costs" of integration are effectively diminished by the presence of a welcoming community. Yet another factor, mentioned briefly above, was easier and more rapid transportation through a spreading railway system, the expansion of maritime transport, and lower costs. Finally, the policies of the host countries were an important factor in emigration: consider the Homestead Act of 1862 which granted land outright to heads of families over 21 years of age who intended to farm the land and who were either US citizens or had requested citizenship.

By the eve of the First World War, Europe had exported tens of millions of its inhabitants overseas, both easing demographic pressure at home and contributing dramatically to the demographic growth and consolidation of the receiving countries. The Western expansion of the US, and the peopling of the interior and the south of Argentina owed much to European emigration. In 1860 cultivated land in the United States, Canada, and Argentina amounted to 66 million hectares as compared to 140 million in Europe (excluding Russia): by 1910, 174 million hectares were being farmed in the former and 147 in the latter. The American expansion should not, however, make us overlook the expansion taking place in the other direction, beyond the Ural Mountains and into inhospitable Siberia. Between 1850 and 1914 – when emigration all but ceased – 5.3 million people settled in Asiatic Russia, 3.5 million of whom arrived between 1897 and 1911. Initially the movement involved a few tens of thousands of people per year, encouraged by the 1861 freeing of the serfs and the progressive saturation of the best farmland; it accelerated enormously in the 1890s with the opening of the Trans-Siberan railway. And then, in 1914, the great era of European expansion came to an end.

7

The End of a Cycle

Demography in the Twentieth Century: Mortality and
Fertility

In the year 2000 the population of Europe will be 730 million. This
is almost four times the population of 1800 (188 million), and 60
percent more than in 1914 (458 million). Considerable though this
growth may be, especially when factoring in the high mortality of
two world wars, it nevertheless conceals a downward trend that
has led European population today to the verge of a standstill.
Population between 1920 and 1930 was growing at an annual rate
of 4.5 million, and between 1950 and 1960 at 6 million annually;
today it has all but ceased to grow (see table 7.1). The cycle of
growth that began with the Industrial Revolution has come full
circle, and an era of abundant human resources has given way to
one of scarcity; in short, we have reached the end of the great demographic transition.

We can identify three distinct periods. The first occupies the years
between the two world wars, and was marked by high First World
War mortality, the end of mass emigration, and relative demographic isolation as migration declined during the Great
Depression. The second phase, ushered in by the demographic
deficit of the Second World War and geopolitical boundary

Table 7.1 Population of selected European countries, 1920–2000

Year	United Kingdom	France	Germany	Italy	Spain	Ussr/Russia (European)	Other countries	Europe
				Population (millions)				
1920	43.7	39.0	52.3	37.4	21.2	139.1	134.4	467.1
1930	46.1	41.6	55.9	40.8	23.4	156.8	147.2	511.8
1940	48.2	41.0	60.1	44.3	25.8	176.4	160.6	556.4
1950	50.6	41.8	68.4	47.1	28.0	156.2	156.6	548.7
1960	52.4	45.7	72.7	50.2	30.5	180.3	173.5	605.3
1970	55.6	50.8	77.7	53.8	33.8	197.2	187.5	656.4
1980	56.3	53.9	78.3	56.4	37.5	209.5	201.1	693.0
1990	57.4	56.7	79.4	57.0	39.3	222.1	209.8	721.7
2000	59.0	59.0	81.7	57.3	39.8	218.8	214.2	729.8
				Average annual rate of growth (%)				
1920–30	0.53	0.65	0.67	0.87	0.99	1.20	0.91	0.91
1930–40	0.45	-0.15	0.72	0.82	0.98	1.18	0.87	0.84
1940–50	0.49	0.19	1.29	0.61	0.82	-1.22	-0.25	-0.14
1950–60	0.35	0.89	0.61	0.64	0.86	1.43	1.02	0.98
1960–70	0.59	1.06	0.67	0.69	1.03	0.90	0.78	0.81
1970–80	0.13	0.59	0.08	0.47	1.04	0.61	0.70	0.54
1980–90	0.19	0.51	0.14	0.11	0.47	0.58	0.42	0.41
1990–2000	0.27	0.40	0.29	0.05	0.13	-0.15	0.21	0.11
1920–2000	0.38	0.52	0.56	0.53	0.79	0.57	0.58	0.56

Note: Europe includes the European territories of the former USSR (Estonia, Lithuania, Latvia, Belarus, Moldavia, Russian Federation, Ukraine). Borders of the various countries are present-day

Sources: From 1950 to 2000: United Nations, *World Population Prospects. The 1994 revision*, New York 1995. For 1920–50, United Nations, *Demographic Yearbook 1955*, New York 1995 and national sources

changes, was one of demographic recovery fed by the economic boom in western European countries, and of renewed international as well as internal migration. The energy and manufacturing crises of the early 1970s marked the end of this phase, together with the decline of migration within Europe and from several nearby countries. The third phase covers the last three decades of the twentieth century and is marked by extremely low fertility, a rapidly aging population, and the gradual closing to migration from outside Europe. The economic and demographic situation of the second period made possible the creation of a generous and promise-filled social welfare state, while the demographic evolution of the third phase has made revisions and reconsiderations necessary.

In the last chapter I examined at length the nature and causes of the nineteenth century transition, and so can fairly briefly describe its development and conclusion, leaving room to reflect on the impact it has had on European society. Five phenomena in particular are worthy of careful attention: the almost uninterrupted, and greater than expected, decline in mortality; the widespread practice of birth control and the plunge in fertility to below replacement levels; the end of mass transoceanic emigration and the beginning of immigration from poor countries; the rapid aging of the population and its economic implications; and finally, changes in social

Table 7.2 Life expectancy (men and women) in major European countries, 1920–94

Country	1920	1930	1950	1970	1994
United Kingdom	57.6	60.8	69.2	72.0	76.8
France	54.0	56.7	66.5	72.4	77.5
Germany	53.6	61.4	67.5	71.0	76.3
Italy	50.0	54.9	66.0	72.1	77.5
Spain	45.8	54.6	63.9	72.9	77.1
Soviet Union	42.9	–	67.3	68.2	64.5

Note: United Kingdom: before 1950, England, after 1950, United Kingdom; Germany: before 1950, borders at the time, after 1950, present-day borders; USSR: before 1950, borders at the time, after 1950, borders of Russian Federation. Values for 1920 refer to 1920–2 (England), 1920–3 (France), 1924–6 (Germany), 1921–2 (Italy), 1926–7 (USSR); values for 1930 refer to 1930–2 (England), 1928–33 (France), 1932–4 (Germany), 1930–2 (Italy); values for 1950 and 1970 refer respectively to 1950–5 and 1970–5.
Sources: Before 1950: Dublin, Lotka, and Spiegelman, *Length of Life*, Ronald Press, New York, 1949. After 1950: United Nations; 1994 (1993 for Spain): national sources

rules and conventions regarding marriage and the stability of procreating couples; traditionally those rules governed reproduction and cohabitation, but today in many cases they no longer apply.

Briefly, mortality has evolved along these lines: over the course of the entire century there has been a continual decline in mortality (for men and women alike) illustrated by an increase in life expectancy at birth (see table 7.2) from about 50 years in 1914 to about 75 years today. There is virtually no break in the decline if we exclude periods of war and the unusual developments in eastern Europe, of which more below. Put another way, life expectancy has increased by close to four months per calendar year, an extraordinary gain, and one which shows no sign of slowing in spite of the fact that today an average life expectancy of 80 years, not long ago considered the biological limit, has been exceeded by many female populations.

Several important aspects of this process of mortality decline deserve mention: (a) until average life expectancy reached 65–70, gains were chiefly the result of declining mortality for both infants and adults, while recent gains have been almost exclusively due to improved survivorship of the elderly; (b) in the earlier phase much of the gain in life expectancy was the result of the gradual control of infectious diseases both through vaccines and pharmacology (sulfa drugs and antibiotics) and disease prevention and improved hygiene; while more recent gains in old-age survivorship have mainly been the result of a lower incidence of noninfectious disease (e.g., cardiovascular) because of better information about their causes, healthier lifestyles, and effective treatment for them; (c) life expectancy has improved more for women (over 82 years in some countries) than for men, and the gap is currently between 6–8 years; and (d) there have been some interesting variations in the geography of life expectancy: significant pre-First World War differences between countries were primarily a function of economic development. Life expectancy in a country like Russia was barely over 35, while in Sweden and England it was well over 50 (see table 6.4, on p.135); over the next 50 to 60 years national life expectancies evened out (in 1970 more or less between 70 and 75), but a gap has reappeared in the last 20 years due to worsening mortality in Russia and other former eastern-bloc countries as against continued progress in the rest of the continent.

Fertility, like mortality, declined steadily over the course of the long nineteenth century, reaching replacement level between the 1930s and the 1950s. In this case, too, fertility decline closely followed the course of economic development: earlier in "advanced" northern and western Europe, and later in predominantly rural Mediterranean zones and in much of Russia, eastern Europe, and the Balkans. In parts of western Europe the birth rate recovered slightly after the Second World War, while in others it leveled off, but from the 1970s it began to fall to an average of 1.5 children per woman in all of Europe, a level well below replacement (see table 7.3).

On the macro level the trend seems straightforward, but naturally it conceals complex mechanisms and models. Though we cannot discuss them at length in these pages, they include the following: (a) a dramatic restructuring of female reproductivity in terms of the number of offspring produced: today, in the countries

Table 7.3   Average number of children per woman in selected European countries, 1921–95

Years	England	France	Germany	Italy	Spain	Soviet Union/ Russia
1921–5	2.39	2.42	2.62	3.50	3.96	–
1926–30	2.01	2.30	2.10	3.30	3.75	6.04
1931–5	1.79	2.16	1.84	3.07	3.50	4.53
1936–40	1.98	2.07	2.24	3.00	2.77	4.66
1941–5	2.39	2.11	1.90	2.56	2.72	–
1946–50	2.19	2.98	2.07	2.77	2.68	3.13
1950–5	2.18	2.73	2.16	2.32	2.52	2.51
1955–60	2.49	2.71	2.30	2.35	2.75	2.62
1961–5	2.81	2.85	2.49	2.55	2.89	2.48
1965–70	2.52	2.61	2.32	2.49	2.93	2.02
1971–5	2.04	2.31	1.64	2.28	2.89	1.98
1975–80	1.72	1.86	1.52	1.92	2.63	1.92
1980–5	1.80	1.87	1.46	1.55	1.86	1.99
1985–90	1.81	1.80	1.43	1.35	1.46	2.10
1995	1.71	1.70	1.24	1.17	1.18	1.39

Note: United Kingdom: 1931–50, England and Wales, after 1950, United Kingdom. Germany: before 1946, borders at the time, after 1946, present-day borders; USSR: before 1950, borders at the time, after 1950, borders of Russian Federation

Sources: 1950–90, United Nations. 1995, national sources (1994 for Russian Federation). Before 1950, Chesnais, *La transition démographique*, PUF, Paris, 1985; for the USSR, E. Andreev, L. Darskij, T. Kharkova, "L'histoire de la population de l'URSS 1920–59," *Annales de Démographie Historique*, 1992

with the lowest fertility, there are more women in a given generation with one or no children than with two or more; while for the generations born in the nineteenth century there were more women with four or more children than with zero to three; (b) a decline in the average age at the birth of a first child corresponding to a decline in the age at marriage between the 1930s and 1960s, followed by a sharp increase in the last few decades, which has both shortened and delayed the childbearing period for women; (c) a rapid rise in children born out of wedlock; (d) significant changes in birth control methods. Though the practice of *coitus interruptus* was responsible for much of European fertility decline, the commercial availability of traditional birth control methods in the first half of the twentieth century (though prohibited by law in much of Europe until fairly recently) and the introduction of modern and secure ones since the 1960s have made possible the precise planning of fertility. At the same time, legalized abortion offers a safe option for correcting planning errors.

Mortality was still a strong selective force at the beginning of this century, so that out of 100 births only about half lived to the end of their reproductive cycles, and these survivors were responsible for the continuation of the species. Today, almost all women (99 percent) survive to the end of their childbearing years, and mortality no longer interferes in the replacement process. Nonetheless, today's 1.5 children per woman cannot guarantee replacement, and so the road to decline is open; European societies accustomed to abundant human resources are finding themselves at the end of the millennium in a much changed situation.

Demography in the Twentieth Century: Migration, Structures, Models

Mass migration was the single most striking demographic event of the nineteenth century, in terms of scale and its implications for the development of several continents. Following the First World War, the conditions that had made it possible changed: demand in the traditional destination countries declined, and demographic slowdown in Europe shrank supply. Yet these changes acted slowly, while other factors – such as war and national migration policies – abruptly halted the migratory waves. Approximately 1.4 million people left Europe every year between 1906 and 1915. After the inevitable slowing due to the war, the figure dropped to about 0.6

million between 1921 and 1930, and barely over 100,000 between
1930 and 1940. Migration grew again in the immediate post-
Second World War period but that trend was short-lived. The most
effective controls to emigration were the restrictions introduced in
the United States and culminating in the 1924 *National Origins Act*
that not only imposed a quota on annual immigration (just over
150,000 down from the 900,000 per year before the First World
War), but was designed in such a way as to penalize the "new immigration," namely that from southern and eastern Europe. Before
the war, for example, Italy was responsible for almost 25 percent
of total immigrants to the US, but the quota reduced this figure to
less than 4 percent. In part because of the Great Depression, other
destination countries also adopted restrictive policies and imposed
quotas: South Africa in 1930, New Zealand in 1931, Australia in
1932, and Brazil in 1934. Whatever the reason – the pressure to
exclude groups deemed ethnically or culturally undesirable,
economic hardship, a feeling that nations created through immigration had reached stability – the era of mass migration, at least
for Europe, had come to an end. Transoceanic emigration did
resume briefly after the Second World War, but less for the purpose
of finding work abroad than for family reunification and the
settling of war refugees. America and Europe, paradoxically, were
more closely linked at the beginning of the twentieth century than
during its second half.

A look at earlier events helps complete this picture. With the
opening of ocean routes to the Americas, Europe was transformed
from a continent of immigration – through the large gateway of the
Eurasian steppes or across the Mediterranean – to one of emigration. The second half of the twentieth century has reintroduced
immigration, partly as the legacy of lost colonial empires and partly
in response to a demand for labor not met by a slowly growing
population increasingly unwilling to do certain types of work.
About 20 million foreigners live in Europe today (excluding
Russia), and over half are non-Europeans: there are north Africans
in France, Spain, and Italy; Turks in Germany; Pakistanis, Indians,
and Caribbeans in Great Britain. While throughout Europe states
have adopted zero immigration policies, there seems little chance
that those policies will change the general course of a phenomenon
that in all likelihood will characterize the twenty-first century.

Age structure is another important demographic phenomenon,
and though we have neglected it in our discussion thus far, for
reasons which will become clear, it is of vital importance in popu-

lation issues today. Age structure itself depends on mortality and fertility: when those factors are more or less constant, as they were in the earlier centuries, then age structure does not change much. Of course stability in this case is relative and no longer holds in the face of age-specific crises or migration. Since fertility and mortality began their decisive decline in the second half of the nineteenth century, that is also when age structure began to change. Fertility decline reduces the relative size of the younger age groups and so increases that of the older, automatically bringing about the "aging" of the population. Increased life expectancy instead has a "net" effect depending on which age groups are affected. If, for instance, life expectancy is equally improved for all age groups, then age structure does not change, but if instead it improves disproportionately for infants or children (as it did up until the middle of this century and beyond), then age structure changes favor that age group and the population becomes "younger." And if life expectancy increases more for the elderly (as it has in the past few decades), then that group grows relative to the others.

Until 1910, changes in the birth and death rates had relatively little effect on the age structure of European populations. Taking the total populations of Great Britain, Germany, France, and Italy we find that from 1870 to 1910, the total population under 15 stayed at about 32 percent, while that over 60 was about 9 percent. After 1910 the percentage of young people began to drop and the percentage of elderly to rise: in 1950 in the same four countries 24 percent of the total population was younger than 15, while the figure for 2000 is about 17 percent ; by 1950 the percentage over 60 had risen to 14 percent and at millennium's end it was up to 20 percent. The average age of the population, 29 in 1910, has risen to 39 in 2000, and the aging process shows no signs of abating.

Even though chronological age is too rigid an indicator of the phases of a human life span, the above statistics indicate a profoundly important transformation in the ratio of generations and age groups, in family structures, and in the distribution of social roles and duties. We shall return to this topic again later in the chapter.

The final point to consider in this background discussion are the changing rules governing reproduction. Traditionally these rules included: marriage as the "locus" of procreation; the stability of that union; and the simultaneous occurrence of separation from one's original family, the formation of a new nuclear family, and the occupation of a fairly fixed economic and social "niche." The once monolithic system, needless to say, has been altered and in some cases undermined in the last few decades, and demographic indicators are clear in this regard: more couples live together without marrying; the divorce rate is higher; there are more and more single-parent families; and there is an ever greater separation between "economically productive" life and "reproductive" life. Because these changes vary widely from country to country, and the picture is constantly changing, I make no attempt to summarize them; which, moreover, would require a long excursion to that micro level we have generally avoided up to this point. Nonetheless, this change in the "rules" of the game will need to be kept in mind when evaluating the importance of the reproductive crisis of the late twentieth century.

Politics

The twentieth century brought with it a new demographic development, the attempt by governments to influence the course of demographic growth and the introduction of true population policies. In truth, this was not an entirely new concept; the mercantilist notion of "*governar es poblar*" was fairly widespread in the seventeenth and eighteenth centuries, and measures more or less designed to encourage large families and stimulate marriage can be traced to that period. Nonetheless, population policies in these earlier centuries primarily consisted in the physical movement of people for the purpose of establishing colonies or occupying new land and border territories. While some of these measures, as we have seen, failed miserably and others succeeded, it was only in the twentieth century that there emerged the idea of truly manipulating demographic events through public measures designed to convince, motivate, discourage, or prohibit certain behaviors. This could never have happened if not for two developments: early in the century it became clear that births were not only being controlled, but planned, and at the same time it was recognized that public health measures were successfully increasing life expectancy. The course of demographic development was no longer at the mercy of natural and unyielding forces of constraint, but could be changed and controlled. In addition, the distressing phenomenon of declining fertility struck many as a sign of weakness in the social fabric rather than the inevitable adjustment to the demographic transition.

Before we discuss population politics, though, it is worth pausing a moment over the brutal consequences of warfare for European populations, both in terms of deaths and the forced relocation of people after national boundaries were redefined. These too were the legacy of "politics" and profoundly marked the demographic history of the twentieth century. Approximately 58 million European men, roughly one-half of the active male population, were mobilized during the five years of the First World War, and about 9 million, or 15.5 percent of those mobilized, did not survive. In addition to soldiers, warfare also claimed civilian lives, both directly and by means of resurgent infectious diseases, the gravity and spread of which was favored by the chaotic conditions created by war; the 1918–19 influenza pandemic, for instance, killed over 2 million. In addition, the war generations suffered the long-term effects of injury and disability and of deprivation. Mass mobilization also lowered the marriage rate and separated husbands and wives, causing a dramatic drop in the wartime birth rate. Attempts have been made to estimate the "growth loss" for various countries by calculating excess deaths and the birth deficit, but they are crude at best, in part because of the rallying of the birth rate in 1919–21, and so estimates reflect the arbitrariness of the hypotheses chosen. Nonetheless, it is estimated that 22 million people died in Europe (excluding Russia) as a result of the war, a figure equal to about 7 percent of the 1914 population. The numbers for Russia are still less exact, and include casualties incurred by the Revolution. Lorimer has estimated that, not including emigration, war and revolution together cost 10 million lost births and 16 million deaths, both military and civilian. Losses in the Second World War were of a similar order, and the estimates – over 20 million – are equally uncertain because of the large share of civilian causalities. The birth deficit for 1939–45, though high, was considerably lower than for 1914–18. The two world wars had a particularly dramatic effect on age structure immediately following the war in those countries that suffered the greatest losses (Germany, Poland, the Soviet Union). The generations born during the war years were small, and the Second World War further reduced the generation born in 1914–18; the age groups corresponding to the ages of the majority of soldiers serving in the two wars were abnormally small (those born in the 1890s, and between 1915 and 1925); and the ratio of men to women was sharply out of balance.

The impact of the two world wars (especially the first) was important not only because it affected the growth, structure, and distribution of European population, but also because it reinforced the general impression that Europe was speeding headlong towards demographic decline, already a source of anxiety in some countries before 1914. Gradually, and in some cases not so gradually, Malthusian doctrines – the fear of population growth not controlled by virtuous "preventive" checks – gave way to the opposite fear of potential demographic decline: a fear of "too many" was replaced by a fear of "too few." The earliest and most dramatic signs came from France, where the birth rate had clearly begun to decline early in the nineteenth century. The defeat by Prussia in 1870 dramatically heightened concern for the diminishing vitality of France: on one side of the Rhine a strong, unified, heavily populated, and steadily growing Germany, and on the other, a defeated France whose slow growth jeopardized the balance of population and so power. Concern about the demographic weakness, or even decline, of France grew, and by the beginning of the next century concrete pronatalist measures were proposed. Belief in the negative consequences of demographic weakness persists still today, in an updated and revised form, and encompasses military, political-diplomatic, cultural, and economic concerns. Briefly, from the military point of view, as long as wars are heavily dependent on the human element, to be numerically smaller than other nations (Anglo-Saxons, Germans, or Slavs) meant the abandonment of expansionist aims, and the search for security through alliances at the risk of encouraging other powers (in particular Germany) to attack France. Demographic feebleness also signified less capacity for colonial expansion, the inability to people new territories and spread French language and culture. The sum of this could not help but have a negative impact on the political importance of France. Low fertility in France and high fertility in other countries attracted immigrants and so weakened French culture and – insofar as immigrants tended to settle in boundary areas – undermined national security. Demographic frailty also weakened the economic system, as reflected in the supply of labor, the capacity to produce and save, and in entrepreneurship.

Anxiety over demographic decline spread slowly throughout Europe following more or less the birth rate decline – the effects of which were exacerbated by the First World War – and reached a peak in the interwar period. The population policies of first fascism, and then Nazism, were nothing more than distorted expressions of fear over demographic decline (which France had already made less sensational attempts to combat) and took root in already fertile ground. These policies included a wide spectrum of demographic measures attempting to modify deeply rooted behaviors concerning procreation, marriage, and even mobility, and were consistent with a totalitarian ideology. Not surprisingly, in addition to Italy and Germany, they also flourished in Vichy France, Japan, and even the Soviet Union, where in the 1930s the "liberal" laws on marriage and procreation of the preceding decade were overturned. Population policy was officially announced in Italy by Mussolini in his Ascension Day speech of 1927:

> I assert that a prerequisite, if not a fundamental aspect, of the political power of a nation, and so of its economic and moral power, is its demographic strength. Let us speak clearly: what are 40 million Italians in the face of 90 million Germans or 200 million Slavs? Look to the west as well: what are 40 million Italians as compared to 40 million French plus a colonial population of another 90 million or compared to 46 million Britons and 450 million colonials? Gentlemen! In order to count for something in the world, Italy must greet the second half of this century with no fewer than 60 million inhabitants.

The first concrete steps were taken in 1926 with the prohibition of the sale of contraceptives, and in 1927 with the bachelor tax (affecting men between 25 and 65), followed by tax deductions for large families, and birth and marriage prizes; the policy was reinvigorated in 1937 by the introduction of no-interest family loans with progressive debt cancellation on the birth of each child, the consolidation of earlier measures, and the introduction of a host of minor ones regarding wages, job preferences for married men and heads of large families, and the organization of propaganda. Nazi population policy, fundamentally racist, was pursued energetically beginning early in the regime. Based on the defense of "Aryan" racial purity, it outlawed "mixed" marriages (between Aryans and non-Aryans, especially Jews) and promoted the sterilization of individuals considered "unsuitable" for reproduction. In addition, the policy was backed up by hefty financial incentives that encouraged marriage, fertility, and large families. I will not deal here with Nazi genocide and the 6–7 million victims it claimed; for it has more to do with the history of criminal madness than the history of policy.

In Germany and Italy, and everywhere that fascist population policies were adopted or imitated, laws were passed to counteract "neo-Malthusianism" and the trend to smaller families: penalties for abortion were increased, and migration to the cities – breeding grounds of neo-Malthusianism – was discouraged or forbidden. There was a great emphasis on country life, and its healthier and more fruitful lifestyle was exalted. Attempts were also made to strengthen the family against the "dangers of individualism and hedonistic egoism." If impossible to revolutionize deeply rooted behaviors, it was at least necessary to ensure that families produced the two or three offspring required for their own replacement. Although independently inspired, there is little doubt that the Catholic Church's stance on the non-permissibility of birth control, communicated in Pius XI's 1930 encyclical *Casti connubii*, seconded fascist propaganda.

Fascist and Nazi policies were, again, charactersitc of the ideologies that produced them. In France, demographically enfeebled as a result of war and the target of intensive immigration, a clear pronatalist stance also emerged. In 1920, antiabortion laws were reinforced and neo-Malthusian propaganda was outlawed; birth control was classified with abortion as threatening "the greater rights of the nation" by depriving France of potential new citizens. In 1932, formerly private family allowances were taken over by the state and became a benefit available to all employed workers. In 1938, the pro-natalist position of the state was reinforced, and in 1939 the *Code de la Famille* (family law) was passed, increasing aid to families, especially those with at least three children. Under Vichy, French population policy came to resemble the fascist policies.

The case of the Soviet Union is highly unusual and complex. The liberal marriage, divorce, and abortion laws introduced following the Revolution were replaced between 1934 and 1944 by a populationist policy that limited abortion and divorce, reinforced the family unit and parental authority, and introduced food allowances for children and family allowances. Stalin announced this new policy in May 1935 in a speech entitled "Man, the most precious resource." Unlike the cases of other European nations, declining fertility could not explain this transformation, for the Soviet birth rate was still high. The explanation instead lay in the devastating demographic consequences of Stalinist policy itself; the end of the New Economic Policy, and the beginning of massive and ambitious industrialization, which fed large-scale urbanization and required stockpiling product from the countryside. In 1927–8 and 1928–9 these efforts at stockpiling fell far short of their goal, and it was necessary to ration bread in the cities.

With the industrial plan on the verge of collapse, two serious decisions were made: the liquidation of the kulaks, the wealthy class of peasants considered the enemies of the Revolution; and forced agricultural collectivization. The kulak resettlement took place in three waves and continued until 1932. According to Molotov, 6 or 7 million people (other estimates are closer to 10 million) were deported, and many did not survive the strenuous journeys or the labor camps, dying from cold, starvation, sickness, violence, or at the hands of firing squads. Rigidly supervised agricultural collectivization instead seemed to be the ideal method to guarantee wheat deliveries from tens of millions of previously independent (and protesting) households.

Wheat stockpiling in 1930 appeared to have been successful thanks to a good harvest, and it was mistakenly believed that even more could be collected in 1931 and 1932. Failure became inevitable, though, as farmers who had been forced to collectivize their estates sold their reserves and their tools, butchered their cattle, sowed little and harvested even less. Forty-five percent of the much reduced 1932 Ukrainian harvest was earmarked for delivery; shortage and famine followed, hitting all the wheat-growing regions, the Volga river area, and the northern Caucasus. The resulting famine caused huge number of deaths, and mortality for the whole of Ukraine tripled in 1933: this was a demographic catastrophe comparable to the most severe old-regime crises. Outside of the Soviet Union, the Great Famine and high mortality were hidden from or denied to the outside world; they were the price of gross planning errors and a project of brutal rural repression. The combination of the December 1926 census and the suppressed January 1937 census (later discovered in archives) plus other demographic data suggests that an extra 9 million people died during the decade of kulak resettlement and agricultural collectivization. Prior to the release of the 1937 census, Stalin, a convert to populationism, had triumphantly announced that the population of the Soviet Union had reached 170 million; he could not then accept the lower census figure of 162 million (which would have uncovered his earlier concealments), and so in February 1937 *Pravda* declared that "the glorious Soviet police had wiped out the viper's nest of traitors in the Soviet statistical apparatus." The politics of power had wiped out close to 10 million people, canceled a census, and eliminated the people responsible for it.

Generally speaking, pronatalist population policies had modest results. Incentives and awards managed to accelerate marriages and births to some extent; especially in Nazi Germany where the investment was the greatest and produced some recovery. It was short-lived though and did not affect the fundamental choices made by married couples. Then the Second World War put an end to them. Yet the era of population politics left at least two negative legacies: first, many European governments maintained bans on free reproductive choice well into the 1970s; and second, the attempt to exorcise the past left the enduring notion that demographic variables are practically neutral and independent from other social phenomena .

Economics

The economic transformation of Europe between 1914 and the early 1990s has been extraordinary, in spite of the great costs of two world wars and much political upheaval. Per-capita income – if we leave out those countries that had socialist regimes for at least half of the century – has grown fivefold, whereas during the already very dynamic preceding century (1820–1913) the increase was less than threefold. While economic growth was particularly strong in the postwar period, 1950–73 (4.3 percent annually), it was also considerable in the decades that included both wars (1.2 percent during 1913–50), and has continued growing at 2 percent during the last two decades (1973–92). To what extent have demographic changes affected economic ones?

Though the relationship between population and economy is complex, several factors emerge clearly. The demographic evolution of the past two centuries has greatly augmented the capacity of populations to make choices – to control mortality and disease, fertility and reproduction, and mobility – that are vital to economic development. Declining mortality, by reducing the risk of premature death and leveling dramatic and unexpected oscillations in mortality, created greater stability in interpersonal relationships and allowed people to establish long-term goals for employment and career, two decidedly positive factors for economic development. In addition to lower mortality, the general state of health significantly improved, particularly in the twentieth century. There were fewer disabling illnesses (malaria, for example, left the victim debilitated and reduced his or her productiveness), less frequently recurring temporary disabilities, and a greater physical efficiency illustrated by, among other things, a pronounced increase in height (roughly 10 cm. for young males between the early nineteenth century and today). In other words, illness became progressively less dominant in people's lives while at the same time physical efficiency was fortified by improvements in diet, medicine, and environment. In the third place, fertility decline cut the amount of time, energy, and resources devoted to childrearing and so allowed these resources (particularly in the form of female employment) to be spent on more directly productive activities. The fourth change was greater mobility thanks to expanding labor markets, faster and more economical communication, and the elimination of institutional barriers (such as different forms of bondage which still persisted in rural Russia, for instance, well after the 1861 liberation of the serfs); all of which allowed human resources to be better allocated, another boost to economic development. Fifth, for the 50 or so years leading up to the 1930s, changes in age structure favored the more productive ages, reducing the ratio of nonproducers (children and the elderly) to producers (adolescents, young- and middle-aged adults). Finally, demographic growth had a positive effect on economies of scale because it led to expanded markets, stimulating the creation of large infrastructures and encouraging entrepreneurship and the invention of "new" knowledge.

Taken together these changes had a strongly positive effect on economic development; and though their contribution was gradual and cannot explain the major cycles of modern economic growth, without a doubt they increased the average level of efficiency of the population. This process unfolded over most, though not all, of the twentieth century; during the last decades, however, the positive impact of demographic evolution on efficiency has been used up and cannot be replicated in the decades to come. Further decline of the already low birth rate will create serious problems; further extension of life expectancy might translate into a disproportionate amount of time marked by ill health and impaired autonomy; and changing age structure is radically reducing the ratio of producers to nonproducers in society and curtailing mobility. Finally, accepting that positive effects have followed upon demographic growth (of course only in certain contexts), these have surely been exhausted by now. Considering the overall "net" impact of demographic change over the past century (and the one before it as well), there have been many benefits derived from increased efficiency, though the returns have been

Table 7.4 Per-capita gross domestic product in European countries, 1913–92 (1990 dollars)

Country	1913	1950	1973	1992	Ratio 1992/1913	Annual percentage variation		
						1913–50	1950–73	1973–92
Austria	3,488	3,731	11,308	17,160	4.9	0.2	4.8	2.2
Belgium	4,130	5,346	11,905	17,165	4.2	0.7	3.5	1.9
Denmark	3,764	6,683	13,416	18,293	4.9	1.6	3.0	1.6
Finland	2,050	4,131	10,768	14,646	7.1	1.9	4.2	1.6
France	3,452	5,221	12,940	17,959	5.2	1.1	3.9	1.7
Germany	3,833	4,281	13,152	19,351	5.0	0.3	4.9	2.0
Italy	2,507	3,425	10,409	16,229	6.5	0.8	4.8	2.3
Netherlands	3,950	5,850	12,763	16,898	4.3	1.1	3.4	1.5
Norway	2,275	4,969	10,229	17,543	7.7	2.1	3.1	2.8
Sweden	3,096	6,738	13,494	16,927	5.5	2.1	3.0	1.2
Switzerland	4,207	8,939	17,953	21,036	5.0	2.0	3.0	0.8
United Kingdom	5,032	6,847	11,992	15,738	3.1	0.8	2.4	1.4
Greece	1,621	1,951	7,779	10,314	6.4	0.5	6.0	1.5
Ireland	2,733	3,518	7,023	11,711	4.3	0.7	3.0	2.7
Portugal	1,354	2,132	7,568	11,130	8.2	1.2	5.5	2.0
Spain	2,255	2,397	8,739	12,498	5.5	0.2	5.6	1.9
Arithmetic mean	3,316	5,077	12,095	16,973	5.9	1.2	4.3	2.0

Source: A. Maddison, Monitoring the World Economy 1820–1992, OECD, Paris, 1995

diminishing in the last 25 years, and have perhaps already become negative.

A look at the three periods we have already identified – the inter-war period, recovery after the Second World War, and the slow down of the last quarter century – helps to clarify the relationship between population and economy.

Between the wars

The First World War, the Great Depression, post-Depression protectionism, and the exclusion of the Soviet Union from the world economy so deeply marked this period that it would be pointless to try to trace the specific effects of demographic phenomena on economy. Keynes offered a general interpretation of inter-war stagnation, linking it to demographic slowdown:

> An increasing population has a very important influence on the demand for capital. Not only does the demand for capital . . . increase more or less in proportion to population. But, business expectations being based much more on present than on prospective demand, an era of increasing population tends to promote optimism, since demand will in general tend to exceed, rather than fall short of, what was hoped for. Moreover a mistake, resulting in a particular type of capital being in temporary over-supply, is in such conditions rapidly corrected. But in an era of declining population the opposite is true. Demand tends to be below what was expected, and a state of over-supply is less easily corrected. Thus a pessimistic atmosphere may ensue.

Demographic deceleration in the 1930s – compared to vigorous growth up to the First World War – may have had just these consequences. In the 50 years that preceded the Great War, demographic growth stimulated the demand for capital investments in construction, the creation of infrastructures, and so on. Between the wars, the exact opposite may have happened, and European economies slowed down. Another relevant demographic factor was the slowing down of demographic growth in urban areas, where the demand for investments in housing, railroads, highways, and industrial structures was high. The European cities that had populations above 500,000 in 1910 had grown in the period 1870–1910 at an annual rate of 2.0 percent, while between 1910 and 1940 growth slowed to 0.9 percent. Other factors may also have had a negative impact: the Great Depression, for example, not only provoked a general backlash of protectionism but also curtailed migration within Europe (as well as intercontinental migrations which we have already discussed), and in some cases, internal migration (anti-urbanism measures), which had strong repercussions on the labor market. This change too was a drastic one compared to the prewar period characterized by great freedom of mobility. Lastly, geodemographic transformations affected the political and economic organization of Europe. Before the First World War (and excluding Russia), five large countries – Great Britain, France, Germany, Austria-Hungary, and Italy – accounted for three-quarters of the population of the continent and dominated the European scene; the rest of the population was divided among Spain and a dozen smaller countries with fewer than 6 million inhabitants each. The Treaty of Versailles transformed the space of Europe into 22 national entities, and cut the number of large countries from five to four with the dismantling of the Austro-Hungarian empire. Europe was further fragmented and economic development suffered from the barriers to international trade and migration.

From reconstruction to the energy crisis

The 25 years between the end of the Second World War and the early 1970s, which saw the exclusion of eastern Europe from the market economy, meanwhile brought strong growth to the west. From the demographic perspective there was an increase in the birth rate that peaked in the mid–1960s, renewed migration (especially strong from southern Europe), and greater general mobility. Economic reconstruction benefited from an unlimited supply of labor that held down the costs of labor and goods. In the stronger countries, immigration allowed commercial interests to self-finance and compete internationally, and promoted mobility between sectors. In weaker countries (Italy, Spain, Portugal, Greece), emigration eased the burden of unemployment and emigrant remittances helped raise standards of living and contributed to economic development. A similar process took place within "dual" countries such as Italy and Spain by means of massive internal migration from south to north.

Age structure also favored the creation in this period of generous state welfare systems that provided pensions and a wide spectrum of social services; as there were far more workers who contributed to the system than aged retirees who withdrew from it.

The last quarter century

While recent demographic history has indeed been marked by demographic slowdown, at the same time the workforce has swelled with the coming-of-age of the fairly large generations born through to the end of the 1960s. Population aging has accelerated, and Europe has closed its borders to immigration. The specific effect of demography on the economy can be seen from two points of view. The first is high unemployment among the young, which some attribute to the entry into the labor market of those large generations cited above, creating a supply of labor that exceeds demand. There is however a problem with this explanation: in North America, where the "baby boom" was much more pronounced than in Europe, unemployment has remained low even though there has been greater competition for jobs among those born in the 1950s and 1960s. The explanation offered is that in North America the adjustment was made by lowering relative wages and, in effect, the standard of living for young workers. In Europe instead, wages have been protected and have remained high, and so the adjustment of supply to demand has been made by means of high unemployment.

Second, the generous welfare state has emerged as the primary victim of the demographic changes of the last few decades. In pension systems, normally pay-as-you-go, the group paying in (workers) continues to decrease substantially with respect to the group that takes out (pensioners). The current difficult adjustments being made, such as raising the retirement age, cutting benefits, and increasing contributions, are the consequence of adopting systems in the postwar period that could not hold up in the face of the demographic changes that have come to pass.

Values

Individuals, couples, and families and their motivations, behaviors, interpersonal relationships, and values have all been left out of this book, which has instead concentrated on the major collective trends of the past millennium. In conclusion, a little reflection is in order regarding the impact that demographic change in this and the previous century has had on personal values linked to birth, death, sickness, solitude, family, and society. The population cycle that began with the Industrial Revolution has profoundly changed the individual journeys that link the two most important events in life: birth and death. Those journeys have multiplied as population has grown and have become considerably longer as the average distance between birth and death has more than doubled. They are journeys, however, much less rich in life events. Our forebears were born into large families with extensive kinship networks, and within this dense context death came like the dropping of a needle from an evergreen, a detachment from a greater whole as compared to today's world in which the individual tends to be more and more isolated in both birth and death. What is more, anyone in the past surviving to middle, or even old, age witnessed birth and death with a repetition that created a familiarity – both painful and joyful – with life events: that familiarity has given way to an anxious estrangement.

To be sure, these changes have deeply affected the way we look at life and death and, as a result, the way we perceive others (about whom there are at once fears of too rapid growth and of decline). Some reflection on these topics may provide insight into the collective phenomena and their numerical representation.

Between the end of the eighteenth and the end of the twentieth centuries, the Western world has gone from a system of inefficiency and disorder to one of economy and order. Societies today can efficiently maintain themselves with a minimum waste of human lives; mortality crises diminished and then disappeared, and death is increasingly less frequent, less precocious, less unexpected. People have gradually become less afraid that something serious, inevitable, and unpredictable is likely to happen this year, or next, or the one after that. Disorder became less frequent and gradually disappeared. There is another even more important aspect of the transition from "disorder" to "order." In old demographic regimes, the likelihood that the natural chronological hierarchy of death would be inverted – that a child would die before its parent or grandparent, younger siblings before older – was high. The higher the mortality and the more frequent the mortality crises, the more serious the inversion of the hierarchy. In Europe in the eighteenth century the probability that a 30-year-old mother would outlive her newborn child over the course of the next 20 years was four in 10; that a 50-year-of-old mother outlive her 20-year-old child over the next 20 years was one in five. Given today's mortality levels, the likelihood of the same occurring is slim indeed. These examples give an idea of the disorder in the natural chronological hierarchy caused by the "unpredictable and capricious unfairness" of death.

Here is some more food for thought. European societies have passed from a state in which death was capricious, unpredictable, and subverted the natural chronological hierarchy, to one in which death is predictable, reliable, orderly. The consequences have been twofold. Modern societies have indeed lost their fear of disorder and the random nature of death, and the resulting stability of inter-personal relationships is a prerequisite for economic development. As Camus observed, "No one will be free so long as there is pestilence." On the other hand, the very rarity of a child dying before his parents makes that event, when it does happen, unbearable and irreparable, and is a source of anxiety and fear in today's world. Chekhov described this scene over a century ago:

> Krilov and his wife were silent and did not cry, as if they felt the total pathos of their situation in their loss [Andrei, their son, has just died from typhoid]: as they had once lost their youth, they now, with the boy, forever lost their right to have children! The white-haired doctor already seemed an old man at 44 years old, and his wife, wizened and ill, was 35. Andrei was their only, but also their last, child.

The modern view of death – rare, remote, and late in coming – has deeply transformed its nature and image. Death is no longer the medieval domestic affair described by Ariès – where the dying person presides over a quasi-public group ritual that includes friends, relatives, and children – but is instead remote and hidden from view.

> The dying person's entourage tried to spare him and hide the gravity of his condition from him . . . The first motivation for the lie was the desire to spare the sick person, to assume the burden of his ordeal. . . . But this sentiment very rapidly was covered over by a different sentiment, a new sentiment characteristic of modernity: one must avoid – no longer for the sake of the dying person, but for society's sake, for the sake of those close to the dying person – the disturbance and the overly strong and unbearable emotion caused by the ugliness of dying and by the very presence of death in the

midst of a happy life, for it is henceforth given that life is always happy or should always seem to be so.

Dying should be dignified, upsetting the equilibrium of family members, friends, and society as little as possible. The death ritual, once presided over by the dying person and in the hands of relatives has become an anonymous institutional event managed by doctors and taking place in the hospital, where it becomes a technical matter.

The demographic rationalization of death – less frequent, coming late in life, and respecting the natural chronological hierarchy – goes hand in hand with a remoteness that is both technical and physical (a hospital death, out of view from family and friends) and psychological (hiding death from the dying). The less familiar death becomes, the greater the effort to remove it and isolate it because of its uniqueness and inevitability. The thought of death, which once impregnated every living moment, is now relegated to a precise and circumscribed phase of life.

In old demographic regimes the disorder of death was accompanied by the unexpectedness and inevitability of disease. We have discussed epidemics at length, but even "normal" mortality was unexpected and dominated by infectious diseases. The gradual control of these, and the concept of recovery from disease – thanks to human intervention – has surely revolutionized our relationship to sickness and death. The degenerative diseases that prevail today, such as cancer or cardiovascular disease, are often foretold and have a long course of illness. A cancer patient who has had surgery or a person suffering from circulatory problems fears the specific action of his disease, even though it may never strike or may only do so after many years. Susan Sontag sees these "new" sorts of illness – tuberculosis in the nineteenth century and cancer in the twentieth – in metaphorical terms:

> In contrast to the great epidemic diseases of the past (bubonic plague, typhus, cholera), which strike each person as a member of an afflicted community, TB was understood as a disease that isolates one from the community. However steep its incidence in a population, TB – like cancer today – always seemed to be a mysterious disease of individuals, a deadly arrow that could strike anyone, that singled out its victims one by one.

Today sickness, even if it does not lead to death, is viewed as a great failure. And the attempt to rationalize failure is perhaps

connected with the tendency to blame illness on individual characteristics or behavior. Sontag, again, explores the implications:
"[W]ith the modern disease (once TB, now cancer), the romantic
idea that the disease expresses the character is invariably extended
to assert that the character causes the disease – because it has not
expressed itself." Both the myth of tuberculosis and, today, that of
cancer regard the individual as responsible for his own illness; TB
was the disease of hypersensibility and passion, while cancer is the
disease of repression and the inability to express oneself. In this way
the burden and responsibility of illness fall on the patient and push
him into isolation. Similarly, a greater risk of heart attack is
attached to one's psychological state or fast-paced and stressful
lifestyle; the burden of the illness is transferred to the patient,
taking the weight of failure and inadequacy away from medical
science. Still more striking, AIDS is our grimmest metaphor for
catastrophe, much greater than syphilis once was: it is disease
which carries with it an implication of "guilt" for its link to anom-
alous sexual behavior and illicit drug use; it is identified
(denounced), drags on through time, and leads to the inevitable
punishment of death.

Medical advances have attenuated the random and lethal nature
of diseases, and prolonged their course; but the inadequacy of those
advances has also contributed to personalizing disease, shifting
responsibility to the patient, and socially isolating him.

The victory of orderliness and predictability in survival has come
at a price, and that price is solitude. Take an elderly man or woman
in the old demographic regime. His or her spouse had most likely
died, but several children survived – two, three, perhaps even four
– who were themselves married with children. Third-degree nieces
and nephews – the children of siblings – and kin of the same degree
from the spouse's side filled out the family tree; and in all, the old
man or woman had a few dozen close relatives. Over time, this
family network is added to or subtracted from through births and
deaths; and some relatives may have migrated, but most have probably not gone very far away.

The same elderly man or woman in today's world may have two
surviving children, who in turn have spouses or companions, and
two, three, or maybe even four grandchildren. There may be living
siblings as well, and their children. There are similarly fewer relatives on the spouse's side, and the resulting family network is less
dense. Greater mobility in recent times will also likely mean that
family members are more geographically dispersed, at distances

that modern communications can only in part bridge. Moreover, this network undergoes less modification over time by births and deaths.

Upon reaching the last phase of life's course, people are more alone than in the past. Less often do the lives of family members follow parallel and intersecting paths, and the solidarity between generations is often sorely tested. Solitude and a keen awareness of "fragility" are two major themes of old age and the price paid for living a long life.

The meaning and significance of birth as well as death has changed. In twentieth-century Europe, the child has moved from the periphery to the center of family life. The history of fertility decline, as we know, coincides with the greater investment of parents, families, and society in children, and the shift from quantity of offspring to quality, measured by well-being, nutrition, health, and learning. Childbirth itself has become an increasingly planned and prepared-for event, a function of family budget, expectations, and conceptions of ideal family size. The timing of a pregnancy has come to reflect future projects and plans, just as the day and hour of childbirth come to conform to doctors' or hospitals' schedules. The biophysical characteristics and the sex of the unborn child are known in advance. The great medicalization of pregnancy and childbirth may indeed be excessive and risks creating new syndromes of anxiety. Up until the end of the 1960s, despite already quite low fertility, couples still practiced fairly imperfect birth control and in the end a fair number of births were unplanned ones: one might say that parents had still left the door open to chance and the unexpected. But since the 1960s and 70s, the availability of reliable birth control methods has allowed for perfectly planned conceptions, and legalized abortion has made it relatively easy to correct any possible errors. Pregnancy and childbirth today are programmed and preordained; some of the unborn child's characteristics are known in advance of birth; medicalization is pervasive. Such a heavy investment in children – even before their birth – raises proportionately high expectations and leads to serious frustrations when those expectations are unmet.

We have reached the end of a population cycle, and not only because the end of the twentieth century marks the terminus of many centuries of growth. A major transformation has also occurred that makes demographic behaviors subject to control, and largely a function of subjective choices. The material quality of old-regime factors of constraint – space, food, disease – that once directly affected demography has given way to an immaterial and less immediate quality. The factors of choice, which were so limited in the old regime, have won the final match. There is more choice, more knowledge, less room for chance, but on the other side of the scale, more responsibility, more fear, and greater worry.

Further Reading

1 Numbers

The example of the *baillages* of Caux, Rouen, and Gisors is taken from J. Dupâquier, "L'autoregulation de la population française (XVIe–XVIIIe siècle)," in *Histoire de la Population Française*, vol. II, *De la Renaissance à 1789*, ed. J. Dupâquier (PUF, Paris, 1989), pp. 415–17. For German industrial *Kreise*, see E. A. Wrigley, *Industrial Growth and Population Change* (Cambridge University Press, Cambridge, 1961), p. 64. The Italian city of Prato is discussed in E. Fiumi, *Demografia, movimento urbanistico e classi sociali in Prato dall'età comunale ai tempi moderni* (Olskhki, Florence, 1968). For general population events in fourteenth- and fifteenth-century Tuscany, see D. Herlihy and C. Klapisch-Zuber, *Les Toscans et leurs familles* (Presses de la Fondation Nationale des Sciences Politiques, Paris, 1978).

The growth potential for different populations is – as far as we know – invariable in time and space. Any differences are essentially cultural: even duration of breastfeeding and frequency of sexual relations, two factors which affect the interval between births and so fertility, depend to a great degree on cultural factors. As far as survivorship goes, current examples demonstrate that even genetically "remote" groups (though even in extreme cases genetic distance is quite small) have practically identical survivorship.

It is a mistake to describe higher mortality as adaptive; higher mortality can instead be selective if it eliminates the weak in favor of the fit ("weak" and "fit" here are used in a generic way) so that the genetic characteristics of the fit are transmitted to future generations and that selection leads to improved survivorship.

For a discussion of immunity and in general on defense mechanisms against infectious diseases, see Sir Macfarlane Burnet, *The Natural History of Infectious Diseases* (Cambridge University Press, Cambridge, 1962).

On the *Domesday Book* population estimates, see J. C. Russell, *British Medieval Population* (University of New Mexico Press, Albuquerque, 1948). Russell uses a hearth equivalent of 3.5 individuals for his estimates though other scholars have used five and six individuals per hearth which leads to 40–70 percent higher estimates. Figure 1.1 is based on the estimates in J.-N. Biraben, "Essai sur le nombre des hommes," in *Population*, 1 (1979). It is reasonable to assume that population estimates for the year 1000 may vary more or less by 50 percent; for 1500 by 20 percent; for 1700 by 10 percent. It is also safe to claim a 5 percent variation for 1800, 2 percent for 1900, and 1 percent for the year 2000. J. Durand ("Historical Estimates of World Population: An Evaluation," in *Population and Development Review*, III (1977) offers the following ranges for Europe including the Soviet Union: year 1000, 36–55 million; 1500, 70–88; 1750, 150–75; 1900, 425–35. The intervals are more limited than those I have proposed and are equal to more or less 20 percent (year 1000); 11 percent (1500); 8 percent (1750); and 1 percent (1900). Within these limits Durand accepts without preference any estimate.

On plague and its disappearance from Europe, see chapter 4 and the relevant notes.

There is room for greater study and definition of the subject of intercontinental migration. For the purposes of this work I have treated as non-European: Arab immigration to Spain and Sicily, Turkish migration to the Balkans, and migration that originated in the steppes between the Caucasus and the Urals, historical meeting point for East and West. For the nineteenth century, I consider both the well-studied European emigration to the Americas, South Africa, and Oceania, but also Russian emigration beyond the Urals.

C. Cipolla, *The Economic History of the World Population* (Penguin, Harmondsworth, 1962). On agricultural productivity, see B. H. Slicher van Bath, "Agriculture in the Vital Revolution," in *The Cambridge Economic History of Europe*, E. E. Rich and C. H. Wilson, eds., (Cambridge University Press, Cambridge, 1977), vol. V, *The Economic*

Organization of Early Modern Europe, p. 81. D. Grigg, *The Transformation of Agriculture in the West* (Basil Blackwell, Oxford, 1992). A. De Maddalena, "Rural Europe, 1500–1750," in *The Fontana Economic History of Europe*, C. M. Cipolla, ed. (Collins, Glasgow, 1974), vol. II, *The Sixteenth and Seventeenth Centuries*. The Slicher van Bath reference is from *The Agrarian History of Western Europe, AD 500–1850* (Arnold, London, 1963), p. 106.

On Crulai, see E. Gautier and L. Henry, *La population de Crulai, paroisse normande* (PUF, Paris, 1958). On macro versus micro paradigms, see M. Livi Bacci, "Macro versus Micro," in *Convergent Issues in Genetics and Demography*, J. Adams, A. Hermalin, D. Lam and P. Smouse, eds. (Oxford University Press, Oxford, 1990).

2   Space

The Malthus citation is from the famous first edition (1798) of his *An Essay on the Principle of Population* (Penguin, Harmondsworth, 1978), p. 104.

In discussing the processes of land occupation, I deliberately do not deal with topics that are strictly tied to the history of agriculture – price cycles, the variable combinations of farmland and pasture, systems of landownership, and the development of agricultural technology – because they are not appropriate to an introductory discussion of the relationship between population and space. For further discussion, consult the indispensable B. H. Slicher van Bath, *The Agrarian History of Western Europe, AD 500–1850* (Edward Arnold, London, 1963).

The Cipolla observation is from C. Cipolla, *The Economic History of the World Population* (Penguin, Harmondsworth, 1962).

Characteristics of European geography are taken from: *World Atlas of Agriculture*, vol. I (De Agostini, Novara, 1969); T. Vidal Bendido, "Europa. Soporte humano privilegiado?," paper presented at the Universidad Internacional Menéndez y Pelayo (Santander, July 1992).

For general information about the settling and peopling of Europe, see the following key works on historical geography: N. J. C. Pounds, *An Historical and Political Geography of Europe* (London, G. G. Harrap, 1947); C. T. Smith, *An Historical Geography of Western Europe before 1800* (Longman, Green and Co, London, 1967); N. J. C. Pounds, *An Historical Geography of Europe* (Cambridge University Press,

Cambridge, 1990); H. C. Darby, "The Clearing of Woodland in Europe," in *Man's Changing the Face of the Earth*, W. L. Thomas, ed. (University of Chicago Press, Chicago, 1956).

For the great Germanic migration east, I have relied on H. Aubin, "German Colonisation Eastwards," in *The Cambridge Economic History of Europe* (Cambridge University Press, Cambridge, 1966), vol. I; W. Kuhn, *Geschichicte der deutschen Ostsiedlung in der Neuzeit*, 2 vols. (Cologne, 1955); C. Higounet, *Les Allemands en Europe centrale et orientale au Moyen Age* (Aubier, Paris, 1989). The Christian *reconquista* is covered in Salvador de Moxó, *Repoblación y sociedad en la España cristiana medieval* (Madrid, 1979), and D. W. Lomax, *La Reconquista* (Editorial Crítica, Barcelona, 1984). For general information, see also R. Koebner, "The Settlement and Colonisation of Europe," in *The Cambridge Economic History of Europe*, vol. 1. In this work I do not discuss the abandonment of land and villages in the wake of the plague and other significant upheavals, but refer the reader to the collection, *Villages désertés et histoire économique XIe–XVIIIe siècles* (SEVPEN, Paris, 1965).

For Germanic migration in the seventeenth and eighteenth centuries, see G. Schmoller, *Die preussische Kolonisation des 17. und 18. Jahrhunderts* (Leipzig), 1886; a summary of Germanic migration is included in H. Fenske, "International Migration: Germany in the Eighteenth Century," *Central European History*, vol. XIII, 4 (Dec. 1980), pp. 332–47. On Catherine the Great's new territories policy, see I. De Madariaga, *Russia in the Age of Catherine the Great* (Yale University Press, New Haven, 1981). For figures on the German population in Russia in 1897, see *Premier Recensement Général de la Population de L'Empire de Russie. Relevé général pour tout l'Empire des résultats du dépouillement des donnés du premier recensement de la population en 1897*, vol. II (St. Petersburg, 1905). An excellent source on expansion and settlement in territories south of the political borders of Russia and Austria is W. McNeill, *Europe's Steppe Frontier: 1500–1800* (University of Chicago Press, Chicago, 1964). For Russian population in the New South between 1724 and 1859, see F. Lorimer, *The Population of the Soviet Union: History and Prospects* (League of Nations, Geneva, 1946), p. 10. The rapid growth of the French Canadians is treated in H. Charbonneau, A. Guillemette, J. Légaré, B. Desjardins, Y. Landry, and F. Nault, *Naissance d'une population* (INED-Presses de l'Université de Montréal, Paris–Montréal, 1987).

The fundamental work on demographic development in the Middle Ages is M. Bloch, *Les charactères originaux de l'histoire rurale française* (Oslo, Aschelong), 1931; See also H. Dubois, "L'essor médiéval," in

Histoire de la population française, vol. 1, J. Dupâquier, ed., *Des origines á la Renaissance* (PUF, Paris, 1988); G. Pinto, "Dalla tarda antichità all metà del XVI secolo," in L. Del Panta, M. Livi Bacci, G. Pinto, and E. Sonnino, *La popolazione italiana dal Medioeveo a oggi* (Laterza, Rome-Bari, 1996); E. Sereni, "Agricoltura e mondo rurale," in *Storia d'Italia*, vol. I (Einuaudi, Turin, 1972); G. Duby, *L'économie rurale et la vie des campagnes dans l'Occident Médiéval*, 2 vols. (Editions Montaigne, Paris, 1962). A useful work that deals with different aspects of the relationship between land availability and population in modern western Europe is D. Grigg, *Population Growth and Agrarian Change: A Historical Perspective* (Cambridge University Press, Cambridge, 1980). Village foundation in Sicily in the sixteenth and seventeenth centuries is discussed in T. Davies, "La colonizzazione feudale della Sicilia nella prima età moderna" in *Storia d'Italia, Annali*, vol. 8, *Insediamenti e territorio*, C. De Seta, ed. (Einaudi, Turin, 1985).

For works on land reclamation, in addition to Grigg (cited above), see H. C. Darby, ed., *An Historical Geography of England before* AD *1800* (Cambridge University Press, Cambridge, 1963) and H. C. Darby, "The draining of the Fens, AD 1600–1800," in H. C. Darby, ed., *A New Historical Geography of England after 1600* (Cambridge University Press, Cambridge, 1976); L. Gambi, "Una 'Patria artificiale' nata governando razionalmente le acque," in Fondazione Basso, *L'ambientazione nella storia d'Italia* (Marsilio,Venice, 1980); M. Aymard, "La fragilità di un'economia avanzata: l'Italia e la trasformazione dell'economia europea," in *Storia dell'economia italiana*, R. Romano ed., vol. II, *L'età moderna: verso la crisi* (Einaudi, Turin, 1991); P. Wagret, *Polderlands* (Methuen, London, 1968).

There are a number of important studies on European urbanization and the growth of the city, among which: R. Mols, *Introduction à la démographie historique des villes d'Europe du XIVe au XVIIIe siècle*, 3 vols. (Duculot & Gembloux, Louvain, 1954–6). I have relied on the following two works for statistical information: J. De Vries, *European Urbanization: 1500–1800* (Harvard University Press, Cambridge, Mass., 1984), and P. Bairoch, J. Batou, and P. Chèvre, *La population des villes européennes de 800 à 1850* (Droz, Geneva, 1988). See also P. Bairoch, *De Jéricho à Mexico* (Gallimard, Paris, 1985). For the section in which I calculate the average latitude and longitude for cities with populations over 50,000, I have relied on data in Bairoch, Patou, and Chèvre, *La population des villes Europpéennes*, but eliminated Russia and the Balkans from my calculations because pre-eighteenth century data for those countries is not reliable.

3 Food

Many of the arguments in this chapter are drawn from my own *Population and Nutrition: An Essay on European Demographic History* (Cambridge University Press, Cambridge, 1991). For the classical economists: A. Smith, *The Wealth of Nations* (Dent & Sons, London, 1964) [1776]; T. R. Malthus, *An Essay on the Principle of Population* (Penguin, Harmondsworth, 1979) [1798]; D. Ricardo, *The Principles of Political Economy and Taxation* (Dent & Sons, London, 1965) [1817]. Authors who argue that the link between nutrition and mortality is fundamental to demographic development are: T. McKeown, *The Modern Rise of Population* (Academic Press, New York, 1976); and R. Fogel, "New sources and new techniques for the study of secular trends in nutritional status, health, mortality, and the process of aging," *Historical Methods*, XXVI, 1 (1993).

For the literature on nutritional and caloric standards: National Academy of Sciences, *Recommended Daily Allowances* (NAS, Washington, D.C., 1980); World Health Organization, "Energy and Protein Requirements," *Technical Report Series*, 724 (WHO, Geneva, 1985). On the relationship between nutrition, infection, and mortality see: R. K. Chandra and P. M. Newberne, *Nutrition, Immunity, and Infection* (Plenum Press, New York, 1977); N. S. Scrimshaw, C. E. Taylor, and J. E. Gordon, "Interaction of Nutrition and Infection," *Monograph Series*, 57 (WHO, Geneva, 1968).

Some general works on nutrition include the following: J. C. Drummond and A. Wilbrahm, *The Englishman's Food: A History of Five Centuries of English Diet* (Jonathan Cape, London, 1939); A. Maurizio, *Histoire de l'alimentation végétale* (Paris, Payot, 1932); J.-J. Hémardinquer, ed., "Pour une histoire de l'alimentation," *Cahier des Annales*, 28 (Paris, 1970); the insert devoted to the "Histoire de la consommation," *Annales ESC*, XXX, 2–3 (1975); H. Neveux, "L'alimentation du XIVe au XVIIIe siècle," in *Revue d'Histoire Economique et Sociale*, LI, 3 (1973); M. Morineau, "Révolution agricole, révolution alimentaire, révolution démographique," *Annales de Démographie Historique* (1974); W. Abel, *Congiuntura agraria e crisi agrarie* (Einaudi, Turin, 1976); F. Braudel, *Civilisation matérielle, économie et capitalisme*, vol. I, *Les structures du quotidien: le possible et l'impossible* (Armand Colin, Paris, 1979); M. S. Mazzi, "Note per una storia dell'alimentazione medievale," *Studi di storia medievale e moderna in onore di E. Sestan*, vol. I (Firenze, 1980); M. Montanari, *The Culture of Food* (Blackwell, Oxford, 1994); R. Smith, "Periods of 'feast and famine':

food supply and long term changes in European mortality, 1200–1800," presented at the Istituto F. Datini for a conference on "Food and Nutrition, 13th to 18th centuries" (Prato, 1996). Though I neither discuss food laws and politics nor eighteenth-century restrictions on the grain trade, both undoubtedly influenced nutrition and food. On this subject, consult A. M. Pult Quaglia, *"Per provvedere ai popoli." Il sistema annonario nella Toscana dei Medici* (Olschki, Firenze, 1990).

The estimates of food budgets and calorie counts are from M. Livi Bacci, *Population, and nutrition,* pp. 130–2.

G. B. Segni, *Trattato sopra la carestia e fame, sue cause, accidenti, previsioni e reggimenti* (Bologna, 1602); J. W. Goethe, *Italian Journey* (North Point Press, San Francisco, 1982).

There is a wealth of literature on agrarian crises, famines, and mortality. Some recommendations include: A. B. Appleby, "Grain prices and subsistence crises in England and France 1590–1740," *Journal of Economic History*, XXXIX, 4 (1979); F. Lebrun, "Les crises de démographie en France aux XVIIe et XVIIIe siècles," *Annales ESC*, XXXV, 2 (1980); W. Abel, *Massenarmut und Hungerkrisen im vorindustriellen Europa* (Verlag Paul Parey, Hamburg, 1974); L. Del Panta, "Cronologia e diffusione delle crisi di mortalità dalla fine del XIV all'inizio del XIX secolo," *Ricerche storiche*, VII, 2 (1977); V. Pérez Moreda, *Las crisis de mortalidad en la España interior, siglos XVI–XIX* (Siglo Veintiuno, Madrid, 1980).

In comparing life expectancy for English peers and the general population, I have used figures from T. H. Hollingsworth, "Mortality in the British Peerage families since 1600," *Population*, XXXII (1977), and A. E. Wrigley and R. Schofield, *The Population History of England, 1541–1871* (Arnold, London, 1981). Figures for life expectancy and mortality levels of other special groups are drawn from: T. H. Hollingsworth, "A demographic study of the British ducal families," *Population Studies*, XI, 1 (1957); S. Peller, "Births and deaths among Europe's ruling families since 1500," in D. V. Glass and D. E. C. Eversley, ed., *Population and History* (Arnold, London, 1965); L. Henry, *Anciennes familles Genevoises* (INED, Paris, 1956); L. Henry and C. Levy, "Ducs et Pairs sous l'ancien régime: characteristiques démographiques d'une caste," *Population*, XV, 5 (1960); S. Salvini, *La mortalità dei gesuiti in Italia nei secoli XVI e XVII* (Dipartimento di Statistica, Florence, 1979). The relative independence of mortality levels in relation to nutrition is supported by the fact that life expectancy in newly established colonies, despite plenty of land and food, was about the same as in Europe.

A comparison between real wages and life expectancy in England is treated in M. Livi Bacci, *Population and nutrition*, p. 102 and figure 17. For more on crises in north-central Italy, see L. Del Panta, *Le epidemie nella storia demografica italiana* (Loescher, Turin, 1980), and on real wages for building workers, see G. Vigo, "Real wages of the working class in Italy: Building workers' wages (14th to 18th century)," *Journal of European Economic History*, 3, 2 (1974).

4   Microbes and Disease

Epistolario di Coluccio Salutati, ed. F. Novati, vols. I–IV (Rome, Forzani, 1891-1905). On the subject of life expectancy, the "inquisitions post mortem" for men drawn up for England by J. C. Russell in "Late Ancient and Medieval Populations," *Transactions of the American Philosophical Society*, new series, vol. 48, part III (Philadelphia, 1958), p. 31, estimates life expectancy at birth for those born before 1276 at 35.3 years; 31.3 for 1276–1300; 29.8 for 1301–25; 27.2 for 1326–50; 17.3 for 1351–75; 20.5 for 1376–1400; 23.8 for 1401–25; and 32.8 for 1426–50.

For English life expectancy, see R. Schofield and A. E. Wrigley, *The Population History of England, 1541–1871* (Arnold, London, 1981), p. 230. On life expectancy in the nineteenth century, see L. I. Dublin, A. J. Lotka, and M. Spiegelman, *Length of Life* (Ronald Press, New York, 1949). Russian life expectancy in 1897 was still only 32.4.

On the incidence of infectious disease in England and Italy in 1871 and 1881, see G. Caselli, "Health transition and cause-specific mortality," in *The Decline of Mortality in Europe*, R. Schofield, D. Reher, and A. Bideau, eds. (Clarendon Press, Oxford, 1991). More detailed comparisons can be found in S. H. Preston, N. Keyfitz, and R. Shoen, *Causes of Death: Life Tables for National Populations* (Seminar Press, New York, 1972). On the problems of identifying causes of death, particularly in the seventeenth, eighteenth, and nineteenth centuries, see the publications for the conference, "The History of Registration of Causes of Death," (Bloomington, Indiana, 1993). The London Bills of Mortality for 1629–36 and 1647–59 are reported in J. Graunt, "Observations on the bills of mortality," *The Economic Writings of Sir William Petty*, C. H. Hull, ed., vol. II (Kelley, New York, 1964) [1899], out-of-text table on p. 406.

On the relationship between the geographical position of Europe and the spread of disease, see: W. H. McNeill, *Plagues and People* (Anchor, Garden City, NY, 1976); E. Le Roy Ladurie, "Un concept: l'unification microbienne du monde (XIVe–XVIIe siècles)," ibid., *Le territoire de l'historien*, vol. II (Paris, 1978); A. W. Crosby, *The Columbian Exchange: Biological and Cultural Consequences of 1492* (Greenwood, Westport, CT, 1972).

The Zinsser citation is from H. Zinsser, *Rats, Lice, and History* (Bantam, New York, 1971) [1935], p. 210.

M. N. Cohen deals with the relationship between population growth and density and the spread of infectious diseases in *Health and the Rise of Civilization* (Yale University Press, New Haven, 1988). The success of an infectious disease in a population where no one is immune ultimately depends on how many secondary infections are produced by the primary one. If the ratio between secondary and primary cases is greater than one, then the infection tends to survive and spread; if the ratio is less than one, then the infection tends to die out. Epidemiologists express this ratio as $R(0)$, well-known to demographers as the net rate of reproduction. One may also assume that $R(0) = bND$, where b is the relative frequency of contact between individuals, N the total population, and D the average length of time a disease is contagious in an individual. It follows that the value of $R(0)$, and so the speed with which an infection spreads, is, among other things, a function of population size, and more importantly, population density, because there are more opportunities for contact in large and dense populations than in small and sparse ones. These theoretical principles are relevant to the problems discussed in this chapter. For further reading, see *Population Biology of Infectious Diseases*, R. M. Anderson and R. M. May, eds. (Springer-Verlag, Berlin, 1982), pp. 121–47.

The classification of transmission of infectious diseases is from F. Macfarlane Burnet, *The Natural History of Infectious Diseases* (Cambridge University Press, Cambridge, 1962), pp. 166-75. The quotes are from Macfarlane Burnet, *The Natural History of Infectious diseases*, p. 41; Zinsser, *Rats*, p. 44; and *Emerging Infections*, J. Lederberg, R. E. Shope, and S. C. Oaks, eds. (National Academy Press, Washington, 1992), p. 84. This last text in particular discusses the conditions for emerging new diseases. In terms of the coadaptation between microbe and host, there do exist exceptions to the general rule: if a microbe, for example, is transported by a vector, it does not matter if the host is killed as long as the microbe is transmitted to another host.

See P. W. Ewald, "L'evoluzione della virulenza," *Le Scienze*, 298 (June 1993).

On the origins of syphilis, see M. D. Grmek, *Les maladies à l'aube de la civilisation occidentale* (Payot, Paris, 1983), pp. 199–226, and Zinsser, *Rats, Lice, and History*, pp. 51–5. The Marcello Cumano excerpt is cited in A. Corradi, *Annali delle epidemie occorse in Italia dalle prime memorie fino al 1850*, vol. I (Forni, Bologna, 1973) [1865–94], p. 351. Fracastoro wrote "Syphilis sive morbus gallicus" in 1530. His observations on the evolution of syphilis and the origin of typhus are part of his 1546 work entitled *De contagione et contagiosis morbis*. A detailed history of syphilis in Europe is found in C. Creighton, *A History of Epidemics in Britain*, vol. I (Frank Cass, London, 1965) [1984], pp. 423–38, and Zinsser, *Rats, Lice, and History*, pp. 51–6. For more on the sweating sickness, see Creighton, *A History of Epidemics in Britain*, vol. I, p. 237–81.

Zinsser's *Rats, Lice, and History* also discusses the history of typhus, and for its origins in Europe, see A. Corradi, *Annali delle epidemie occorse in Italia*, vol. 1, pp. 370-4. On the epidemiological/demographic aspects of the disease, see L. Del Panta, *Le epidemie nella storia demografica italiana* (Loescher, Turin, 1980), pp. 54–62. The Macfarlane Burnet reference to typhus is again from *The Natural History of Infectious Diseases*, p. 191.

There is no end to what has been written about plague. I have already cited historical studies by Corradi and Creighton, the work of Del Panta, McNeill and Zinsser, and must add the following important work which I refer to throughout the chapter: J.-N. Biraben, *Les hommes et la peste en France et dans les pays européens et méditerranéens*, 2 vols. (Mouton, Paris, 1975). On the epidemiology of plague, see Wu Lien-Teh, *A Treatise on Pneumonic Plague* (League of Nations, Geneva, 1926); Wu Lien-Teh, J. W. H. Chun, R. Pollitzer, and C. Y. Wu, *Plague: A Manual for Medical and Public Health Workers* (Shanghai, 1936). Wu Lien-Teh was the physician and microbiologist who directed public health measures during the 1910 outbreak of plague in Manchuria. Also see R. Pollitzer, *Plague* (WHO, Geneva, 1953); J. V. D. Shrewsbury, *A History of Bubonic Plague in the British Isles* (Cambridge, Cambridge University Press, 1970). The essays in the supplement "The plague reconsidered," *Local Population Studies* (1977) offer an excellent review of the literature of plague studies.

The Campeggio diary entry is in Creighton, *A History of Epidemics in Britain*, vol. I, p. 292. I once again draw on Biraben, Creighton, and Del Panta for my discussion of the chronology and spread of plague and also use the following: J. T. Alexander, *Bubonic Plague in Early Modern Russia* (Johns Hopkins University Press, Baltimore, 1980); E. A. Eckert, "Boundary formation and diffusion of plague: Swiss epidemics from 1562 to 1669," *Annales de Démographie Historique* (1978); V. Pérez Moreda, *Las crisis de mortalidad en la España interior* (Siglo XXI, Madrid, 1980). On the retreat of plague in the Mediterranean, see G. Restifo, *Le ultime piaghe* (Selene, Milan, 1994).

Almost all of the above-cited works express useful, if hypothetical, ideas on the disappearance of plague in Europe. Additional reading specifically on this topic includes: A. B. Appleby, "The disappearance of the plague: A continuing puzzle," *The Economic History Review*, new series, XXXIII, 2 (May 1980); P. Slack, *The Impact of Plague in Tudor and Stuart England* (London, 1985). Carlo Cipolla discusses the organization and role of health offices in Italy in, *Fighting the Plague in Seventeenth Century Italy* (University of Wisconsin Press, Madison, 1981); ibid., *Public Health and the Medical Profession in the Renaissance* (Cambridge University Press, Cambridge, 1976). The account of the activities of the Florence health office is taken from documents in the Archivio di Stato, Florence, *filze* 191–4.

For discussion of demographic decline in the century after plague, see the historical demographic work on the late medieval period. The idea that that mortality was not entirely due to plague has recently been sustained only (maybe) by J. W. Shrewsbury, *A History of Bubonic Plague*. For demographic decline in Italy, see L. Del Panta, M. Livi Bacci, G. Pinto, and E. Sonnino, *La popolazione italiana dal Medioevo a oggi* (Laterza, Rome-Bari, 1996), p. 54. For France, see H. Dubois, "La dépression (XIVe et XVe siècles)," *Histoire de la Population Française*, J. Dupâquier, ed., vol. I, *Des origines à la Renaissance* (PUF, Paris, 1988). For England, see J. C. Russell, "The preplague population of England," *Journal of British Studies*, V, 2 (1996); for Norway and Scandinavia in general, see O. J. Benedictow, *Plague in the Late Medieval Nordic Countries* (Middelalderforlaget, Oslo, 1992). T. H. Hollingsworth treats the subject of the insufficient reproductivity of the English in the fourteenth and fifteeenth centuries in *Historical Demography* (London, 1969).

The frequency and severity of plague in Tuscany is discussed in L. Del Panta, *Le epidemie nella storia demografica italiana*, p. 132, and M. Livi Bacci, *La société italienne devant les crises de mortalité* (Dipartimento di Statistica, Florence, 1978), pp. 37–42. Estimates of demographic losses due to plague in seventeenth-century France are from Biraben, *Les Hommes et la peste en France*, pp. 306–10; for the Kingdom of Naples, Corradi, *Annali delle epidemie occorse in Italia*, vol. II, p. 185; for north-central Italy, Cipolla cited in Del Panta, *Le epidemie*, p. 151.

Population losses in cities are taken from the following: for Moscow, J. T. Alexander, *Bubonic Plague in early modern Russia*, p. 327; for Marseilles, Aix, Toulon, and Barcelona, Biraben, *Les hommes et la peste en France*, vol. I.

R. Pollitzer speculates on resistance to plague in rat populations in his *Plague*, chapter 9.

The "oriental" origins of typhus are discussed in Zinsser, *Rats, Lice, and History*, pp. 201–2. Both Corradi, *Annali delle epidemie occorse in Italia*, and Del Panta, *Le epidemie nella storia demografica Italiana*, pp. 147–50, 163–6, 211–19, discuss typhus epidemics in Italy. On famine, nutrition, and epidemics, see J. D. Post, "Food shortage, nutrition, and epidemic disease in the subsistence crises of preindustrial Europe," *Food and Foodways*, vol. I (1987). The following works deal with smallpox: C. W. Dixon, *Smallpox* (Churchill, London, 1962); Creighton, *A History of Epidemics in Britain*, pp. 466–9; Del Panta, *Le epidemie nella storia demografica italiana*, pp. 63–73, 219–25; A. Mercer, *Disease, Mobility and Population in Transition* (Leicester University Press, London, 1990). For Bernoulli's thoughts on smallpox, see S. Peller, *Quantitative Research in Human Biology and Medicine* (John Wright, Bristol, 1967), p. 55. Long-term life expectancy cycles in England are examined in Wrigley and Schofield, *The Population History of England*; in France in J. Vallin, "Mortality in Europe from 1720 to 1914," in *The Decline of Mortality in Europe*, R. Schofield, D. Reher, and A. Bideau, eds. (Clarendon Press, Oxford, 1991); in Italy in M. Breschi, L. Pozzi, and R. Rettaroli, "Analogie e differenze nella crescita della popolazione italiana, 1750–1911," *Bollettino di Demografia Storica*, 20 (1994).

The frequency of mortality crises is the subject of the following works: M. W. Flinn, "The stabilization of mortality in pre-industrial western Europe," *Journal of European Economic History*, 3 (1974); L. Del Panta, *Le epidemie nella storia demografica italiana*; V. Pérez Moreda, *Las crisis de mortalidad*; A. Perrenoud, "The attenuation of mortality crises and the decline of mortality," in *The Decline of Mortality in Europe*, R. Schofield, D. Reher, and A. Bideau, eds. (Clarendon Press, Oxford, 1991).

For the relationship between the severity of a crisis and the possibility of reproductive recovery for generations that have not yet reached child-bearing age, see L. Del Panta and M. Livi Bacci, "Chronique, diffusion et intensité des crises de mortalité en Italie, 1600–1850," *Population*, special issue (December 1977).

5 Systems

An illustration of the "systems" model discussed in this text and shown in table 5.1 in simplified version is found in G. De Santis and M. Livi Bacci, "La reproduction des populations," *Population*, 5 (1997).

The empirical data for the model are from the following sources: for France, the numbers are taken from a series of articles published as part of an INED study, and in particular, L. Henry, "Fécondité des mariages dans le quart sud-ouest de la France de 1720 à 1829," part I, *Annales ESC*, 3 (1972); part II, *Annales ESC*, 4–5 (1972); L. Henry and H. Houdaille, "La fécondité des mariages dans le quart nord-ouest de la France de 1670 à 1829," *Population*, 4–5, 1973; J. Houdaille, "La fécondité des mariages de 1670 à 1829 dans le quart nord-est de la France," *Annales de Démographie Historique* (1976); L. Henry, "Fécondité des mariages dans le quart sud-est de la France de 1670 à 1829," *Population*, 4–5 (1978); L. Henry and J. Houdaille, "Célibat et âge au mariage aux XVIIIe et XIXe siècles en France," part I, *Population*, 1 (1978); part II, *Population*, 2 (1979); Y. Blayo, "La mortalité en France de 1740 à 1829," *Population*, special issue (Nov. 1975). On Crulai, see E. Gautier and L. Henry, *La population de Crulai, paroisse normande* (INED-PUF, Paris, 1958). On Rouen, see J.-P. Bardet, *Rouen aux XVIIe et XVIIIe siècles* (Sedes, Paris, 1983).

The data for England are taken from A. E. Wrigley and R. Schofield, *The Population History of England, 1541–1871* (Arnold, London, 1981); ibid., "English Population History from Family Reconstitution: Summary Results 1600–1799," *Population Studies*, XXXVII (1983), pp. 157–84.

Data for Germany are from J. Knodel, "Demographic Transitions in German Villages," in *The Decline of Fertility in Europe*, A. J. Coale and S. Cotts Watkins, eds. (Princeton University Press, Princeton, 1986).

On the differences in demographic systems, aside from works already cited, see the following: on Russia, A. J. Coale, B. Anderson, and E. Harm, *Human Fertility in Russia since the Nineteenth Century* (Princeton University Press, Princeton, 1979); on Italy, L. Del Panta, "Dalla metà del Settecento ai nostri giorni," in L. Del Panta, M. Livi Bacci, G. Pinto, and E. Sonnino, *La popolazione italiana dal Medioevo a oggi* (Laterza, Rome-Bari, 1996), pp. 137–43. The dominant demographic system in fifteenth-century Florence is described in C. A. Corsini, "La demografia fiorentina nell'età di Lorenzo il Magnifico," in *La Toscana al tempo di Lorenzo il Magnifico*, vol. III (Pacini, Pisa, 1992). The Della Pergola citation is from S. Della Pergola, *La trasformazione demografica della diaspora ebraica* (Loescher, Torino, 1983), p. 61.

The Malthus citation is from T. R. Malthus, *A Summary View of the Principle of Population* (John Murray, London, 1830). The Cantillon is from 1775 and is included in F. Lebrun, "Le mariage et la famille," in *Histoire de la Population Française*, J. Dupâquier, ed., vol. II, *De la Renaissance à 1789* (PUF, Paris, 1988), p. 303. The seminal work on European marriage systems is J. Hajnal, "European marriage patterns in historical perspective," in D. V. Glass and D. E. C. Eversley, eds., *Population in History* (Arnold, London, 1965), followed by J. Hajnal, "Two kinds of preindustrial household formation system," *Population and Development Review*, VIII, 3 (1982). M. W. Flinn gives a good overview in *The European Demographic System 1500–1820* (Harvester Press, Brighton, 1981). There are many local studies for early modern Europe although few deal with large populations or broad time periods. Among the latter, for England see Wrigley and Schofield, *The Population History of England;* for France, Henry and Houdaille, "Célibat et âge au marriage" and F. Lebrun, "Le mariage et la famille"; for Spain and Portugal, R. Rowland, "Sistemas matrimoniales en la Peninsula Ibérica (siglos XVI–XIX): Una perspectiva regional," in V. Pérez Moreda and D. Reher, eds., *Demografía Histórica en España* (El Arquero, Madrid, n.d.); D. Reher, *Town and Country in Pre-Industrial Spain* (Cambridge University Press, Cambridge, 1990). On Italy see R. Rettaroli, "L'età al matrimonio," in M. Barbagli and D. I. Kertzer, eds., *Storia della famiglia italiana 1750–1950* (Il Mulino, Bologna, 1992). For a long-term study of Tuscany, see M. Breschi and R. Rettaroli, "La nuzialità in Toscana, secoli XIV–XIX," in *Le Italie demografiche. Saggi di demografia storica* (Udine, 1995). With regard to Germany, see Knodel, "Demographic Transitions in German Villages," in *The Decline of Fertility in Europe*, A. J. Coale and S. Cotts Watkins, eds. (Princeton University Press, Princeton, 1986); for Flanders, see C. Vandenbroeke, "Le cas Flamand: évolution sociale et comportements démographiques aux XVIIe–XIXe siècles," *Annales ESC*, XXXIX, 5 (1984). Other more specific works include: G. Delille, *Famille et propriété dans le Royaume de Naples (XVe–XIXe siècle)* (Ecole Française de Rome - EHESS, Rome/Paris, 1995). Data for Hungary is taken from the personal correspondence of R. Andorka. L. Del Panta and M. Livi Bacci, "Le componenti naturali dell'evoluzione demografica nell'Italia del Settecento," in Società italiana di demografia storica, *La Popolazione italiana nel settecento* (CLUEB, Bologna, 1980); J. Schlumbohm, "Social differences in age at marriage: examples from rural Germany during the XVIIIth and XIXth centuries," in *Historiens et populations. Liber Amicorum Etienne Hélin* (Société Belge de Démographie, Louvain-la-Neuve, 1991); W. Lutz, *Finnish Fertility since 1722* (The Population Research Institute, Helsinki, 1987).

For discussion of nuptiality in the Middle Ages, in addition to Hajnal, "European marriage patterns," see the critical inquiry by R. M. Smith, "The people of Tuscany and their families in the fifteenth century: Medieval or Mediterranean?," *Journal of Family History* (Spring 1981). For Tuscany, a fudamental source is D. Herlihy and C. Klapisch-Zuber, *Les Toscans et leurs familles* (Presses de la Fondation Nationale des Sciences Politiques, Paris, 1978); see also F. Leverotti, *Popolazione, famiglie, insediamento. Le sei miglia lucchesi nel XIV e XV secolo* (Pacini, Pisa, 1992). For France, once again C. Klapisch-Zuber, "Parenté et mariage," in *Histoire de la Population Française*, vol. I.

Illegitimate fertility and premarital conceptions are discussed in Flinn, *The European Demographic System*. On natural fertility, see E. van de Walle, "De la nature à la fécondité naturelle," *Annales de Démographie Historique* (1988); H. Leridon, *"Fécondité naturelle et espacement des naissances,"* ibid. For a discussion of legitimate fertility, in addition to the Flinn's overview, see the above-cited studies on England, France, and Germany. In addition, for France see A. Bideau and J.-P. Bardet, "Une géographie très contrastée," *Histoire de la Population Française*, vol. II, pp. 366–7. On Italy, see M. Breschi and M. Livi Bacci, "Italian fertility: A historical account," *Journal of Family History*, XV, 4 (1990). For Sweden, E. Hofsten and H. Lundström, *Swedish Population History* (National Central Bureau of Statistics, Stockholm, 1976); for Flanders, C. Vandenbroeke, "Caractéristiques de la nuptialité et de la fécondité en Flandre et en Brabant au XVIIIe–XIXe siècles," *Annales de Démographie Historique* (1977). Spanish fertility is disccussed in Reher, *Town and Country in Pre-Industrial Spain*, p. 91; also Reher, *La familia en España. Pasado y presente* (Alianza Editorial, Madrid, 1995).

Much of the discussion of infant mortality is from M. Livi Bacci, *Population and Nutrition* (Cambridge University Press, Cambridge, 1991), pp. 75–8; for additional references see that work's bibliography. French regional mortality is discussed in J. Houdaille, "La mortalitè des enfants dans la France rurale de 1690 à 1799," *Population*, XXXIX, 1 (1984). For mortality in England, see Wrigley and Schofield, *The Population History of England*; for Germany, A. E. Imhof, "The amazing simultaneousness of the big differences and the boom in the 19th century," in T. Bengtsson, G. Fridlizius, and R. Ohlsson, eds., *Pre-Industrial Population Change* (Almquist & Wiksell, Stockholm, 1984); for Finland, O. Turpeinen, "Infectious diseases and regional differences in Finnish death rates 1749-73," *Population Studies*, XXXII, 3 (1978).

Areas of occupational immigration are treated in J. Lucassen, *Migrant Labour in Europe 1600-1900: The Drift to the North* (Croom Helm, London, 1987); C. A. Corsini, "Le migrazioni stagionali dei lavoratori italiani del periodio napoleonico (1810–12)," in AA.VV., *Saggi di demografia storica* (Dipartimento di statistica, Florence, 1969). A wealth of information is found in the essays edited by A. Eiras Roel and O. Rey Castelao, *Les migrations internes et à moyenne distance en Europe*, 2 vols. (Xunta de Galicia, Santiago de Compostela, 1994). Also see L. Page Moch, *Moving Europeans* (Indiana University Press, Bloomington, 1992).

Long-distance migration is discussed in the proceedings of the XVII International Conference for Historical Sciences, (Madrid, 1990), and in the proceedings of the *Settimana Datini*, especially a paper by J. Dupâquier, "Macro-migrations en Europe (XVIe–XVIIIe siècles)." For Italy, see the collection "Rassegna storiografica sui fenomeni migratori a lungo raggio in Italia dal basso medievo al secondo dopoguerra," *Bollettino di Demografia storica*, XIII (1990). The expulsion of the *moriscos* and the Jews from Spain is covered in V. Pérez Moreda, "La Población Española," in M. Artola, ed., *Enciclopedia de Historia de España*, vol. I, *Economía y sociedad* (Alianza Editorial, Madrid, 1988), pp. 396–8; J. Nadal, *La población española, siglos XVI a XX* (Ariel, Barcelona, 1984), p. 49. The numbers of Huguenots expelled from France is discussed in J.-P. Poussou, "Mobilité et migrations," *Histoire de la Population Française*, vol. II, pp. 129-32.

The following resources discuss transoceanic migration by country: for Spain, see Nadal, *La población española*, pp. 54–64; A. M. Macias Hernández, ed., *La emigración española a América. Actas del II Congreso de la ADEH*, vol. I (Instituto de Cultura Gil Albert, Alicante, 1990); for Portugal, R. Rowland, "Emigración, estructura y región en Portugal (siglos XVI–XIX)," in Macias Hernández, ed., *La emigración Española; for* England, Wrigley and Schofield, *The Population History of England*, pp. 219–29; for France, Poussou, "Mobilité et Migrations" pp. 124–9; for Holland, J. Lucassen, "Dutch migrations (1500–1900)," paper presented at the International Conference for Historical Sciences, (Madrid, 1990); for Germany, H. Fenske, "International migration: Germany in the eighteenth century," *Central European History*, XIII, 4 (Dec. 1980). The figures for European settlers in America at the end of the eighteenth century are from C. McEvedy and R. Jones, *Atlas of World Population History* (Penguin, Harmondsworth, 1980), p. 279.

The section on Ireland is based on the following sources: K. H. Connell, *The Population of Ireland (1745–1845)* (Clarendon Press, Oxford, 1950); L. A. Clarkson, "Irish population revisited," in *Irish Population, Economy and Society: Essays in Honour of the Late K. H. Connell* (Clarendon Press, Oxford, 1981); J. Mokyr and C. O'Grada, "New developments in Irish population history, 1700–1850," *The Economic History Review*, new series, XXVII (1984); C. O'Grada, *Ireland before and after the Famine* (Manchester University Press, Manchester, 1993). For the Netherlands, see J. de Vries and A. van der Woude, *The First Modern Economy. Success, Failure and Perseverance of the Dutch Economy* (Cambridge University Press, Cambridge, 1998); J. De Vries, *The Dutch Rural Economy in the Golden Age* (Yale University Press, New Haven, 1974); ibid., "The population and economy of pre-industrial Netherlands," *Journal of Interdisciplinary History*, XV (1985).

For Spain, see V. Pérez Moreda, "La evolución demográfica española en el siglo XVII," a paper presented at the Conference of the Italian Society of Historical Demography, "La popolazione italiana nel seicento" (Florence, November 1996); and for Italy, M. Breschi and L. Del Panta, "I meccanismi dell'evoluzione demografica del Seicento: mortalità e fecondità," a paper presented at the same conference.

6　*The Great Transformation (1800–1914)*

C. Cipolla discusses the availability of energy in C. Cipolla, *The Economic History of the World Population* (Penguin, Harmondsworth, 1962). Per-capita income figures are drawn from A. Maddison, *Monitoring the World Economy, 1820–1922* (OECD, Paris, 1995). The estimates are made by converting GDP into a constant currency – in this case, 1990 international dollars – according to purchasing power parity (PPP), making it possible to make comparisons between different countries at different time periods.

The percentage of the population engaged in agriculture is discussed in Cipolla, *Economic History*; P. Bairoch, "Agriculture and the industrial revolution," in C. Cipolla, ed., *The Fontana Economic History of Europe*, vol. III, *The Industrial Revolution* (Collins, Glasgow, 1973); and B. R. Mitchell, *European Historical Statistics, 1750–1975* (Macmillan, London, 1980).

Agricultural development and productivity and the agrarian revolution are treated by F. Dovring, "The transformation of European agriculture," in H. Habakkuk and M. Postan, eds., *The Cambridge Economic History of Europe*, vol. VI, *The Industrial Revolutions and After* (Cambridge University Press, Cambridge, 1965); Bairoch, "Agriculture and the industrial revolution"; ibid., "The impact of crop yields, agricultural productivity and transport costs on urban growth between 1800 and 1910," in A. van der Woude, J. de Vries, and A. Hayami, eds., *Urbanization in History* (Oxford University Press, Oxford, 1990); and D. Grigg, *The Transformation of Agriculture in the West* (Basil Blackwell, Oxford, 1992).

The measure of total fertility (TFR) used in table 6.5 represents the average number of children born per woman during childbearing years in the absence of mortality, that is if no member of the generation dies before 50. Because this calculation does not take mortality into consideration, it is useful for making comparisons between fertility levels of different populations.

The estimates of net population loss due to emigration give a general idea of the phenomenon and are drawn from G. Sundbärg, *Aperçus statistiques internationaux* (Imprimerie Royale, Stockholm, 1908).

On the topic of the demographic transition, see M. Reinhard, A. Armengaud, and J. Dupâquier, *Histoire générale de la population mondiale* (Montchrestien, Paris, 1968); A. Armengaud, "Population in Europe, 1700–1914," in C. Cipolla, ed., *Economic History*, vol. III. For a more specialized discussion, see J.-C. Chesnais, *La transition démographique* (PUF, Paris, 1985); while a classical statement is that of F. Notestein, "Population, the long view," in T. W. Schultz, ed., *Food for the World* (University of Chicago Press, Chicago, 1945). An updated interpretation is given by A. J. Coale in "The demographic transition reconsidered," in *International Population Conference* (IUSSP, Liège, 1973), and a critical one in S. Szreter, "The idea of the demographic transition and the study of fertility change: A critical intellectual history," *Population and Development Review*, XIX, 4 (1993).

The Ariès citation is from *Histoire des populations françaises* (Seuil, Paris, 1971), pp. 378–9. Nineteenth-century mortality decline is discussed in R. Schofield, D. Reher, and A. Bideau, eds., *The Decline of Mortality in Europe* (Clarendon Press, Oxford, 1991); J. Stolnitz, "A century of international mortality trends," *Population Studies*, IX (1955); L. I. Dublin, A. J. Lotka, and M. Spiegelman, *Length of Life* (Ronald Press, New York, 1949).

J. D. Post discusses the 1816-17 subsistence crisis in *The Last Great Subsistence Crisis in the Western World* (Johns Hopkins University Press, Baltimore/London, 1977). The statistics on the grain trade are from Mitchell, *European Historical Statistics*. The Irish Famine is discussed by R. D. Edward and T. D. Williams in *The Great Famine* (New York University Press, New York, 1957); J. Mokyr, *Why Ireland Starved: A Quantitative and Analytical History of the Irish Economy, 1800–1850* (Allen and Unwin, London, 1983). The Finnish problems during the 1860s are described in K. J. Pitkanen, *Deprivation and Disease* (Finnish Demographic Society, Helsinki, 1993). For Russia, see A. Blum, *Naître, vivre et mourir en Union Soviétique* (Plon, Paris, 1994).

The nutritional theory is advanced in T. McKeown, *The Modern Rise of Population* (Arnold, London, 1976). It is discussed in M. Livi Bacci, *Population and Nutrition: An Essay on European Demographic History* (Cambridge University Press, Cambridge, 1991). Also, W. Michinton, "Patterns of Demand 1750–1914," in C. Cipolla, ed., *Economic History*.

Disease in the nineteenth century is treated in the two essays on cholera (P. Bourdelais, "Cholera: A victory for medicine?") and turberculosis (B. Puranen, "Tuberculosis and the decline of mortality in Sweden") in the collection edited by Schofield, Reher and Bideau, *The Decline of Mortality in Europe*. On causes of death, see S. H. Preston, N. Keyfitz, and R. Schoen, *Causes of Death: Life Table for National Populations* (Seminar Press, New York, 1973). On malaria, the citation is from F. Bonelli, "La malaria en Italie," in *Actes du Colloque international de démographie historique, Liège 1964* (Editions M. Th. Gémin, Paris, 1965). For malaria in Europe, see L. J. Bruce-Chwatt and J. de Zulueta, *The Rise and Fall of Malaria in Europe* (Oxford University Press, Oxford, 1980). Differences in the incidence of malaria in swampy and non-swampy areas is discussed in M. J. Dobson, "Malaria in England: A geographical and historical perspective," *Parassitolgia*, XXXVI (1994), pp. 35–60. On pellagra, see the Ministry of Agriculture, Industry, and Commerce, "La pellagra in Italia," *Annali di Agricoltura*, XVIII (1879); M. Livi Bacci, "Fertility, nutrition and pellagra: Italy during the vital revolution," *Journal of Interdisciplinary History*, XVI, 3 (1986).

The role of medicine in declining mortality is discussed in T. McKeown, *The Modern Rise of Population;* R. H. Shryock, *The Development of Modern Medicine* (Knopf, New York, 1947); B.-P. Lécuyer and J.-N. Biraben, "L'hygiene publique et la révolution pastorienne," in *Histoire de la Population Française*, J. Dupâquier, ed., vol. III, *De 1789 à 1914* (PUF, Paris, 1988).

Trends in infant mortality are discussed in P.-M. Boulanger and D. Tabutin, eds., *La mortalité des enfants dans le monde et dans l'histoire* (Ordina, Liège, 1980); C. A. Corsini and P. Viazzo, eds., *The Decline of Infant Mortality in Europe – 1800–1950: Four National Case Studies* (UNICEF/ICDC, Florence, 1993); ibid., *The Decline of Infant and Child Mortality* (Nijhof, The Hague, 1997). On the relationship between mortality and fertility, see S. H. Preston, ed., *The Effects of Infant and Child Mortality on Fertility* (Academic Press, New York, 1981).

Infant mortality statistics are taken from Mitchell, *European Historical Statistics*. In addition to the studies by W. Farr (*Vital Statistics: A Memorial Volume of Selections from the Reports and Writings of William Farr*, N. A. Humpreys, ed. (London, 1885)), high infant mortality in English cities is discussed in R. Woods, N. Williams, and C. Galley, "Infant Mortality in England, 1550–1950"; and in Corsini and Viazzo, *The Decline of Infant Mortality*. The stages in the fight against infant mortality is the topic of a paper by C. Rollet, "La lutte contre la mortalité infantile dans le passé: essai de comparaison internationale," presented at the "Séminaire sur la mortalité des enfants dans le passé" (Montréal, 1992). The acts from the Montreal conference include a number of important papers.

Declining fertility in Europe is the topic of P. Festy, *La fécondité des pays occidentaux de 1870 à 1970* (PUF, Paris, 1979) and J.-C. Chesnais, *La transition demographique* (PUF, Paris, 1985). The European Fertility Project (EPF) is a geographically detailed, country-by-country comparative study that uses standardized criteria in order to make international comparisons. Directed by A. J. Coale (Princeton University), the project has published a series of national monographs and a final volume: A. J. Coale and S. Cotts Watkins, eds., *The Decline of Fertility in Europe* (Princeton University Press, Princeton, 1986). The monographs are published by Princeton University Press and include: A. J. Coale, B. Anderson, E. Harm, *Human Fertility in Russia since the Nineteenth Century* (1979); J. Knodel, *The Decline of Fertility in Germany, 1871–1939* (1974); R. J. Lesthaeghe, *The Decline of Belgian Fertility, 1800–1970* (1977); M. Livi Bacci, *A Century of Portugese Fertility* (1971); ibid., *A History of Italian Fertility during the Last Two Centuries* (1977); M. Teitelbaum, *The British Fertility Decline: Demographic Transition in the Crucible of the Industrial Revolution* (1984); E. van de Walle, *The Female Population in France in the Nineteenth Century* (1974).

For fertility control practiced by special groups, see M. Livi Bacci, "Social-group forerunners of fertility control in Europe," in Coale and Cotts Watkins, eds., *The Decline of Fertility in Europe.*

The history of contraception and the Roman Penitentiary inquiries are discussed in J. T. Noonan, *Contraception* (Harvard University Press, Cambridge, Mass., 1965).

The rates of marriage, spinsterhood, and bachelorhood in the nineteenth century, and their relationship to fertility is covered in Festy, *La fécondité des pays Orientaux,* and also in J. Hajnal, "European marriage patterns in perspective," in D. V. Glass and D. E. C. Eversely, eds., *Population and History* (Arnold, London, 1965). Hajnal's research is amply cited in chapter 5.

Measurements of legitimate fertility, along with other important equations for illegitimate fertility and nuptiality, were introduced by A. J. Coale in the EFP, cited above. The highest level of legitimate fertility ever registered was that of Canadian Hutterites (married between 1921–30), farming Anabaptists opposed to birth control; mothers breastfed for an established number of months and general health was excellent.

Statistics for urban and rural fertility in Italy are from M. Livi Bacci, *A History of Italian Fertility*; also, A. Sharlin, "Urban–rural differences in fertility in Europe during the demographic transition," in Coale and Cotts Watkins, eds., *The Decline of Fertility in Europe.*

French fertility and the possible causes of its decline are discussed in J.-P. Bardet, "Le constat; Les incertitudes de l'explication," in *Histoire de la Population Française,* vol. III. For the contrast between France and England, see A. E. Wrigley, "The fall of marital fertility in nineteenth century France. Exemplar or exception?," *European Journal of Population,* part 1, I, 1 (1985); part 2, I, 2–3 (1985).

An fundamental source for international migration statistics is I. Ferenczi and W. F. Wilcox, *International Migrations,* 2 vols. (NBER, New York, 1929–31). Other important works on the topic are: M. R. Davie, *World Immigration* (Macmillan, New York, 1936); T. J. Hatton and J. G. Williamson, "International Migration and World Development: A Historical Perspective," in *Historical Paper,* no. 41 (NBER, Cambridge, Mass., 1992); ibid., "What Drove the Mass Migrations from Europe in the Late Nineteenth Century?," in *Historical Paper,* no. 43 (NBER, Cambridge, Mass., 1992). On English migration, see S. S. Johnson, *A History of Emigration from the United Kingdom to North*

America: 1763–1912 (F. Cass, London, 1913 [1966]); on German migration, K. J. Bade, "German emigration to the United States and continental immigration to Germany in the late nineteenth and early twentieth century," *Central European History*, XIII, 4 (Dec. 1980); on Italy, F. Coletti, *Dell'emigrazione italiana* (Hoepli, Milan, 1911); and on Russia, V. V. Obolensky-Ossinsky, "Emigration from and immigration into Russia," in Ferenczi and Wilcox, *International Migrations*. On frontier history, see R. A. Billington, *Westward Expansion. A History of the American Frontier* (Macmillan, New York, 1967).

Increased productivity of labor in agriculture is analyzed in Bairoch, *The Impact*. Population figures for major cities are from Mitchell, *European Historical Statistics*. The increase in cultivated surface area in Russia between 1883 and 1887 and 1904 and 1909 was approximately 41 percent; see also F. Lorimer, *The Population of the Soviet Union: History and Prospects* (League of Nations, Geneva, 1946), p. 211.

7   The End of a Cycle

The following are important references for the demography of twentieth-century Europe: D. Kirk, *Europe's Population in the Interwar Years* (League of Nations, Princeton University Press, Princeton, NJ, 1946); M. Reinhard, A. Armengaud, and J. Dupâquier, *Histoire générale de la population mondiale* (Montchrestien, Paris, 1968); M. Livi Bacci, *La trasformazione demografica delle società europee* (Loescher, Turin, 1977); J.-C. Chesnais, *La transition démographique*; and D. Noin and R. Woods, eds., *The Changing Population of Europe* (Basil Blackwell, Oxford, 1993). A complete set of statistics for the primary demographic variables of different European countries for the period 1950–95 is included in United Nations, *World Population Prospects. The 1996 Revision* (New York, 1997). Mortality, fertility, and international migration are specifically covered in the general reference works cited for chapter 6, many of which also include the twentieth century.

The characteristics of the recent transition, and in particular, unmarried couples, out-of-wedlock births, the instability of families, and the incidence of divorce are discussed in the following works: D. van de Kaa, "The second demographic transition revisited: theories and expectations," a paper presented at the conference *Population Change and European Society*, European University, Florence, Italy, 1988; R. J. Lesthaeghe, "The second demographic transition in western countries:

an interpretation," presented at the conference *Gender and Family Change*, IRP-IUSSP, Rome, Italy, 1992; L. Roussel, *La famille incertaine* (Odile Jacob, Paris, 1989).

The estimates given for First World War casualties are from the International Labor Organization and are found in A. Landry, *Traité de démographie* (Payot, Paris, 1949), p. 202. For Russian and Soviet estimates, F. Lorimer, *The Population of the Soviet Union: History and Prospects* (League of Nations, Geneva, 1946); A. Blum, *Naître, vivre et mourir en Union Soviétique* (Plon, Paris, 1994). On the cultural and political repercussions of demographic slowing down in Europe, see M. Teitelbaum and J. Winter, *The Fear of Population Decline* (Academic Press, Orlando, 1985); J. Spengler, *France Faces Depopulation* (Duke University Press, Durham, 1938). On European population policies, see D. V. Glass, *Population Policies and Movements in Europe* (Clarendon Press, Oxford, 1940). For Italy, see C. Ipsen, *Dictating Demography: The Problem of Population in Fascist Italy* (Cambridge University Press, Cambridge, 1996); ISTAT, "L'azione promossa dal Governo nazionale in favore dell'incremento demografico," in *Annali di Statistica*, 7th series, VII (Rome, 1943). For Germany, see Reinhard, Armengaud, and Dupâquier, *Histoire Générale*. For the Soviet Union, see Blum, *Naître vivre et mourir*. On the 1932–3 famine and its demographic effect, see M. Livi Bacci, "On the human cost of collectivization in the Soviet Union," *Population and Development Review*, XIX, 4 (1993).

The relationship between demographics and economics is discussed in the following works: A. Maddison, *Monitoring the World Economy, 1820–1992* (OECD, Paris, 1995); S. Kuznets, *Modern Economic Growth* (Yale University Press, New Haven, 1966); ibid., *Population, Capital and Growth: Selected Essays* (Norton, New York, 1973); C. P. Kindleberger, *Europe's Postwar Growth* (Harvard University Press, Cambridge, Mass., 1967). I also discuss this relationship in Livi Bacci, *A Concise History of World Population* (Basil Blackwell, Oxford, 1997). The Keynes reference is from "Some economic consequences of a declining population," *Eugenics Review*, XIX (April 1937). For periodization, see G. Tapinos, *La démographie* (Fallois, Paris, 1996).

The effect that demographic changes have had on values is the topic of my contribution entitled "Demografia della paura," in S. Riscossa, ed., *Le paure del mondo industriale* (Laterza, Rome-Bari, 1990). The references in the discussion are as follows: A. Camus, *La peste* (Gallimard, Paris, 1947), p. 42; the "unpredictable and capricious unfairness" of death is an expression of Thomas Mann's from *Buddenbrooks*; A. Checkhov, translated from the Italian version of the short story

"Enemies"; P. Ariès, *Western Attitudes toward Death: from the Middle Ages to the Present* (Johns Hopkins Press, Baltimore, 1974), pp. 86–7; S. Sontag, *Illness as Metaphor* (Farrar, Straus & Giroux, New York, 1978), pp. 37–8, p. 46. See also Sontag's discussion of AIDS and J. Delumeau, *La peur en occident* (Fayard, Paris, 1978).

Index

Note: major European countries do not have their own headings but appear as subheadings throughout.

Aachen, 2
Abel, W., 49
abortion, 5, 169, 188
adaptation, 4, 65–6, 68, 70
age at birth of first child, 169
age at marriage, 96–8, 100, 101–7,
    123–4, 152, 169
  Balkans, 103
  England, 103, 105, 107
  Flanders, 105
  Florence, 106
  France, 103, 105–6
  Germany, 103, 105
  Italy, 104, 105
  Netherlands, 103
  Portugal, 103–4
  Russia, 103
  Scandinavia, 103
  Spain, 103, 105
age at weaning, 115
age structure, 170–1, 173, 179, 182–3
agricultural productivity *see*
   productivity, agricultural
agricultural revolution, 130–2, 140

agricultural societies, 13, 21, 30,
   129–32
agriculture: growing season, 20
AIDS, 64, 67, 187
Aix-en-Provence, 83
Americas, 6–7, 158–60, 163
   see also migration
Amsterdam, 75, 118
Andalusia, 74, 119
Andorka, R., 103
Antwerp, 48
Aquitaine, 31
Aragon, 119
Ariès, P., 140, 185–6
Arles, Bishop of, 56
Arnsberg, 2
Aubin, H., 25, 26
Augusta, 83
Aymard, M., 34
Azov, 29

baby boom, 183
bachelorhood, 100, 101
Bairoch, P., 130–1, 161

Baltic lands, 22
Barcelona, 79, 83
Baret, J.-P., 157
Bavaria, 98
Bernoulli, D., 87
Biraben, J.-N., 74, 82
birth control, 5, 99, 131, 137–9,
    151–8, 166, 169, 188
    France, 156–7
birth rates *see* fertility
Black Death, 25, 32, 72–3
    see also plague
Black Sea, 72
Bonelli, F., 145
Borromeo College, 46, 56
Brandenburg, 27
Brazil, 120
bread *see* grains
breastfeeding, 5, 108–9, 112, 114–16,
    147–50
Bremen, 144
buboes, 71
buckwheat, 143
Burnet, Macfarlane, 65

Caen, 46
Cagliari, 78
Calais, 68
calorie counts, 46–9
Cambridge University, 96
Campeggio, 70
Camus, A., 185
cancer, 186–7
Cantillon, 100
capitalism, 105
cardiovascular disease, 186–7
Casal, G., 146
Castile, 24, 117, 119
Castile y León, 119
Catalonia, 117
Catherine the Great, 28
Caux, 1
censuses, 100
Charles VIII, 63, 67, 74
Chekhov, A., 185
children,
    childbirth, 188
    childcare, 116
    childrearing, 140, 147–50, 179
    cost of, 137

cholera, 63, 64, 67, 142, 143–4, 147
Cipolla, C., 13–14, 19, 74, 82
Civitavecchia, 78
climate, 3–4, 19–20
coal, 127
collectivization, agricultural, 177
colonization *see* migration
colostrum, 114–15
conception, premarital, 108
Connell, K. H., 122–4
contraception *see* birth control
cordons sanitaires, 75, 77, 79
corn, 143, 146
Corsica, 118
cretinism, 43
Crimea, 29
crops: new, 131, 143
    see also individual crops
Crulai, 16–17, 97
Cumano, M., 67
Cyprus, 69, 85

Danube river, 22, 29
Danzig, 75
death rates *see* mortality; life
    expectancy
demographic pressure, 160–2
demographic transition, 137–9, 157–8
dengue fever, 67
de Vries, J., 36, 124
diarrhea, 44, 64
diet *see* nutrition
diphtheria, 45, 64, 147
diseases, 3–4, 14–15, 43–5, 52, 55,
    62–90, 143–7, 167, 178–9,
    186–7
    gastrointestinal, 45, 64–5
    respiratory, 45, 64–5
    sexually transmitted, 64
    vector transmitted, 64–7
    see also individual diseases
divorce, 172
Domesday Book, 5, 30
Dupâquier, J., 121
Dusseldorf, 2
Dutch East India Company, 124
dysentery, 64

East Anglia, 117
Ebola, 67

economic development, 137–9, 145, 167–8, 178–83
Edict of Nantes, 119
emigration *see* migration
energy, 3–4, 13–14, 19, 127
Erik of Sweden, 46, 56
Estremadura, 119
Europe
  geography, 19–21, 63
  mountains, 20–1
  seas, 20

families: single-parent, 172
family reconstitution, 16–17, 96, 100, 108
famine *see* subsistence crises
Farr reports, 149
Felicini, J., 78
Fenske, H., 28
Ferdinand III, 23
fertility, 92–4, 96–9, 100, 103, 107–12, 134–5, 148, 166, 167–9, 174, 179, 188
  decline, 137–9, 151–8, 171, 172
  England, 109
  Europe, 103
  Flanders, 109
  France, 109–12, 153
  Germany, 109–12
  Ireland, 153
  Italy, 155
  Russia, 153
  Sweden, 109
  see also natural fertility; marital fertility
fertility rate *see* rates
Flanders, 21
fleas, 71–2, 76–7, 83
Flinn, M., 90
Florence, 78–9, 106
Floridablanca, 105
food budgets, 46–7, 56
Fortescue, J., 50
foundation effect, 25, 27, 28
foundling homes, 115, 150
Fracastoro, 68, 69
Frederick II, 28
French Revolution, 156
Friesland, 98

Galicia, 120
Gautier, E., 16–17
Genoa, 73, 78–9
geography *see* Europe
Gisors, 1
Goethe, W., 51
goiter, 43
grain trade,
  Brandenberg, 27
  England, 27
  Germany, 141
  Netherlands, 27
  Russia, 141
grains and bread, 47–9, 51–2, 55, 56, 142–3
Granada, 23, 69, 85
Graunt, J., 43, 68, 80, 83
Great Depression, 182
Great Famine (Ireland), 2, 11, 52, 123, 141
Grigg, D., 161
gross domestic product, 128–9
Guadalquivir Valley, 24

Hajnal, J., 102–3, 105–7
Hamburg, 144
Harald the Fairhaired, 25
harvest-to-sowing ratio, 14, 21
Hebrides, 160
height, 143, 179
Henry, L., 16–17, 57, 97, 108
Herlihy, D., 106
HIV *see* AIDS
Hong Kong, 71, 72
Huguenots, 119
hygiene, personal and public, 77–80, 140, 142, 178–9
  Barcelona, 79
  England, 79–80
  Italy, 77–9
  Russia, 79
  Scotland, 79

illegitimacy, 99, 107–8
immigration *see* migration
immune system: infant, 114–15
income:
  family, 142
  per capita, 128–9, 140, 178
India, 72

industrialization, 6, 144, 147, 157, 161–2
Industrial Revolution, 127, 130, 161
infant abandonment, 150–1
infant mortality, 112–16, 145, 147–51
  Belgium, 148
  Denmark, 148
  England, 113, 148–9
  Finland, 114
  France, 113, 148–9
  Germany, 149
  Italy, 149
  Moscow, 113
  Sweden, 149
influenza, 64, 173
inheritance, 101
intensification, 30–5, 35–9

James I, 86
Jenner, E., 87, 142
Jews, 119, 152

Keynes, J. M., 181
King, G., 39, 50
kinship, 187–8
Klapisch, C., 106
Knodel, J., 97
Koch, W., 140, 143, 147
Kuhn, W., 25
kulak, 177
kwarshiorkor, 43

land and land use, 3–4, 7, 13–14, 30–5, 39
  England, 34–5
  Netherlands, 32–4
  Po Valley, 34–5
landnamabok, 25
land reclamation *see* land and land use
Languedoc, 79, 84
Lassa fever, 67
Latium, 118
Lebrun, F., 105
lice, 68–9, 80, 147
life expectancy, 61–2, 89–90, 96–8, 129, 135–6, 140, 142, 148, 167, 171, 179

England, 58, 61–2
Italy, 62
Liguria, 78
Lombardy, 150
London, 68, 70, 75, 80, 83, 117, 118
Lorimer, F., 173
Lucca, 78
Lyme disease, 67

McKeown, T., 142
McNeill, W., 29
Maddison, A., 128
Madrid, 117
Magnus, Duke, 46
malaria, 45, 65, 67, 88–9, 98, 144, 145–6, 147
Malthus, T. R., 18, 41, 99–100, 103
Malthusian model, 41–2
marasma, 43
Marcigny, Convent of, 56
Maréchal de Saxe, 17
Maremma, 27
Maria Theresa, 29
marital fertility, 152–5
marriage *see* nuptiality
Marseilles, 75, 83
Maximilian I, 67
Mazzarino, Cardinal, 46, 56
measles, 64, 147
meat, 48–51, 142–3
meconium, 115
menopause, 108
Messina, 72, 75, 79
Meuvret, J. 51
microbes, 67–72
migration, 5, 7, 11, 13, 20, 21–30, 52, 96–8, 116–22, 119, 136–7, 139, 141, 158–63, 179, 182
  Albania, 118
  Americas, 119, 120–1
  Argentina, 159, 163
  Australia, 159
  Austria, 22, 29
  Austria-Hungary, 158
  Brazil, 159
  Canada, 159
  Cuba, 159
  England, 117–18
  Europe, 21–30, 164–6, 169–70

migration *(continued)*
  France, 117, 118, 119, 121
  French Canada, 27
  Galicia, 118
  Germanic peoples, 22–3, 25–7, 28, 118
  Germany, 121, 158
  Great Britain, 120–1, 158
  Greenland, 25
  Hungary, 22, 28
  Iberia, 117, 119
  Iceland, 25
  Ireland, 124, 158
  Italy, 118, 158, 170
  Netherlands, 117–18, 121, 124–5
  New Zealand, 159
  North Sea, 117
  Norway, 158
  Poland, 28, 158
  Portugal, 158
  Prussia, 28
  Russia, 28–9, 121, 137, 158
  Scandinavia, 25
  Scotland, 118
  Siberia, 137, 163
  Silesia, 28
  Spain, 23–4, 27, 158
  Sweden, 158
  Switzerland, 118
  Tuscany, 27
  United States, 159–60, 163, 170
  Uruguay, 159
  Volga river valley, 28
Milan, 78, 150
Mirabeau, V. R., 17
Molotov, Vyacheslav, 177
Montesquieu, C.-J., 17
Morineau, M., 47
moriscos, 119
mortality, 62–3, 70, 80–4, 85, 89–90, 92–4, 96–9, 100, 111, 122, 135, 169, 184–7
  Benedictines, 57
  decline, 112–13, 130–1, 137–9, 140–7, 166–7, 178
  Denmark, 57
  England, 56–7, 89–90
  France, 90
  Geneva, 57
  Italy, 89–90

Jesuits, 57
  and nutrition, 42, 43–5, 51–60
  Russian, 135
  Soviet Union, 177
  Sweden, 90
  see also infant mortality; life expectancy; population growth and decline
Moscow, 75, 83
Münster, 2
Murcia, 119
Mussolini, B., 175

Naples, 67, 78, 82, 150
Napoleonic wars, 63
National Origins Act, 170
natural fertility, 108–12, 124, 152
Neolithic Revolution, 127
New Economic Policy (Soviet Union), 176
New Russia, 28–9
Normandy, 31, 156
Novara, 67
nuptiality, 4, 93–5, 96–8, 99–107, 122–4, 137, 139, 152, 157–8, 167, 171–2, 173
nutrition and diet, 3–4, 14, 42–60, 114, 130–1, 140, 142–3
  England, 50, 53–5
  France, 47, 51, 53–5
  Germany, 53
  Iberia, 53
  Italy, 51, 53
  Netherlands, 53
  Scotland, 53
  Sweden, 53
old regime, demographic, 12–16
Orkney Islands, 25

Papal State, 78
parasites, 65–6, 68–9, 71–2, 76–7, 80
  see also microbes
paratyphoid fever, 64
Paris, 79, 117, 150
Pasteur, L., 140
pasteurization, 149
pellagra, 43, 144, 146
Peller, S., 57
percentage never married, 100, 101, 104, 107

Pinto, G., 31
Pius XI, 176
plague, 2, 6, 7, 45, 58, 59, 61, 63,
    64–5, 67, 69, 70–84, 87, 125,
    143, 147
  Justinian, 72
  pneumonic, 71–2, 83
policies: migration, 162–3, 169–70
policies: population, 172–8
  Fascist, 175–6
  France, 174, 176
  Japan, 175
  Nazi, 175–6, 178
  Soviet, 176–7
Pomerania, 22, 25
population: aging, 166
  see also age structure
population anxiety, 174–6
population density, 64
population doubling, 10–12
population growth and decline, 63–4
  Aix-en-Provence, 83
  Augusta, 83
  Baltics, 12
  Barcelona, 83
  eastern Europe, 2
  England, 2, 5, 7–11, 15–16, 81, 96,
    98
  Europe, 1–2, 5–12, 15–16, 81, 96,
    126, 133–7, 160, 164–6, 169,
    173
  France, 7–11, 17, 81–2, 96–8, 133,
    174
  Germany, 7–11, 12, 97–8, 174
  Iberia, 98
  Ireland, 2, 7–11, 98, 123, 141
  Italy, 7–11, 82–3, 98–9, 133
  Jews, 99
  London, 83
  Marseilles, 83
  Moscow, 83
  Naples, 82
  Netherlands, 2, 7–11, 33, 124
  Norway, 7–11, 81
  Poland, 12
  Russia, 7–12, 98, 133
  Scandinavia, 12
  Scotland, 11
  Soviet Union, 177
  Spain, 7–11, 133

Sweden, 7–11
Toulon, 83
Tuscany, 81–2
United Kingdom, 133
population growth rate *see* rates
Portugal, 120
potato, 122–4, 141, 143
Potemkin, 29
Po Valley, 21, 118
Prato, 2, 105–6
prices *see* wages
productivity, agricultural, 14, 129–32,
    137, 140, 161
pronatalism, 174–8
Protestant Reformation, 105
Provence, 75, 79, 84, 117
Prussia, 22, 25, 28, 79

quarantines, 74, 75, 77–80

rates,
  fertility, 109–11
  population growth, 13, 62, 92–3,
    100
  total fertility, 134–5, 151, 168
rats, 71–2, 76–7, 80, 83–4
reconquista, 23–4
Reggio Calabria, 73, 75
Reher, D., 111
reproduction, biological potential for,
    3
reproductivity, 92–3, 122
residence system,
  neolocal, 101
  patrilocal, 101
Rhine, 75
Ricardo, D., 41
Richard III, 68
rickets, 43
rickettia, 68
Rocky Mountains, 72
Rollet, C., 149
Rome, 78–9, 118
Ross, R., 147
Rouen, 1, 97, 156
Russell, J. C., 107
Russo-Turkish war, 29

St. Lawrence River Valley, 27
Salutati, C., 61

Sardinia, 78
Saxony, 22
scarlet fever, 147
Schofield, R., 121, 122
scurvy, 43
Sereni, E., 32
settlement patterns, 3–4, 7, 13, 25, 30–2
  England, 30
  France, 31
  Italy, 30–2
Seville, 24
sexual relations: frequency of, 108
Shetland Islands, 25
Sicily, 32
Silesia, 22, 25, 28
Slavs, 22, 26
Slicher van Bath, 14, 15, 31
smallpox, 45, 64, 85–8, 142, 143, 146
Smith, A., 30, 40–1
Sontag, S., 186–7
Soranus, 114
space, 3–4
Spedale degli Innocenti, 150
spinsterhood, 100, 101
Stalin, J., 176–7
standard-of-living, 128–9, 144
Stockholm, 144
subsistence crises, 6, 40–1, 51–5, 85, 140–2, 147, 177
  Finland, 141
  Russia, 142
surplus labor, 131–2
survivorship, 93, 97–8, 125
sweating sickness, 68, 70, 87
syphilis, 63, 64, 67–8
systems: demographic, 5, 16, 87, 91–125, 127, 138–9
  England, 139
  France, 139
  Ireland, 122–4, 139
  Netherlands, 124–5
  Scandinavia, 139

Tartars, 29
technological progress, 14
Thirty Years War, 6, 16, 53–5, 63, 85–6
Thuringia, 22
Toulon, 83
Toutain, 47, 51
Treaty of Versailles, 182
tuberculosis, 64, 67, 144–5, 147, 186–7
tularemia, 67
Tuscany, 27, 78, 98–9, 118, 145, 150
typhoid fever, 64, 147
typhus, 45, 52, 63, 65, 68–70, 74, 77, 84–5, 87, 142, 143, 147

Urals, 7
urbanization, 35–9, 137–9, 144, 147, 149, 156, 161–2, 181
urban latitude, 38–9

Valencia, 119
van der Woude, A., 124
Vexin, 156
Viareggio, 78
virgin populations, 87
Volga River, 76

wages and prices, 15, 16, 51–9, 122, 143, 161
  England, 54–5, 58
  France, 54–5
  Tuscany, 54–5, 58
Westphalia, 117
wet nurse, 156
World War I, 133, 159, 173–4
World War II, 173, 178
Wrigley, A., 96, 121, 122

yellow fever, 63, 65, 144
Yersin, A., 71
yersinia pestis, 71, 84
Young, A., 123

Zinsser, H., 63, 66, 84

Lightning Source UK Ltd.
Milton Keynes UK
23 February 2010

150514UK00002B/69/P